The Instructional Use of Learning Objects

D1736422

David A. Wiley, Editor

Agency for Instructional Technology

Association for
Educational Communications & Technology

$29.95US

Published by
Agency for Instructional Technology
and
Association for Educational Communications & Technology
Box A
Bloomington, Indiana 47402-0120

©2002 by individual chapter authors

Printed version ©2002 by AIT/AECT
All rights reserved.
This material may be distributed only subject to the terms and conditions set forth in the Open Publication License. (Information available upon request from the author or publisher.)

No part of the printed version protected by this copyright notice may be reproduced or utilized for commercial purposes in any form or by any means, electronic or mechanical, including photocopying, recording, or by any information storage and retrieval system, without permission from the copyright owner.

AIT Customer Service: 1-800-457-4509
Internet: www.ait.net

First Edition

ISBN: 0-7842-0892-1

Library of Congress Control Number: 2001091342

David A. Wiley, *Editor*
Deneise Self Hueston, *Copy Editor; Text & Cover Designer*
Michael F. Sullivan, *Executive Director, AIT, Publisher*
Phil Harris, *Executive Director, AECT, Co-Publisher*

Printed by Tichenor Printing, Bloomington, Indiana

Contents

Acknowledgments

For their undying support during this and
other labors of love, my affection and heartfelt thanks
go to my immediate family:
Elaine, David Enoch, and Megumi.

My gratitude also goes to my academic family for
their enculturation and inspiration:
my "mom" Laurie Nelson, "grandfather" Charlie Reigeluth,
and "great-grandpaw" David Merrill.

—David A. Wiley

1.0 Learning Objects Explained

Connecting Learning Objects to Instructional Design Theory: A Definition, a Metaphor, and a Taxonomy

David A. Wiley
(Utah State University)

The purpose of this chapter is to introduce an instructional technology concept known commonly as the "learning object." First a review of the literature is presented as groundwork for a working definition of the term. A brief discussion of instructional design theory is followed by an attempt to connect the learning objects approach to existing instructional design theory, then the general lack of such connective efforts is contrasted with the financial and technical activity generated by the learning objects notion. The Lego™ metaphor frequently used to describe learning objects is critically examined and a successor metaphor is nominated. A taxonomy of learning object types is presented as a foundation for continued research on learning objects and related instructional design theories. Finally, the connection of instructional design theory to taxonomy is demonstrated, and the benefits of this approach are briefly espoused. This introduction should provide the reader with a context for interpreting the remaining chapters of this book.

What Is a Learning Object?

Technology is an agent of change, and major technological innovations can result in entire paradigm shifts. The computer network known as the Internet is one such innovation. After effecting sweeping changes in the way people communicate and do business, the Internet is poised to bring about a paradigm shift in the way people learn. Consequently, a major change may also be coming in the way educational materials are designed, developed, and delivered to those who wish to learn. The instructional technology called "learning objects" (LTSC, 2000a) currently leads other candidates as the technology of choice for the next generation of instructional design, development, and delivery (Hodgins, 2000; Urdan & Weggen, 2000; Gibbons, Nelson, & Richards, 2002). This is because of its potential for reusability, generativity, adaptability, and scalability.

Learning objects are elements of a new type of computer-based instruction grounded in the object-oriented paradigm of computer science. Object-orientation highly values the creation of components (called "objects") that can be reused in multiple contexts (Dahl & Nygaard, 1966). The fundamental idea behind learning objects is that instructional designers can build small (relative to the size of an entire course) instructional components that can be reused a number of times in different learning contexts. Additionally, learning objects are generally understood to be digital entities deliverable over the Internet. This means that any number of people can access and use learning objects simultaneously. (Traditional instructional media, such as an overhead or a video tape, only exist in one place at a time.) Moreover, individuals who incorporate learning objects can collaborate on and benefit immediately from new versions. These are significant differences between learning objects and previously existing instructional media.

Supporting the notion of small, reusable chunks of instructional media, Reigeluth and Nelson (1997) suggest that when teachers first gain access to instructional materials, they often break these materials down into constituent parts. Teachers then reassemble these parts in ways that support each individual's instructional goals. This suggests one reason why reusable instructional components (learning objects) may provide instructional benefits: if instructors received instructional resources as individual components, the initial step of decomposition could be bypassed, potentially increasing the speed and efficiency of instructional development.

To facilitate the widespread adoption of the learning objects approach, the Learning Technology Standards Committee (LTSC) of the Institute of Electrical and Electronics Engineers (IEEE) was formed in 1996 to develop and promote instructional technology standards (LTSC, 2000a). Without such standards, universities, corporations, and other organizations around the world would have no way of assuring the interoperability of their instructional technologies, specifically their learning objects. A similar project called the Alliance of Remote Instructional Authoring and Distribution Networks for Europe (ARIADNE) had already started with the financial support of the European Union Commission (ARIADNE, 2000). At the same time, another venture called the Instructional Management Systems (IMS) Project was just beginning in the United States, with funding from Educom (IMS, 2000a). Each of these and other organizations (e.g., ADL, 2000) began developing technical standards to support the broad deployment of learning objects. Many of these local standards efforts have representatives on the LTSC.

The Learning Technology Standards Committee chose the term "learning objects" (possibly from Wayne Hodgins' 1994 use of the term in the title of the CedMA working group called "Learning Architectures, API's, and

Learning Objects") to describe these small instructional components; the LTSC also established a working group and provided a working definition:

> Learning Objects are defined here as any entity, digital or non-digital, which can be used, re-used or referenced during technology-supported learning. Examples of technology-supported learning include computer-based training systems, interactive learning environments, intelligent computer-aided instruction systems, distance learning systems, and collaborative learning environments. Examples of Learning Objects include multimedia content, instructional content, learning objectives, instructional software and software tools, and persons, organizations, or events referenced during technology supported learning. (LOM, 2000)

This definition is extremely broad and upon examination fails to exclude any person, place, thing, or idea that has existed at anytime in the history of the universe, since any of these could be "referenced during technology supported learning." Accordingly, different groups outside the Learning Technology Standards Committee have created different terms that generally narrow the scope of the canonical definition down to something more specific. Other groups have refined the definition but continue to use the term "learning object." Confusingly, these additional terms and differently-defined "learning objects" are all Learning Technology Standards Committee "learning objects" in the strictest sense.

The proliferation of definitions for the term "learning object" makes communication confusing and difficult. For example, computer-based training (CBT) vendor NETg, Inc., uses the term "NETg learning object" but applies a three-part definition: a learning objective, a unit of instruction that teaches the objective, and a unit of assessment that measures the objective (L'Allier, 1998). Another CBT vendor, Asymetrix, defines learning objects in terms of programming characteristics. "ToolBook II learning objects—pre-scripted elements that simplify programming . . . provide instantaneous programming power" (Asymetrix, 2000). The NSF-funded Educational Objects Economy takes a technical approach, only accepting Java Applets as learning objects (EOE, 2000). It would seem that there are almost as many definitions of the term as there are people employing it.

In addition to the various definitions of the term "learning object," other terms that imply the general intention to take an object-oriented approach to computer-assisted instruction confuse the issue further. David Merrill uses the term "knowledge objects" (Merrill, Li, & Jones, 1991). Merrill is also writing a book on the topic of object-oriented approaches to instruction to be called "Components of Instruction" (personal communication, March 21, 2000), which is sure to introduce yet another term, "instructional component," into the instructional design vernacular. The previously mentioned ARIADNE project uses the term "pedagogical documents" (ARIADNE, 2000). The NSF-funded Educational Software Components of Tomorrow (ESCOT) project uses the term "educational software components" (ESCOT, 2000), while the Multimedia Educational Resource for Learning and On-Line Teaching project (MERLOT) uses the terminology "online learning materials" (MERLOT, 2000). Finally, the Apple Learning Interchange simply terms them "resources" (ALI, 2000). Depressingly, while each of these is something different, they all conform to the Learning Technology Standards Committee's learning object definition. An in-depth review of the precise meanings of each of these terms would not add to the main point of this discussion. The field is still struggling to come to grips with the question, *"What is a learning object?"*

The Learning Technology Standards Committee definition seems too broad to be useful, since most instructional technologists would not consider the historical event "the war of 1812" or the historical figure "Joan of Arc" to be learning objects. At the same time, the creation of yet another term may only add to the confusion. *So, what is a learning object?* While the creation of a satisfactory definition of the term "learning object" will probably consume the better part of the author's career, a working definition must be presented before the discussion can proceed. Therefore, this chapter defines a learning object as *"any digital resource that can be reused to support learning."* This definition includes anything that can be delivered across the network on demand, be it large or small. Examples of smaller reusable digital resources include digital images or photos, live data feeds (like stock tickers), live or prerecorded video or audio snippets, small bits of text, animations, and smaller Web-delivered applications (like a Java calculator). Examples of larger reusable digital resources include entire Web pages that combine text, images, and other media or applications to deliver complete experiences (a complete instructional event). This definition of learning object, *"any digital resource that can be reused to support learning,"* is proposed for two reasons.

First, this definition is sufficiently narrow to define a reasonably homogeneous set of things: reusable digital resources. At the same time, the definition is broad enough to include the estimated 15 terabytes of information available on the publicly accessible Internet (Internet Newsroom, 1999).

Second, this chapter's proposed definition is based on the LTSC definition (and defines a proper subset of learning objects as defined by the LTSC), making issues of compatibility of learning objects as defined within this chapter, and learning objects as defined by the LTSC, explicit. The proposed definition captures what the author feels to be the critical attributes of a learning object ("reusable," "digital," "resource," and "learning"), as does the LTSC definition.

With that compatibility stated, this chapter's proposed definition differs from the LTSC definition in two important ways.

First, this definition explicitly rejects non-digital resources (by dropping the word and dropping the idea of a learning object being simply "reference"-able). This chapter's definition also rejects non-reusable resources (by dropping the phrase "used or" which seems to imply the acceptance of single use). The definition of learning object presented in this chapter does not include actual people, historical events, books (in the traditional sense of the term), or other discrete, physical objects. The definition also drops the phrase "technology supported" which is now implicit, because all learning objects are digital.

Second, the phrase "to support" has here been substituted in place of "during" (found in the LTSC definition). Use of an object *during* learning doesn't connect its use to learning. The LTSC definition implies that nothing more than contiguity of an object's use and the occurrence of learning is sufficient, meaning that a banner advertisement atop an online course Web page would be a legitimate learning object. The definition adopted for this chapter emphasizes the purposeful use (by either an instructional designer, an instructor, or a student) of these objects to support learning.

Armed with a working definition of learning objects, discussion about the instructional use of learning objects can proceed.

Instructional Design Theory and Learning Objects

Instructional design theories have been overviewed frequently in the literature (Dijkstra, Seel, Schott, & Tennyson, 1997; Reigeluth 1983, 1999b; Tennyson, Schott, Seel, & Dijkstra, 1997). Reigeluth (1999a) defines instructional design theory as follows:

> [I]nstructional design theories are design oriented, they describe methods of instruction and the situations in which those methods should be used, the methods can be broken into simpler component methods, and the methods are probabilistic. (p. 7)

Reigeluth's current definition of design theory as prescriptive theory follows earlier definitions of design theory (Simon, 1969; Snelbecker, 1974; Reigeluth, 1983). Because the very definition of "theory" in some fields is "descriptive," design theories are commonly confused with other types of theories that they are not, including learning theory and curriculum theory (Reigeluth, 1999a).

Instructional design theory, or instructional strategies and criteria for their application, must play a large role in the application of learning objects if they are to succeed in facilitating learning. This statement echoes Reigeluth and

Frick's (1999) call: "more [instructional design] theories are sorely needed to provide guidance for . . . the use of new information technology tools" (p. 633). The following discussion takes a step in this direction, by recasting two of the largest learning objects issues—*combination* and *granularity*—in instructional design terms.

Combination

Groups like the Learning Technology Standards Committee exist to promote international discussion around the technology standards necessary to support learning object based instruction. While many people are talking about the financial opportunities that may come into existence because of learning object development, there is astonishingly little conversation around the instructional design implications of learning objects.

Indicative of this lack of thought about instructional design is item 7(d) of the Learning Objects Metadata (LOM) Working Group's Project Authorization Request (PAR) form (LTSC, 2000b). The Learning Objects Metadata Working Group is a Learning Technology Standards Committee working group. The PAR is the mechanism by which IEEE projects are officially requested and approved, and must contain statements detailing the project's scope and purpose. Section 7 of the PAR deals with the purpose of the proposed project, and item (d) in the Learning Objects Metadata Working Group's PAR (LOM, 2000) reads as follows:

> To enable computer agents to automatically and dynamically compose personalized lessons for an individual learner.

As the Learning Object Metadata standard neared finalization in early 2000, some questions were raised regarding the current standard's ability to achieve this purpose. Apparently no one had considered the role of instructional design in composing and personalizing lessons. If the reader will pardon a short digression, at this point a brief discussion of metadata, the focus of the Learning Object Metadata Working Group's efforts, is necessary.

Metadata, literally "data about data," is descriptive information about a resource. For example, the card catalog in a public library is a collection of metadata. In the case of the card catalog, the metadata is the information stored on the cards about the author, title, and publication date of the book or resource in question. The labels on cans of soup are another example of metadata: they contain a list of ingredients, the name of the soup, the production facility where the soup was canned, and other information. In both the case of the library book and the can of soup, metadata allows you to locate an item very quickly, without investigating all the individual items through which you are searching. Imagine trying to locate *Paradise Lost* by sifting through every book in the library, or looking for chicken soup by opening every can of soup in the store and inspecting contents! The Learning Objects Metadata Working Group is trying to create metadata for learning objects (such as title, author, version, format) so that people and computers will be able to find objects by searching, as opposed to browsing the entire digital library one object at a time until they find one that suffices.

The problem with 7(d) arose when people began to actually consider what it meant for a computer to "automatically and dynamically compose personalized lessons." This meant taking individual learning objects and combining them in a way that made instructional sense, or in instructional design terminology, "sequencing" learning objects. It seemed clear to some people that in order for a computer to make sequencing or any other instructional design decisions, the computer must have access to instructional design information to support the decision-making process. The problem was that no instructional design information was included in the metadata specified by the current version of the Learning Objects Metadata Working Group standard.

The lack of instructional design discussion at this standards-setting level of conversation about learning objects is disturbing, because it might indicate a trend. One can easily imagine technology implementers asking, *"If the standards bodies haven't worried about sequencing, why should we?"* Once technology or software that does not support an instructionally-grounded approach to learning object sequencing is completed and shipped to the average teacher, why would he or she respond any differently? This sets the stage for learning objects to be used simply to glorify online instruction, the way clip-art and dingbats are used in a frequently unprincipled manner to decorate elementary school newsletters. Wiley (1999) called this "the new CAI—'Clip Art Instruction'" (p. 6). Obviously, instructionally-grounded sequencing decisions are at the heart of the instructionally successful use of learning objects.

Granularity

Discussion of the problem of combining learning objects in terms of "sequencing" leads to another connection between learning objects and instructional design theory. The most difficult problem facing the designers of learning objects is that of "granularity" (Wiley et al., 1999). How big should a learning object be? As stated above, the Learning Technology Standards Committee's definition leaves room for an entire curriculum to be viewed as a learning object, but such a large object view diminishes the possibility of learning object reuse. Reuse is the core of the learning object notion, as generativity, adaptivity, and other –ivities are all facilitated by the property of reuse. This is why a more restrictive definition has been proposed in this chapter.

Lest the answer seems too straightforward, because learning objects commonly require the creation of metadata (which can mean filling out a form of some twenty-odd fields like "Semantic Density"), designating every individual graphic and paragraph of text within a curriculum as a "learning object" can be prohibitively expensive. From an efficiency point of view, the decision regarding learning object granularity can be viewed as a trade-off between the possible benefits of reuse and the expense of cataloging. From an instructional point of view, alternatively, the decision between how much or how little to include in a learning object can be viewed as a problem of *scope*. While reality dictates that financial and other factors must be considered, if learning is to have its greatest chance of occurring, decisions regarding the scope of learning objects must also be made in an instructionally-grounded, principled manner.

Viewed in this way, the major issues facing would-be employers of learning objects (granularity and combination) turn out to be perhaps the two considerations known best to instructional designers: scope and sequence. There are a number of existing instructional design theories providing explicit scope and sequencing support that, while not intended to be, are applicable to learning objects. Reigeluth's Elaboration Theory (Reigeluth, 1999b), van Merriënboer's Four-Component Instructional Design model (van Merriënboer, 1997), and Gibbons and his colleagues' Work Model Synthesis approach (Gibbons et al., 1995) come to mind, among others. Wiley (2000) recently synthesized these and other instructional design theories into a learning object-specific instructional design theory, called Learning Object Design and Sequencing Theory.

Interest in the Learning Objects Idea

Even without a strong commitment to instructional principles on the part of standards bodies, there has been a considerable investment in the idea of learning objects. The IMS Project, which develops and promotes compliance with technical specifications for online learning, was until recently funded by memberships. The highest level of participation, "Contributing Member," was associated with an annual fee of $50,000, retroactive to the project's beginning. Over 30 vendors, universities, and other organizations belonged to this program (IMS, 2000b) whose membership list reads like a who's who of software developers and high-powered organizations: Microsoft, Oracle, Sun, Macromedia, Apple, IBM, UNISYS, the U.S. Department of Defense, the U.S. Department of Labor, the California State Universities, International Thomson Publishing, and Educational Testing Service, to name a few. The next level of membership down, the "Developers Network," has over 200 members, most of which are universities.

Additionally, a report released by the investment banking firm W. R. Hambrect contains more than the common predictions for the future of online learning—for example, the report says the online learning market will reach $11.5 billon by 2003 (Urdan & Weggen, 2000). As evidenced in this report, even brokers are talking about learning objects and encouraging investors to make sure that the e-learning companies they buy rely on this technology:

> [Online learning content] development cycles are predicted to shorten by 20% every year to two or three weeks by 2004. This imperative will drive more template-based designs and fewer custom graphics. Learning objects will be created in smaller chunks and reusable formats. As a consequence, the industry will become more efficient and competitive . . . We are convinced that the move to defined, open standards is crucial to the continuing successful adoption of e-learning, especially as it begins to transition beyond early adopters into the rapid growth phase of the market. Authoring tools will need to operate across different platforms and communicate with other tools used to build learning systems. Content and courseware must be reusable, interoperable, and easily manageable at many different levels of complexity throughout the online instructional environment. Enterprise learning systems have to accommodate numerous and varied learner requirements, needs, and objectives. Corporate customers need to be able to easily track content created by multiple content providers through one training management system and search vast local or distributed catalogs of content to identify learning objects or modules on a particular topic. The race for education technology standards is on. (Urdan & Weggen, 2000, p. 16)

Whether or not the learning object paradigm is grounded in the best instructional theory currently available, there can be little doubt that the United States and the world (the ARIADNE coalition has a similar list of European members) are about to be flooded with learning object-based tools. Microsoft has already released a toolset it touts as "the first commercial application of work being delivered by the Instructional Management System (IMS) Project" (Microsoft, 2000). Recognition, adoption, and the potential for future support for the learning objects idea is significant, and includes some of the biggest players in software, higher education, and even investment. Learning objects seem to be poised to become *the* instructional technology of online learning. However, technical standards and venture capital are not enough to promote learning. In order to promote learning, technology use should be guided by instructional principles.

The Post-Lego™ Learning Object

From its genesis, the learning object community has used metaphors to explain the learning objects concept to the uninitiated. Learning objects and their behaviors have been likened to Legos™, Lincoln Logs™, and other children's toys in a twofold effort to (1) communicate the basic learning objects idea, and (2) put a friendly, familiar face on a new instructional technology. These analogies continue to serve their intended purpose of giving those new to the idea an easy way of understanding what we are trying to do: that is, to create small pieces of instruction (Legos™) that can be assembled (stacked together) into some larger instructional structure (castle) and reused in other instructional structures (e.g., a spaceship). Unfortunately, this metaphor has taken on a life of its own. Instead of serving as a quick and dirty introduction to an area of work, this overly simplistic way of talking about things seems to have become the method of expression of choice for those working at the very edge of our field—even when speaking to each other. This point was driven home recently at a conference of a professional educational technology organization, where the Lego™ metaphor was referred to in every presentation on learning objects, even those on related topics such as metadata.

The problem with this ingraining of the Lego™ metaphor is the potential degree to which it could control and limit the way people think about learning objects. Consider the following properties of a Lego™ block:

- Any Lego™ block is combinable with any other Lego™ block.
- Lego™ blocks can be assembled in any manner you choose.
- Lego™ blocks are so fun and simple that even children can put them together.

This metaphor conveys the implicit assumption that these three properties are also properties of learning objects, needlessly restricting some people's views of what a learning object could potentially be and do. It is the author's belief that a system of learning objects with these three properties cannot produce anything more instructionally useful than Legos™ themselves can produce. If what results from the combination of learning objects is not instructionally useful, the combination has failed regardless of whatever else it may do. The recommendation of another metaphor seems necessary.

Instead of making something artificial (like a Lego™) the international symbol for learning objects, let us try something that occurs naturally, something about which we already know a great deal. This might jump start our understanding of learning objects and the way they are put together into instructionally meaningful units. Let us try the *atom* as a new metaphor.

An atom is a small *"thing"* that can be combined and recombined with other atoms to form larger *"things."* This seems to capture the major meaning conveyed by the Lego™ metaphor. However, the atomic metaphor departs from the Lego™ metaphor in some extremely significant ways:

- Not every atom is combinable with every other atom.
- Atoms can only be assembled in certain structures prescribed by their own internal structure.
- Some training is required in order to assemble atoms.

The implications of these differences are significant. The task of creating a useful, real-world learning object system is complicated enough without the requirement inherited from Lego™-type thinking that each and every learning object be compatible (or combinable) with every other learning object. This requirement is naïve and over-simplistic, and if enforced may keep learning objects from ever being instructionally useful.

The task of creating a useful learning object system is also hindered by the idea that learning objects need to be combinable in any manner one chooses. (According to *http://www.lego.com/,* six of the standard 2x4 Lego™ blocks can be combined in 102,981,500 ways.) This is what is currently touted as "theory neutrality." Software vendors and standards bodies describe their learning object-related work as being "instructional theory neutral." Were this the case, all would be well in learning object land. Problematically, a more accurate description of such products might be: "instructional theory agnostic," or in other words, *"We don't know if you're employing an instructional theory or not, and we don't care."* To reiterate, it is very likely that the combination of learning objects in the absence of any instructional theory will result in larger structures that fail to be instructionally useful.

The task of creating a useful learning object system seems to be stuck in the idea that anyone should be able to open a box of learning objects and have fun assembling them with their three-year-old. While the assembly of learning objects should not be made any more difficult than necessary, the notion that any system developed should be so simple that anyone could successfully use it without training seems overly restrictive. It prevents learning object-based instructional design research from reaching Simon's (1969) ideal of being "intellectually tough, analytic, formalizable, and teachable." It seems to prevent the field from making any cumulative, scientific progress.

Worse yet, the three Lego™ properties of learning objects point toward a possible trend: the tendency to treat learning objects like components of a knowledge management system (perhaps the term "information objects" would be more appropriate). While no two people may ever reach a common definition of instruction, most would agree that instruction is more than information, as Merrill is so fond of reminding us. This type of thinking manifests itself, for example, when people equate learning objects with "content objects" to the exclusion of "logic objects" and "application objects."

While pushing a metaphor is risky business, because all metaphors break down at some point, metaphors can be useful as properly contextualized educational exercises. So, if we take the atom as the new learning object metaphor, questions that once were difficult to answer become transparent. For example, take the question mentioned previously, *"What degree of granularity is the most appropriate for instructionally effective learning object combination?"* One answer can be found by examining the atom metaphor more closely.

It is commonly accepted that atoms are not the smallest bits of stuff in the universe. Atoms are, in fact, combinations of smaller bits (neutrons, protons, and electrons), which are combinations of smaller bits (baryons and mesons), which are combinations of even smaller bits (quarks, anti-quarks, and gluons). It is the particular manner in which the top-level bits (neutrons, protons, and electrons) are combined in an individual atom that determines which other atoms a particular atom can bond with. In other words, it is the structure of the combination that determines what other structures the combination is compatible with, much the way the shape of a puzzle piece determines where in the puzzle it must be placed.

Applying this to learning objects, apparently learning objects of a finer grain size (smaller bits) may be combined into structures that promote one learning object's combination with a second object, while the same structure prevents the first object's combination with a third. Suggested by the atom metaphor, the level of aggregation at which learning objects display this structural bonding characteristic is one answer to the question: *"What degree of granularity is the most appropriate for instructionally effective learning object combination?"* From a constructivist point of view which promotes learning within a rich context (Duffy & Cunningham, 1996), one interpretation could be that learning objects should be internally contextualized to a certain degree—a degree that promotes their contextualization (combination) with a closed set of other learning objects, while simultaneously preventing combination with other learning objects.

Atomic bonding is a fairly precise science, and although the theories that explain it are well understood (albeit probabilistically) at the macro-level of neutrons, protons, and electrons, atomic bonding is less well understood at the smaller bits level. While the smaller bits are an area of curiosity and investigation, this does not prevent fruitful work from occurring at the macro-level. Similarly, instructional design theories function probabilistically at a high level, while less is understood about the exact details of the smaller instructional bits. Here again, however, fruitful work continues to occur at the higher level while lower-level explorations are being carried out. It should be obvious at this point that a person without understanding of instructional design has no more hope of successfully combining learning objects into instruction than a person without an understanding of chemistry has of successfully forming a crystal. Rather than thinking about Legos™ or Lincoln Logs™, perhaps our minds should be pointed toward something like a "learning crystal," in which individual learning objects are combined into an instructionally useful, and to some degree *inherent*, structure.

The Role of Taxonomic Development

The discussion of learning object characteristics, such as sequence, scope, and structure, leads one to consider what different types of learning objects might exist. In other words, can types of learning objects be meaningfully differentiated? Taxonomic development has historically accompanied instructional design theories (Bloom, 1956; Gagné, Briggs, & Wager, 1992), and is recommended by Richey (1986) and Nelson (1998) in their instructional design theory development approaches. According to Richey (1986), the development of conceptual models such as taxonomies serves to "identify and organize the relevant variables; defining, explaining, and describing relationships among the variables" (pp. 26–27).

While object categorizations exist specific to particular instructional design theories, such as Merrill's sets of process, entity, and activity classifications (Merrill, Li, & Jones, 1991), a general learning object taxonomy compatible with multiple instructional design theories does not exist. The lack of such a broadly applicable taxonomy significantly hinders the application of the learning object to existing instructional design theories, as current practice has been to create theory-specific taxonomies to support each implementation (Merrill, Li, & Jones, 1991; L'Allier, 1998). This has considerably increased the time, resources, and effort necessary to employ learning objects. The rest of this chapter will present a general taxonomy of learning object types.

A Taxonomy of Learning Object Types

All learning objects have certain qualities. It is the difference in the degree to which (or manner in which) they exhibit these qualities that makes one type of learning object different from another. The following taxonomy differentiates between five learning object types. Examples of these five object types are given below, followed by the taxonomy, which explicates their differences and similarities.

- *Fundamental*—For example, a JPEG of a hand playing a chord on a piano keyboard.
- *Combined-closed*—For example, a video of a hand playing an arpeggiated chord on a piano keyboard with accompanying audio.
- *Combined-open*—For example, a Web page dynamically combining the previously mentioned JPEG and QuickTime file together with textual material "on the fly."

- *Generative-presentation*—For example, a JAVA applet capable of graphically generating a set of staff, clef, and notes, which then positions them appropriately to present a chord identification problem to a student.
- *Generative-instructional*—For example, an EXECUTE instructional transaction shell (Merrill, 1999), which both instructs and provides practice for any type of procedure, for example, the process of chord root, quality, and inversion identification.

Distinguishing between learning object types is a matter of identifying the manner in which the object to be classified exhibits certain characteristics. These characteristics are critical attributes and are stable across environmentally disparate instances (e.g., the properties remain the same whether or not the learning objects reside in a digital library).

Table 1 presents this taxonomy. The purpose of the taxonomy is to differentiate possible types of learning objects available *for use in instructional design*. This taxonomy is not exhaustive in that it includes only learning object types that facilitate high degrees of reuse. Other types of learning objects that hamper or practically prevent reuse (e.g., an entire digital textbook created in a format that prevents any of the individual media from being reused outside of the textbook context), have been purposefully excluded. Finally, this taxonomy's value characteristics (such as High, Medium, and Low) are purposefully fuzzy, since the taxonomy is meant to facilitate inter-object comparison, and not to provide independent metrics for classifying learning objects out of context (such as file size in kilobytes). Related to Table 1, what follows is a more in-depth discussion of each of the characteristics of learning objects and a discussion of the learning object types themselves.

   Learning object characteristics. The characteristics in Table 1 are described below.

- *Number of elements combined*—Describes the number of individual elements (such as video clips, images, etc.) combined in order to make the learning object.
- *Type of elements contained*—Describes the type of learning objects that may be combined to form a new learning object.
- *Reusable component objects*—Describes whether or not a learning object's constituent objects may be individually accessed and reused in new learning contexts.
- *Common function*—Describes the manner in which the learning object type is generally used.
- *Extra-object dependence*—Describes whether the learning object needs information (such as location on the network) about learning objects other than itself.
- *Type of logic contained in object*—Describes the common function of algorithms and procedures within the learning object.

Table 1. Preliminary Taxonomy of Learning Object Types

Learning Object Characteristic	Fundamental Learning Object	Combined-Closed Learning Object	Combined-Open Learning Object	Generative-Presentation Learning Object	Generative-Instructional Learning Object
Number of elements combined	One	Few	Many	Few - Many	Few - Many
Type of elements contained	Single	Single, Combined-Closed	All	Single, Combined-Closed, Generative-Presentation	Single, Combined-Closed, Generative-Presentation
Reusable component objects	(Not applicable)	No	Yes	Yes / No	Yes / No
Common function	Exhibit, display	Pre-designed instruction or practice	Pre-designed instruction and/or practice	Exhibit, display	Computer-generated instruction and/or practice
Extra-object dependence	No	No	Yes	Yes / No	Yes
Type of logic contained in object	(Not applicable)	None, or answer sheet-based item scoring	None, or domain-specific instructional & assessment strategies	Domain-specific presentation strategies	Domain-independent presentation, instruction, & assessment strategies
Potential for inter-contextual reuse	High	Medium	Low	Medium	High
Potential for intra-contextual reuse	Low	Low	Medium	High	High

- *Potential for inter-contextual reuse*—Describes the number of different learning contexts in which the learning object might be used (that is, the object's potential for reuse in different content areas or domains).

- *Potential for intra-contextual reuse*—Describes the number of times the learning object might be reused within the same content area or domain.

Learning object type definitions. The five types of learning objects have been exemplified and their characteristics have been described. While the creation of strict definitions for these types is an ongoing effort, the author's current best thinking with regard to definitions of each type is captured below.

- *Fundamental*—An individual digital resource uncombined with any other, the fundamental learning object is generally a visual (or other) aid that serves an exhibit or example function (Wiley & Nelson, 1998).

- *Combined-closed*—A small number of digital resources combined at design time by the learning object's creator, whose constituent learning objects are not individually accessible for reuse (recoverable) from the combined-closed learning object itself. A video clip exemplifies this definition, as still images and an audio track are combined in a manner which renders these constituent pieces unrecoverable (or at least difficult to recover). The combined-closed learning object may contain limited logic (e.g., the ability to perform answer sheet-referenced item scoring) but should not contain complex internal logic (e.g., the capacity to intelligently grade a set of item forms or case types), since this valuable capability would not be reusable with other learning objects. Combined-closed learning objects are generally single purpose—they provide either instruction or practice.

- *Combined-open*—A larger number of digital resources combined by a computer in real-time when a request for the object is made, whose constituent learning objects are directly accessible for reuse (recoverable) from the combined-open object. A Web page exemplifies this definition, as its component images, video clips, text, and other media exist in reusable format and are combined into a learning object at request-time. Combined-open learning objects frequently combine related instruction and practice, providing combined-closed and fundamental objects in order to create a complete instructional unit.

- *Generative-presentation*—Logic and structure for combining or generating and combining lower-level learning objects (fundamental and combined-closed types). Generative-presentation learning objects can either draw on network-accessible objects and combine them, or generate (e.g., draw) objects and combine them to create presentations for use in reference, instruction, practice, and testing.(Generative-presentation learning objects must be able to pass messages to other objects with assessment logic when used in practice or testing.) While generative-presentation learning objects have high intra-contextual reusability (they can be used over and over again in similar contexts), they have relatively low inter-contextual reusability (use in domains other than that for which they were designed).

- *Generative-instructional*—Logic and structure for combining learning objects (fundamental, combined-closed types, and generative-presentation) and evaluating student interactions with those combinations, created to support the instantiation of abstract instructional strategies (such as "remember and perform a series of steps"). The transaction shells of Merrill's Instructional Transaction Theory (Merrill, 1999) would be classified as generative-instructional learning objects. The generative-instructional learning object is high in both intra-contextual and inter-contextual reusability.

Connecting Learning Objects to Instructional Design Theory

The main theme of this chapter has been that instructional design theory must be incorporated in any learning object implementation that aspires to facilitate learning. The taxonomy of learning object types presented in this chapter is instructional design theory-neutral, making it compatible with practically any instructional design theory. (The taxonomy's explicit references to domain-dependent and domain-independent presentation, instruction, and assessment logic, which must come from somewhere, keep it from being instructional theory agnostic.)

Wiley (2000) posited and presented three components of a successful learning object implementation: an instructional design theory, a learning object taxonomy, and "prescriptive linking material" that connects instructional design theory to taxonomy, providing such guidance as "for this type of learning goal, use this type of learning object." In addition to providing a worked example of this process, Wiley (2000) also presented design guidelines for the five learning object types.

Previously, any person or organization who wanted to employ learning objects in their instructional design and delivery was required to either create their own taxonomy of learning object types or work in an *ad hoc,* frequently higgledy-piggledy manner. Taxonomy development requires significant effort above and beyond normal instructional design and development, and is certainly one cause of the current poverty of instructionally-grounded practical applications of learning objects. However, any instructional designer may potentially connect the instructional design theory of their choice to the theory-neutral taxonomy presented in this chapter via the creation of "prescriptive linking material," a considerably simpler exercise than the creation of a new taxonomy. It is the author's desire that the development of the learning object taxonomy presented herein will (1) speed the practical adoption of the learning object approach; (2) allow the simplified application of any instructional design theory to the learning object approach; and (3) provide a common ground for future research on the instructional technology called "learning objects." Over time, application of the "prescriptive linking material" approach and scrutiny of the taxonomy will help both improve significantly.

Conclusion

Like any other instructional technology, learning objects must partici- pate in a principled partnership with instructional design theory if they are to succeed in facilitating learning. This chapter has presented a possible partnership structure. If learning objects ever live up to their press and provide the founda- tion for an adaptive, generative, scalable learning architecture, teaching and learn- ing as we know them are certain to be revolutionized. However, this revolution will never occur unless more voices speak out regarding the explicitly instructional use of learning objects—the automated or by-hand spatial or temporal juxtapo- sition of learning objects intended to facilitate learning. These voices must pene- trate the din of metadata, data interchange protocol, tool/agent communication, and other technical standards conversations. While instructional design theory may not be as "sexy" as bleeding-edge technology, there must be concentrated effort made to understand the instructional issues inherent in the learning objects notion. The potential of learning objects as an instructional technology is great, but will never be realized without a balanced effort in technology and instruc- tional design areas. *We need more theorists.*

Acknowledgments

The development of this chapter was funded in part by NSF grant #DUE-0085855 and the Edumetrics Institute. *You may reach David Wiley at: Utah State University, Emma Eccles Jones Education 227, Logan, UT 84322-2830, (435) 797-7562; wiley@cc.usu.edu.*

References

ADL. (2000). *Advanced distributed learning network.* Web site [online]. Available: http://www.adlnet.org/

ALI. (2000). *Apple learning interchange.* Web site [online]. Available: http://ali.apple.com/

ARIADNE. (2000). *Alliance of remote instructional authoring and distribution networks for Europe.* Web site [online]. Available: http://ariadne.unil.ch/

Asymetrix. (2000). *Customer case study: Venturist, Inc.* [online]. Available: http://www.asymetrix.com/solutions/casestudies/venturist.html

Bloom, B. S. (1956). *Taxonomy of educational objectives, handbook 1: Cognitive domain.* New York: Longmans Green.

Dahl, O. J., & Nygaard, K. (1966). SIMULA - An algol based simulation language. *Communications of the ACM, 9* (9), p. 671–678.

Dijkstra, S., Seel, N., Schott, F., & Tennyson, R. (Eds.). (1997). *Instructional design: International perspectives.* Vol. 2. Mahwah, NJ: Lawrence Erlbaum Associates.

Duffy, T. M., & Cunningham, D. J. (1996). Constructivism: Implications for the design and delivery of instruction. In D. H. Jonassen (Ed.), *Handbook of research for educational communications and technology* (p. 170–198). New York: Simon & Schuster/Macmillan.

EOE. (2000). *Educational objects economy.* Web site [online]. Available: http://www.eoe.org/eoe.htm

ESCOT. (2000). *Educational software components of tomorrow.* Web site [online]. Available: http://www.escot.org/

Gagné, R., Briggs, L., & Wager, W. (1992). *Principles of instructional design* (4th ed.). Fort Worth, TX: HBJ College.

Gibbons, A. S., Bunderson, C.V., Olsen, J. B., & Rogers, J. (1995). Work models: Still beyond instructional objectives. *Machine-Mediated Learning, 5*(3&4), 221-236.

Gibbons, A. S., Nelson, J., & Richards, R. (2002). The nature and origin of instructional objects. In D. A. Wiley (Ed.), *The instructional use of learning objects.* Bloomington, IN: Agency for Instructional Technology and Association for Educational Communications and Technology.

Hodgins, Wayne. (2000). *Into the future* [online]. Available: http://www.learnativity.com/download/MP7.PDF

IMS. (2000-a). *Instructional management systems project.* Web site [online]. Available: http://imsproject.org/

IMS. (2000-b). *Instructional management systems project.* Web site [online]. Available: http://imsproject.org/imMembers.html

Internet Newsroom. (1999). *Internet growing too fast for search engines* [online]. Available: http://www.editors-service.com/articlearchive/search99.html

L'Allier, J. J. (1998). *NETg's precision skilling: The linking of occupational skills descriptors to training interventions* [online]. Available: http://www.netg.com/research/pskillpaper.htm

LOM. (2000). *LOM working draft v4.1* [online]. Available: http://ltsc.ieee.org/doc/wg12/LOMv4.1.htm

LTSC. (2000a). *Learning technology standards committee.* Web site [online]. Available: http://ltsc.ieee.org/

LTSC. (2000b). *IEEE standards board: Project authorization request (PAR) form* [online]. Available: http://ltsc.ieee.org/par-lo.htm

MERLOT. (2000). *Multimedia educational resource for learning and online teaching* Web site [online]. Available: http://www.merlot.org/

Merrill, M. D. (1999). Instructional transaction theory (ITT): Instructional design based on knowledge objects. In C. M. Reigeluth (Ed.), *Instructional design theories and models: A new paradigm of instructional theory* (pp. 397–424). Hillsdale, NJ: Lawrence Erlbaum Associates.

Merrill, M. D., Li, Z., & Jones, M. (1991). Instructional transaction theory: An introduction. *Educational Technology, 31*(6), 7–12.

Microsoft. (2000). *Resources: Learning resource interchange* [online]. Available: http://www.microsoft.com/eLearn/resources/LRN/

Nelson, L. M. (1998). *Collaborative problem solving: An instructional theory for learning through small group interaction.* Unpublished doctoral dissertation, Indiana University.

Reigeluth, C. M. (1983). Instructional design: What is it and why is it? In C. M. Reigeluth (Ed.), *Instructional design theories and models: An overview of their current status* (pp. 3–36). Hillsdale, NJ: Lawrence Erlbaum Associates.

Reigeluth, C. M. (1999a). The elaboration theory: Guidance for scope and sequence decisions. In C. M. Reigeluth (Ed.), *Instructional design theories and models: A new paradigm of instructional theory* (pp. 425–453). Hillsdale, NJ: Lawrence Erlbaum Associates.

Reigeluth, C. M. (1999b). What is instructional design theory and how is it changing? In C. M. Reigeluth (Ed.), *Instructional design theories and models: A new paradigm of instructional theory* (pp. 5–29). Hillsdale, NJ: Lawrence Erlbaum Associates.

Reigeluth, C. M., & Frick, T. W. (1999). Formative research: A methodology for creating and improving design theories. In C. M. Reigeluth (Ed.), *Instructional design theories and models: A new paradigm of instructional theory* (pp. 633–651). Hillsdale, NJ: Lawrence Erlbaum Associates.

Reigeluth, C. M., & Nelson, L. M. (1997). A new paradigm of ISD? In R. C. Branch & B. B. Minor (Eds.), *Educational media and technology yearbook* (Vol. 22, pp. 24–35). Englewood, CO: Libraries Unlimited.

Richey, R. C. (1986). *The theoretical and conceptual bases of instructional design.* London: Kogan Page.

Simon, H. A. (1969). *Sciences of the artificial.* Cambridge, MA: MIT Press.

Snelbecker, G. E. (1974). *Learning theory, instructional theory, and psychoeducational theory.* New York: McGraw-Hill.

Snow, R. E. (1971). Theory construction for research on teaching. In R. M. W. Travers (Ed.), *Second handbook of research on teaching*. Chicago: Rand McNally.

Tennyson, R., Schott, F., Seel, N., & Dijkstra, S. (Eds.). (1997). *Instructional design: International perspectives*. Vol. 1. Mahwah, NJ: Lawrence Erlbaum Associates.

Urdan, T. A., & Weggen, C. C. (2000). *Corporate e-learning: Exploring a new frontier* [online]. Available: http://wrhambrecht.com/research/coverage/elearning/ir/ir_explore.pdf

van Merriënboer, J. J. G. (1997). *Training complex cognitive skills: A four-component instructional design model for technical training*. Englewood Cliffs, NJ: Educational Technology Publications.

Wiley, D. A. (1999). *Learning objects and the new CAI: So what do I do with a learning object?* [online]. Available: http://wiley.ed.usu.edu/docs/instruct-arch.pdf

Wiley, D. A. (2000). *Learning object design and sequencing theory*. Unpublished doctoral dissertation, Brigham Young University. Available: http://davidwiley.com/papers/dissertation/dissertation.pdf

Wiley, D. A., & Nelson, L. M. (1998). *The fundamental object* [online]. Available: http://wiley.ed.usu.edu/docs/fundamental.html

Wiley, D. A., South, J. B., Bassett, J., Nelson, L. M., Seawright, L. L., Peterson, T., & Monson, D. W. (1999). Three common properties of efficient online instructional support systems. *The ALN Magazine, 3*(2) [online]. Available: http://www.aln.org/alnweb/magazine/Vol3_issue2/wiley.htm

The Nature and Origin of Instructional Objects[1]

Andrew S. Gibbons & Jon Nelson (Utah State University) &
Robert Richards (Idaho National Engineering and Environmental Laboratory)

Introduction

This chapter examines the nature and origin of a construct we term the instructional object. Rather than being a single definable object, it is a complex and multifaceted emerging technological construct—one piece of a larger technological puzzle. The general outlines of the puzzle piece are taking shape concurrently in the several disciplines from which the practices of instructional technology are derived—computer science, information technology, intelligent tutoring systems, and instructional psychology. The terminology used to describe this new idea reflects its multiple origins, its diverse motivations, and its newness. In the literature, what we will refer to as the "instructional object" is termed variously "instructional object," "educational object," "learning object," "knowledge object," "intelligent object," and "data object." Our work is most heavily influenced by the work of Spohrer and his associates on educational object economies (Spohrer, Sumner, & Shum, 1998).

Much has been written about instructional objects but little about how objects originate. This chapter examines instructional objects in the context of a complex instructional design space. We propose the dimensions of this space and to use that as a background for relating together the multiple definitions of the instructional object. We then try to situate the new construct within a context of design activities that differs from traditional design process views. We finish by describing criteria and methodology guidelines for generating objects.

As the instructional object continues to take on definition and proportions, and as work in many fields converges, we believe instructional objects in some form will become a major factor in the growth and proliferation of computer-based instruction and performance-support technology.

Analysis and Instructional Objects

The long-range purpose of this research is to consolidate a theory of instructional design that uses the "model" as a central design construct. Such a base will support systematic future research into product varieties, product architectures, production efficiencies, and specialized productivity tools. By doing so, we hope to link the practice of instructional designers with new design constructs implied by current views of instruction that are shifting toward student-centered, situated, problem-based, and model-centered experiences—ones that are also shaped by the demands of scaling and production efficiency.

We believe that this discussion is timely. Even as the instructional use of the World Wide Web is being promoted with increasing urgency, there are serious questions concerning whether it is fully provided with design concepts, architectures, and tools that fit it for service as a channel for instructing rather than merely informing (Fairweather & Gibbons, 2000). At the same time, instructional design theorists are questioning the assumptions underlying existing design methodologies that are proving brittle in the face of challenges posed by the newer instructional modes (Gordon & Zemke, 2000; Reigeluth, 1999; Edmonds, Branch, & Mukherjee, 1994; Rowland, 1993). The instructional object has been proposed within different specialty fields for its productivity benefits, for its standardization benefits, and as a means of making design accessible to a growing army of untrained developers. As the design process evolves a theoretic base, we feel it important to ask how that theory base can be related to instructional objects.

Standards and CBI Technology

The industry that focuses on the design, development, and delivery of computerized instruction is currently undergoing a period of standard-setting focused on the distribution of instructional experiences over the Internet and World Wide Web. The instructional object—indexed by metadata—has great potential as a common building block for a diverse range of technology-based instructional products. Massive efforts involving hundreds of practitioners, suppliers, and consumers are contributing to object standards that will allow this building block to become the basic unit of commerce in instruction and performance support (Hill, 1998).

It is hard to resist comparing these events with events in the history of the steel-making technology. When Frederick Taylor showed in the opening years of the twentieth century that reliable recipes for steel could be placed into the hands of relatively untrained furnace operators (Misa, 1995), an army of new and less-trained but fully competent furnace operators began to take over the mills. Greater quantities of steel (industrial scale) could be produced at more precisely controlled levels of quality. Three key events in the expansion of steel making involved epochs of standard-setting carried out by three different standards coalitions. Over several decades, these coalitions arbitrated the measures of product quality for rail steel, structural steel, and automotive steel, respectively. With each new standard, the industry progressed and expanded. This in turn led to even more rapid expansion and diversification of the use of steel in other products.

Steel standards paved the way for: (1) the achievement of more precise and predictable control over steel manufacturing processes; (2) a standard-based product that could be tailored to the needs of the user; and (3) the ability to scale production to industrial proportions using the new processes (Misa, 1995). Without these developments, steel quality would still be highly variable, steel products would have a much narrower range, and steel making would still be essentially an idiosyncratic craft practiced by highly trained and apprenticed furnace operators.

The Nature of Instructional Objects

We define instructional objects in a later section of this chapter by relating them to an architecture for model-centered instructional products. As we use the term in this chapter, instructional objects refer to any element of that architecture that can be independently drawn into a momentary assembly in order to create an instructional event. Instructional objects can include problem environments, interactive models, instructional problems or problem sets, instructional function modules, modular routines for instructional augmentation (coaching, feedback, etc.), instructional message elements, modular routines for representation of information, or logic modules related to instructional purposes (management, recording, selecting, etc.).

The literature in a number of disciplines that contribute to instructional technology describes objects that perform some subset of the functions required of the different kinds of instructional objects:

- objects involved in database structuring
- objects for the storage of expert system knowledge
- objects for document format control
- objects used for development process control
- modular, portable expert tutors
- objects representing computer logic modules for use by non-programmers
- objects for machine discovery of knowledge
- objects for instructional design
- objects containing informational or message content
- objects for knowledge capture
- objects that support decision making
- objects for data management

All of these types of objects and more are needed to implement instruction through the real-time assembly of objects. Gerard (1969) in a surprisingly visionary statement early in the history of computer-based instruction describes how "curricular units can be made smaller and combined, like standardized Meccano [mechanical building set] parts, into a great variety of particular programs custom-made for each learner" (pp. 29–30). Thirty years later, the value and practicality of this idea is becoming apparent.

Basic Issues

To set the stage for the discussion of instructional object origins, it is essential to touch briefly on two issues related generally to the design and development of technology-based instruction:

- the goals of computerized instruction: adaptivity, generativity, and scalability;
- the structure of the technological design space.

The Goals of Computerized Instruction: Adaptivity, Generativity, and Scalability

From the earliest days of computer-based instruction as a technology, the goal has clearly been to create instruction that was: (1) *adaptive* to the individual, (2) *generative* rather than pre-composed, and (3) *scalable* to industrial production levels without proportional increases in cost.

Nowhere are these ideals more clearly stated than in *Computer-Assisted Instruction: A Book of Readings* (1969a), a ground-breaking and in many ways still-current volume edited by Atkinson and Wilson. Virtually all of the chapters selected for the book build on the three themes: adaptivity, generativity, and scalability.

Adaptivity. Atkinson and Wilson credit the rapid rate of growth (before 1969) in CAI in part "to the rich and intriguing potential of computer-assisted instruction for answering today's most pressing need in education—the individualization of instruction" (Atkinson & Wilson, 1969b, p. 3). They distinguish CAI that is adaptive from that which is not, attributing the difference to "response sensitive strategy." Suppes (1969) foresees "a kind of individualized instruction once possible only for a few members of the aristocracy" that can "be made available to all students at all levels of abilities" (p. 41). This durable argument is being used currently to promote instructional object standards (Graves, 1994).

Suppes (1969) describes how computers will "free students from the drudgery of doing exactly similar tasks unadjusted and untailored to their individual needs" (p. 47). Stolurow (1969), describing models of teaching, explains:

[A model of teaching] . . . must be cybernetic, or response-sensitive, if it is adaptive. A model for adaptive, or personalized, instruction specifies a set of response-dependent rules to be used by a teacher, or a teaching system, in making decisions about the nature of the subsequent events to be used in teaching a student. (pp. 69–70)

He introduces an "ideographic" instructional model that designs for "possibilities" rather than plans for specific paths: "we need ways to describe the alternatives and we need to identify useful variables" (p. 78). Stolurow makes the important distinction "between branching and contingency or response-produced organization [of instruction]" (p. 79). These and many other things that could be cited from the Atkinson and Wilson volume make it clear that adaptivity was a closely-held early goal of computer-based instruction. Incidentally, these and other statements in the book make it clear that CAI was not envisioned by these pioneers as simply computerized programmed instruction.

Generativity. Generativity refers to the ability of computerized instruction to create instructional messages and interactions by combining primitive message and interaction elements rather than by storing pre-composed messages and interaction logics. The contributors to Atkinson and Wilson describe mainly pre-composed instructional forms because in the early days of CAI there were no tools to support generativity, but many Atkinson and Wilson paper authors emphasize future tooling for generativity.

Suppes (1969), who later produced math problem generation tools himself, describes three levels of interaction between students and instructional programs, all of them subject to some degree of generativity: (1) individualized drill-and-practice, (2) tutorial systems that "approximate the interaction a patient tutor would have with an individual student," and (3) dialogue systems "permitting the student to conduct a genuine dialogue with the computer" (pp. 42–44).

Silberman (1969) describes the use of the computer to generate practice exercises (p. 53). Stolurow, describing the instructional rules of an adaptive system said:

These rules [for controlling presentation of information, posing of a problem, acceptance of a response, judging the response, and giving feedback] also can be called organizing rules; they are the rules of an instructional grammar. Eventually we should develop generative grammars for instruction. (p. 76)

Scalability. The authors of the Atkinson and Wilson volume were sensitive to the (then) highly visible costs of computer-assisted instruction. Their solutions to scalability were projections of lower computer costs, expectations for larger multi-terminal systems, and calculations of product cost spread over large numbers of users. The connective and distributive technology of the day was the time-shared monolithic centralized mainframe system and (then) high-cost and low-quality telephone lines.

The goals of *adaptivity, generativity,* and *scalability* that prevailed in 1969 are still key targets. These goals were adopted by researchers in intelligent tutoring systems, and they are clearly evident in the writings of that group of researchers, especially in the occasional summaries of the field and its evolving theory and method (Wenger, 1987; Psotka, Massey, & Mutter, 1988; Poulson & Richardson, 1988; Burns, Parlett, & Redfield, 1991; Noor, 1999).

Burns and Parlett (1991) tell us to, "Make no mistake. ITSs are trying to achieve one-on-one instruction, and therein lies the complexity and the necessary flexibility of any potentially honest ITS design."

Today the tutorial systems and dialogue systems described by Suppes still represent cutting edge goals for intelligent tutoring systems. Generativity is still clearly a part of the basic game plan. This is evident in the goals of the Department of Defense Advanced Distributed Learning System Initiative (Advanced Distributed Learning Initiative, no date). As Burns and Parlett (1991) explain,

> ITS designers have set up their own holy grail. The grail is, as you might have guessed, the capability for a large-scale, multiuser knowledge base to generate coherent definitions and explanations. It goes without saying that if a student has a reasonable question, then an ITS should have an answer. (p. 6)

The personal computer, the network, and rapidly proliferating communications connectivity have become the standard. Because of this, our focus on scalability has shifted from delivery costs to development costs. One of the forces behind the instructional objects phenomenon is the prospect of lowering product costs through a number of mechanisms: reusability, standardized connectivity, modularity to optimize transmission from central stores, and standardized manufacture.

The Structure of the Technological Design Space: The Convergence Zone

Technologies often develop first as *ad hoc* systems of practice that later must be grounded in technological theory and form a mutually contributory exchange with scientific theory. Instructional technology is seeking its theoretical foundations more vigorously now than ever before (Merrill, 1994; Reigeluth, 1999; Hannafin et al., 1997). We believe that several clues to developing a more robust theoretical basis for instructional technology can come from studying technology as a type of knowledge-seeking activity and from studying the technological process.

Technology consists of human work accomplished within a "convergence zone" where conceptual artifacts (designed structures, construct architectures) are given specific form with materials, information, and force-information transfer mechanisms. In this convergence zone, conceptual artifacts are linked with material or event artifacts that express a specific intention. In a discussion of the World Wide Web and Model-Centered Instruction, Gibbons and his associates (Gibbons, Lawless, Anderson, & Duffin, 2000) describe this convergence zone in terms of conceptual instructional constructs being realized using the programming constructs of a particular software tool.

> This is the place where the designer's abstract instructional constructs and the concrete logic constructs supplied by the development tool come together to produce an actual product. At this point, the abstract event constructs are given expression—if possible—by the constructs supplied by the development tool.

Burns and Parlett (1991) provide a glimpse of this boundary world:

> Proposed architectures for representing teaching knowledge in ITSs can be described in terms of how knowledge is understood by experts and how it can be represented by programmers in sets of domain-independent tutoring strategies. (pp. 5–6)

Herbert Simon, in *Sciences of the Artificial,* describes this convergence zone between the abstract world and the concrete world as a key to understanding technological activity in general:

> I have shown that a science of artificial phenomena is always in imminent danger of dissolving and vanishing. The peculiar properties of the artifact lie on the thin interface between the natural laws within and the natural laws without. What can we say about it? What is there to study besides the boundary sciences—those that govern the means and the task environment?

> The artificial world is centered precisely on this interface between the outer and inner environments; it is concerned with attaining goals by adapting the former to the latter. The proper study of those who are concerned with the artificial is the way in which that adaptation of means to environments is brought about—and central to that is the process of design itself. The professional schools will reassume their professional responsibilities just to the degree that they can discover a science of design, a body of intellectually tough, analytic, partly formalizable, partly empirical, teachable doctrine about the design process. (pp. 131–132)

Simon emphasizes the fragility of the connections across the interface between conceptual and real: the interface is difficult to imagine in the abstract, and it is not surprising that many designers—especially novice ones—focus their attention mainly on the material result of designing rather than on its conceptual precursors. In fact, as we explain in a later section of this chapter, the focus of designers on a particular set of design constructs allows classification of designers into a number of broad classes.

Dimensions of the Design Space

Technologists who succeed in visualizing this conceptual-material boundary can be baffled by its complexity. Designs are never the simple, unitary conceptions that we describe in textbook terms. Instead, they are multilayered constructions of mechanism and functionality whose interconnections require several transformational links to reach across the conceptual-material boundary. Links and layers both must articulate in designs such that interference between layers is minimized and the future adaptability of the artifact to changing conditions is maximized—the factor that gives the artifact survivability. Automated design systems provide principled guidance for those decisions that cannot be automated and default values for those that can.

Brand (1994) describes the principle of layering in designs by describing the layered design of building—in what he calls the "6-S" sequence:

- *Site*—This is the geographical setting, the urban location, and the legally defined lot, whose boundaries and context outlast generations of ephemeral buildings. "Site is eternal, " Duffy agrees.

- *Structure*—The foundation and load-bearing elements are perilous and expensive to change, so people don't. These are the buildings. Structural life ranges from 30 to 300 years (but few buildings make it past 60, for other reasons).

- *Skin*—Exterior surfaces now change every 20 years or so, to keep with fashion and technology, or for wholesale repair. Recent focus on energy costs has led to reengineered *skins* that are air-tight and better insulated.

- *Services*—These are the working guts of a building: communications wiring, electrical wiring, plumbing, sprinkler system, HVAC (heating, ventilating, air conditioning), and moving parts like elevators and escalators. They wear out or obsolesce every 7 to 15 years. Many buildings are demolished early if their outdated systems are too deeply embedded to replace easily.

- *Space Plan*—The interior layout—where walls, ceilings, floors, and doors go. Turbulent commercial space can change every three years or so; exceptionally quiet homes might wait 30 years.

- *Stuff*—Chairs, desks, phones, pictures, kitchen appliances, lamps, hair brushes; all the things that twitch around daily to monthly. Furniture is called *mobilia* in Italian for good reason. (p. 13)

The aging of layers at different rates suggests that layers should be designed to "slip" past each other so that when they require change, update, renewal, or revision on different time cycles that can be accomplished without razing the whole structure. Brand relates the essential interconnections between these layers to the longevity of the artifact:

> A design imperative emerges. An adaptive building has to allow slippage between the differently-paced systems of Site, Structure, Skin, Services, Space plan, and Stuff. Otherwise the slow systems block the flow of the quick ones, and the quick ones tear up the slow ones with their constant change. Embedding the systems together may look efficient at first, but over time it is the opposite, and destructive as well. (p. 20)

Brand explains that "the 6-S sequence is precisely followed in both design and construction." Each layer of a design presents a separate design sub-problem to the designer. Layers must possess their own design integrity, but the structures of each layer must articulate with the structures of the other layers.

Figure 1 suggests the degree of multi-staging and multi-layering at Simon's technology-producing "interface" by illustrating:

1. design layers (the vertical dimension of the figure) as they might be defined for instructional designers;
2. the progressive sequence of integrations or construct-to-construct links (the horizontal dimension of the figure) through which the original conception of a design emerges into an actual artifact; and
3. the interconnections (angled lines) between the layers of a design show that each layer can be articulated with every other layer.

As a design progresses from the conceptual stage to the real artifact stage, the integration of the layers increases to the point where abstract design and concrete product layers can barely be distinguished. Thus the structure and service layers of a building disappear behind covering walls and exterior skin; thus the model and media-logic layers of an instructional artifact disappear behind the strategy and surface representation layers. Since the tangible surface layers of a design are what we experience, it is not surprising that new designers fail to see the multiple layers of structure that are actually designed. This is typical with building designs, and it is especially typical with instructional designs.

Instructional designers can be classified generally in terms of the constructs they envision within a design—the constructs therefore that they are most liable to use to create the central structures of their designs:

- *Media*-centric designers tend to concentrate on media-related constructs and their arrangement (e.g., manuals, pages, cuts, transitions, synchronizations, etc.).

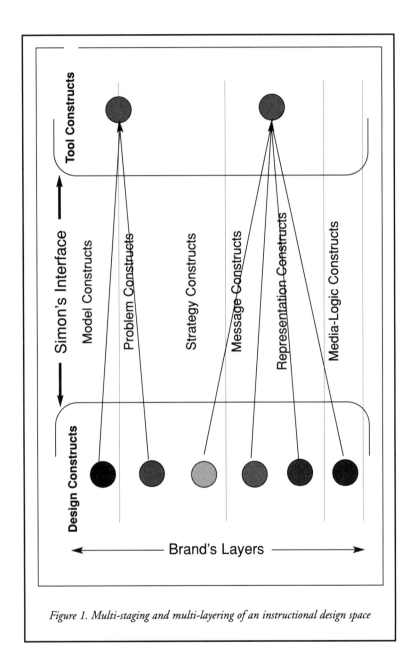

Figure 1. Multi-staging and multi-layering of an instructional design space

- *Message*-centric designers tend to constructs related to "telling" the instructional message in a way that supports its rapid uptake and integration with prior knowledge (e.g., analogy, advance organizer, use of conceptual figures, dramatization, etc.).

- *Strategy*-centric designers prefer to place structures and sequences of strategic elements at the center of their designs (e.g., message componentization, interaction patterns, interaction types, etc.).

- *Model*-centric designers tend to build their designs around central, interactive models of environments, cause-effect systems, and performance expertise and supplement them with focusing problems and instructional augmentations.

Designers tend to move through these "centrisms" as personal experience accumulates and the value of new, less visible, subtler constructs becomes apparent to them. With each move to a new viewpoint the designer gains the use of the new design constructs without giving up the old ones, so this change results in the accumulation of fundamental design building blocks.

When instructional objects are used in design, they are constructs within Simon's design space. They can theoretically be media, message, strategy, or model objects or any combination of these interacting across several layers. They can represent a functional instructional product having a many-layered design or a single element that can be integrated at the time of instruction into products to supply some modular functionality in a cooperative way.

The Origin of Instructional Objects

Prior to the notion of instructional objects, descriptions of the instructional design process have been couched in the terminology of other kinds of constructs considered to be produced at some point during design.

Figure 2 depicts the traditional ISD process in relation to Simon's technology interface. Design is typically seen as deriving from each other, in succession, structural elements that permit requirements tracing of design elements back to a foundation of analysis elements. In Figure 2 this chain of analysis and design constructs begins with tasks obtained through task analysis that are used as a base for deriving objectives, which are in turn used as a base for deriving work models (including instructional events, see Gibbons, Bunderson, Olsen, & Robertson, 1995).

The "Ts" on the diagram indicate rule-guided transformations using the base construct to obtain a resultant construct. Links not marked with a "T" consist of attaching qualities or properties to an already-existing construct. The diagram could be more detailed, but in its present form it illustrates how a progression of analysis constructs (tasks, objectives) eventually links forward to design constructs (work models, instructional events) which constitute the design. At

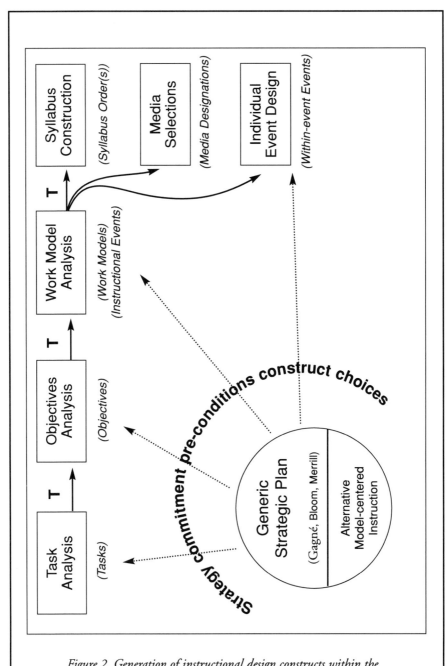

*Figure 2. Generation of instructional design constructs within the
abstract side of the design space, showing the preconditioning
of constructs by instructional assumptions*

this point designers bridge across Simon's gap by linking the constructs that make up the design with media and tool constructs (logic structures, media structures, representations, concrete objects).

Conceptions of the design process are idiosyncratic to designers. Different designers link different constructs through different derivational chains. The goal of Figure 2 is to show how a typical designer view can be related to several generations of abstract constructs on one side of Simon's gap that link from the abstract realm into a concrete realm whose constructs are traceable. A different version of the design process would produce a diagram similar to Figure 2 that linked different elements. All of Figure 2 fits within the leftmost third of Figure 1, so all of the structures shown in Figure 2 are abstract. Development steps that build the bridge to tool and media constructs may give rise to directly corresponding media and tool objects through a process called "alignment" (see Duffin & Gibbons, in preparation).

Regardless of the specific constructs used by a designer, their mapping across Simon's technology gap can be accomplished in the same manner. Thus, Simon's description of this interface describes an underlying design space, and this allows design methodologies to be compared—on the basis of the constructual elements used in linkages on both sides of the gap. Instructional objects have constructual existence on both sides: they represent a particular alignment of abstract design, abstract media, and concrete tool constructs.

The Influence of Instructional Views on Design Constructs

Figure 2 also depicts how the designer's preconceptions regarding instructional methods pre-condition the choice of analysis and design constructs derived on the left side of the gap. A designer subscribing to behavioral principles will derive analysis elements consisting of operant chains and individual operant units. These will link forward to produce a traceable lineage of compatible derived elements. One inclined toward structured strategic approaches to instruction will derive elements that correspond to the taxonomy underlying the particular strategic viewpoint. A Gagné advocate will produce tasks and objectives that correspond with Gagné's learning types; a Bloom advocate will produce analysis units that correspond with Bloom's. Merrill's transaction types (Merrill et al., 1996) serve a similar function. Many designers or design teams, rather than adhering to the constructs of a particular theorist, construct their own categorization schemes. Often these are conditioned by the subject matter being instructed and consist of blends of both theoretic and practically-motivated classes of constructs. These pre-condition the analysis constructs derived and subsequently the chain of constructs that result.

The designer's instructional assumptions thus exercise a subtle but real influence in ways not always fully recognized by everyday designers. The strategic viewpoint acts as a DNA-like pattern, and if it is applied consistently throughout analysis and design can afford the designer product consistency and development efficiency. If the designer is not influenced by a particular strategic viewpoint, the analysis and design constructs linked by derivation can consist of message-delivery constructs or media delivery constructs. In this way Figure 2 can also be related to the four "centrisms" described earlier.

The process of mapping of constructs first within the abstract side of the technological design space and then across the gap to the concrete side is robust to an enormous variety of personally-held instructional design models. It is possible to identify, even in the work of designers who deny having a consistent single approach to design, a pattern of constructs and derivative relationships that bridge the abstraction-concretion gap. We propose that this type of designer is most common because most designers encounter a broad range of design problem types, and construct output from analysis can differ from project to project. It follows logically that this would involve at least some variation in the form and derivation links for those output constructs as well.

In the face of calls for design models adapted specifically to the needs of educators or industrial designers, the view of design we are outlining provides a vehicle for understanding differences. This applies as well to the notion of tailored design processes, partial or local design processes, and process descriptions adapted to the needs of a particular project. It is also possible to see how in iterative design-development processes one of the things that can evolve throughout the project is the nature of the design and analysis constructs themselves.

Implications for Instructional Objects

The constructs used in a design space and their derivative relationships are the key to understanding the origins and structures of any design. The instructional object enters this design space as a potentially powerful construct that must find its place within a fabric of derivative relationships with other constructs. The problem of instructional objects, then, as well as being one of defining the object construct and its internals, involves placing the instructional object within the context of the design process.

For this reason we are interested in pre-design analysis. For the remainder of this chapter, we will outline a model-centered analysis process in terms of its creation of constructs within the design space. We will also show how the analysis product links within the design space and eventually to media and tool constructs. Prior to a discussion of analysis and design constructs, it is necessary to describe the strategic viewpoint of model-centered instruction that preconditions the selection and relation of analysis constructs in this chapter.

Model-Centered Instruction

Model-centered instruction (Gibbons, 1998; in press) is a design theory based on the following principles:

- *Experience*—Learners should be given opportunity to interact with models of three types: environment, cause-effect system, and expert performance.

- *Problem solving*—Interaction with models should be focused through carefully selected problems, expressed in terms of the model, with solutions being performed by the learner, by a peer, or by an expert.

- *Denaturing*—Models are denatured by the medium used to express them. Designers must select the level of denaturing that matches the learner's existing knowledge level.

- *Sequence*—Problems should be arranged in a carefully constructed sequence.

- *Goal orientation*—Problems should be appropriate for the attainment of specific instructional goals.

- *Resourcing*—The learner should be given problem-solving information resources, materials, and tools within a solution environment.

- *Instructional augmentation*—The learner should be given support during problem solving in the form of dynamic, specialized, designed instructional features.

This theory is described in more detail in several sources (Gibbons, 1998; Gibbons & Fairweather, 1998, in press; Gibbons, Fairweather, Anderson, & Merrill, 1997; Gibbons, Lawless, Anderson, & Duffin, 2000).

A current general trend toward model-centered designs is typified by Montague (1988):

> The primary idea is that the instructional environment must represent to the learner the context of the environment in which what is learned will be or could be used. Knowledge learned will then be appropriate for use and students learn to think and act in appropriate ways. Transfer should be direct and strong.

> The design of the learning environments thus may include clever combinations of various means for representing tasks and information to students, for eliciting appropriate thought and planning to carry out actions, for assessing errors in thought and planning and correcting them. I take the view that the task of the designer of instruction is to provide the student with the necessary tools and conditions for learning. That is to say, the student needs to learn the appropriate language and concepts to use to understand situations in which what is learned is used and how to operate in them. She or he needs to know a multitude of proper facts and when and how to use them. Then, the student needs to learn how to put the information, facts, situations, and performance-skill together in appropriate contexts. This performance- or use-orientation is meant to contrast with formal, topic-oriented teaching that focuses on formal, general

knowledge and skills abstracted from their uses and taught as isolated topics. Performance- or use-orientation in teaching embeds the knowledge and skills to be learned in functional context of their use. This is not a trivial distinction. It has serious implications for the kind of learning that takes place, and how to make it happen. (pp. 125–126)

In the model-centric view of instruction, the "model" and the "instructional problem" are assumed as central constructs of design. These model-centered constructs can be linked directly to media and tool constructs. They are identified through a method of pre-design analysis that we call the Model-Centered Analysis Process (MCAP) that captures both analysis and design constructs at the same time, linking them in a closely-aligned relationship. The model-centered analysis generates an output linkable directly to instructional objects. The MCAP was defined on the basis of a thorough review of the pre-design analysis literature by Gibbons, Nelson, and Richards (2000a, 2000b).

The analysis method is intended to be generally useful by all instructional creators (instructors, designers) regardless of the specific instructional medium used. We have deliberately structured the analysis process so that the analysis method applies to the full range of instructional applications. This includes classroom instructors teaching individual lessons, multimedia designers creating short-course products, and intelligent tutoring system designers, particularly those situating their training in realistic performance settings using problems as a structuring principle.

Theory, Artifacts, and Pre-Design Analysis

The prescriptive nature of technological theory requires that a designer know the desired goal state and invites the designer to employ consistent structuring techniques as a means of reaching it. Our review of pre-design analysis literature compared examples of existing analysis methods in terms of: (1) input constructs, (2) transformation rules, and (3) output constructs.

Figure 3 shows the analysis process deriving from a body of expertise an artifact representing some event or content structure. This artifact bears the structural imprint of the expertise and acts as a kind of information store. It in turn can transmit its structure and information to other design artifacts. In the same way a chain of chemical intermediaries during cell metabolism stores and transfers information or energy for later use in forms that cannot be directly metabolized themselves.

At some point in this forward motion of transmittal, the structure is impressed on an instructional artifact to create a form that can be "metabolized." We show this transformation in Figure 3 as design process *transformations,* and we have labeled the resulting artifact as the *artifact of intervention.* One assumption of Figure 3 is that intervention can take place at an *intervention point* that has been

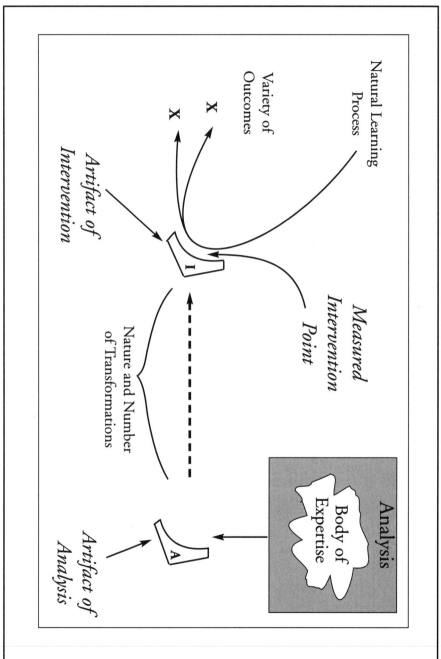

Figure 3. A technological theory of analysis

measured as an appropriate, perhaps optimal, point for the application of that artifactual intervention.

We describe a methodology that produces artifacts containing problem event structures that can be transformed into a variety of artifacts capable of expression in a variety of forms in a variety of media, through a variety of media constructs. When these media constructs are brought into contact with the learning processes of a student, the course of learning is influenced. The chain of deriving these structures is short, and contrary to past formal views of analysis and design, the order of creation of linked artifacts is reversible and two-way.

The Resonant Structure

Figure 4 shows that the output of the MCAP methodology is a design element—the problem structure—and that this element is related to three classes of analytic elements: environment elements, cause-effect system elements, and elements of expert performance. The arrows in Figure 4 show relationships that create a property we call resonance. The principle of resonance is that any type element of the analysis may be used as an entry point for the systematic derivation of the remaining elements of the other types. For instance, the identification of an environment element leads directly to the identification of system process elements, related expert performance elements, and eventually to problems that involve all of these. Likewise, the identification of a problem allows the designer to work backward to define the environment, system, and expert performance requirements necessary to stage that problem for students. The basic unit of MCAP analysis is this resonant structure.

This resonant relationship exists for all four of the Figure 4 elements in all of the directions indicated by arrows. The implication is that analysis does not necessarily proceed in a top-down manner as is true in most analysis methodologies, but that the analyst may move laterally among design elements in a pattern more compatible with a subject-matter expert's stream of thought. We believe that even traditional forms of analysis proceed more or less in this fashion, even during analyses that are putatively "top-down." The analysis begins at some initial anchor point and works outward in all directions, sometimes working upward to a new anchor.

Figure 5 shows that each of the element types from Figure 4 participates in a hierarchy of elements of its own kind. These hierarchies can be projected, as it were, on the views of a modeling language. This modeling language, which we have termed an Analysis Modeling Language (AML), is patterned after the Unified Modeling Language (UML) used by programmers to design complex object systems (Booch, Rumbaugh, & Jacobsen, 1999).

This modeling language offers four projected views of a body of expertise: a view of performance environments, a view of cause-effect systems

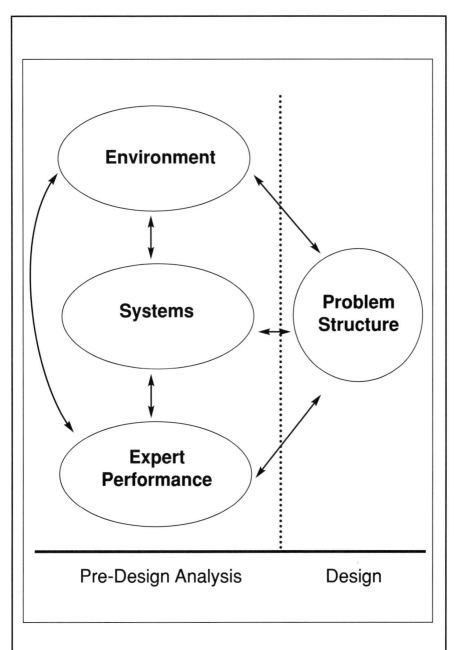

Figure 4. The resonant structure of model-centered analysis

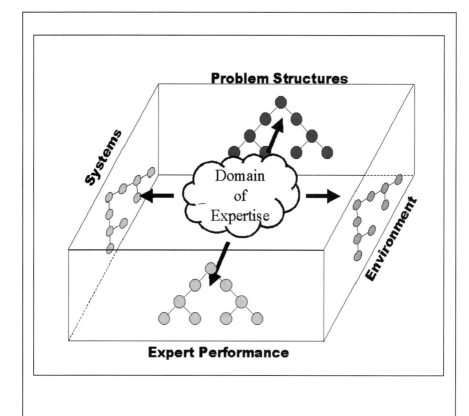

*Figure 5. An Analysis Modeling Language providing
multiple views into a body of expertise*

hosted within the environments, and expert performances performed on the cause-effect systems within the environments. The fourth view into the body of expertise consists of situated problem structures from everyday settings that can be used for instructional design purposes. Problems in the problem view are linked with the elements from the other views in resonant relationships.

The benefit of representing the analysis as a set of views linked internally is that the relationships between elements within a view are preserved and can be used to further the analysis. The principle of resonance allows the analyst to move between views, filling in the hierarchy on each of the views. The analyst is also enabled to work within a single view, generating upward and downward from individual elements according to the logic of that individual hierarchy.

For instance, an analyst, having defined a system process, may break the process into its sub-processes showing them hierarchically on the same view and then move to a different view, say the expert performance view, to identify tasks related to the control or use of the sub-processes that were identified in the first view. This may in turn suggest appropriate training problems to the analyst, so the analyst may move to the problem view and record these problems.

The Organization of the Views

The hierarchies of each view differ according to a logic unique to that view:

- The *environment* view hierarchy breaks the environment into locations that can be navigated by paths. Environment locations are normally nested within each other, and diagrams are often the best representation of their interrelation. However, a simple outline form can capture this relationship also. Paths between locations must be captured in a supplemental form when an outline is used.

- The *system view* contains three hierarchies under a single head: (1) a raw component hierarchy, (2) a functional subsystems hierarchy, and (3) a system process hierarchy. Examples of these relationships include: (1) the division of an automobile engine into physical components determined by proximity or juxtaposition; (2) the division of an automobile engine into sometimes physically isolated parts that form functional subsystems, such as a fuel system, and cooling system; and (3) a separate hierarchy describing processes carried out as forces and information operate and are transformed within the system defined by (1) and (2). The system view in most cases will also include a view of the product produced by expert performance and/or the tools used to produce the product.

- The *expert performance* view decomposes complex, multistep performances into progressively simpler performance units according to a parts-of or varieties-of principle. Several systems for cognitive task analysis have been developed that perform this kind of breakdown. Moreover, traditional task analysis accomplishes this type of a breakdown but to a lesser degree of detail and without including key decision-making steps. The expert performance view also decomposes goals that represent states of the systems being acted upon.

- The *problem structure* view contains a hierarchy of problem structures systematically derivable from the contents of the other views using the parameterized semantic string as a generating device (see description below). This view arranges problems in a multidimensional space according to field values in the string structure. As strings take on more specific modifiers they move downward in the hierarchy.

The environment, system, and expert performance views are composed of analytic elements. The problem structure view is composed of design (synthesized) elements that have an analytic function, hence the connection of the problem view to the other three. This makes the set of views, taken together, a bridge between analysis and design.

Entering Analysis from Multiple Points

The principle of resonance allows for multiple entry points into the analysis. The analyst can begin by collecting environment elements, system elements, elements of expert performance, or problem structure elements and organizing them into views, and once information is gathered for one analysis view, resonance automatically leads the designer to questions that populate each of the other views.

Problem structures. Analysis can begin with a set of constructs normally considered to be on the design side of the analysis-design watershed. This view of analysis means that as analysts we can begin by asking the SME what they think are appropriate performance problems (job situations, common crises, use cases, etc.) for instruction as a means of moving analysis ahead, using constructs from the subject-matter expert (SME)'s world that are already familiar. As an SME begins to generate examples of performance problems, the instructional designer must translate the statements into a semantic string form, either at the time of analysis or in a follow-up documentation period. The instructional designer must also use the resonant relationships principle to identify elements of performance, systems, and environment implicit within problem statements and record them in their respective views. Additional problems can be generated from initial problems by formalizing problem statements into semantic string form and systematically varying string slot contents to create new problem forms.

Expert performance structures. Currently there exists a number of tools for both elicitation and recording of expert performance. This area has been the special focus of analysis in the past for both traditional task analysis (TTA) and cognitive task analysis (CTA). TTA has tended to proceed by fragmenting a higher-level task into lower-level components. CTA has tended to look for sequences of tasks, including reasoning and decision-making steps—especially those related to specific characteristics of the operated system. Performance analysis in MCAP incorporates both of these principles, with emphasis on the hierarchical arrangement of tasks because of the generative principle it establishes for continuing analysis using existing tasks to generate new ones.

To expedite analysis with the SME, a use case approach is appropriate for identifying both task fragments and the decisions that join them into longer sequences of performance. A sufficient number of use cases gathered quickly can provide the analyst with a great deal of analysis detail, and in cases of restricted development time can provide a rapid analysis alternative because use cases constitute a basis for problem sets.

Environment structures. An environment is a system that is not within the immediate scope of instruction. In instruction that uses progressions of models as a method (White & Frederiksen, 1990), what is initially environment eventually emerges into the details of the systems being instructed. Therefore, environment is a relative and dynamic construct. If a particular system is not at the forefront of instruction, in the context of a specific problem, it can be considered the environment or the background for the problem. Environment provides both setting elements and pathing elements for the processes described in the system view of MCAP. An environment description can be quite detailed, and most SMEs tend to accept this as a standard. However, Lesgold (1999) and Kieras (1988) have recommended that both environment and system definitions need to be limited to useful definitions from the student's point of view to avoid including irrelevant, unusable information in instruction.

A good starting point for eliciting elements of the environment is to ask the SME for all of the settings where systems exist or performances are required. One way of capturing the environment is as a diagram using AML. Representing an environment graphically helps both SME and instructional designer ensure completeness in the environment view and to use the environment view to extend other views by path tracing.

System structures. Understanding the processes within a system is a prerequisite to explaining behavior and outcomes with respect to that system. A significant source of operator error is the lack of a complete and accurate system model in the learner. It is clear that good system models are the basis for effective expert performance and that as expertise grows the nature of the expert's system models changes correspondingly (Chi, Glaser, & Farr, 1988; Psotka, Massey, & Mutter, 1988). From our review of the literature we found a number of instructional products that did not succeed as well as they could have because they lacked system process that could be separately articulated. MYCIN (Clancey, 1984), for instance, could not give explanations of expert systems decisions without system models. Instruction that can convey to the learner a complete model of the processes that occur within the scope of instruction can provide the learner with a complete explanation of why certain phenomena were observed.

In system process analysis three things must be identified: initiating events, internal processes, and terminating indications. Events that initiate a system process consist of a user action or another process acting from without. Internal processes are represented in a number of ways: as sequential steps, as flow diagrams, or as principles (rules) that control the flow of events.

System structures are captured in the form of: (1) a hierarchy of system components, (2) a hierarchy of functional units made up of individual components, and (3) a tracing of the processes on the face of (1) and (2) on top of the environment description. Process tracings form a multidimensional hierarchical form but are best captured as individual tracings, normally related to expert performance elements.

The Semantic String as a Construct for Problem Structure Expression

We feel the model-centered architecture and the model-centered analysis process to be highly relevant to a discussion of instructional objects and their nature and origin because any element of the architecture and any element identified during the analysis may be treated as a type of instructional object. This is consonant with the wide range of objects of different kinds (i.e., instructional, knowledge, learning, etc.) mentioned early in this chapter. Moreover, we feel the problem to be a key structuring object type that allows the designer to connect analysis directly with design and designs directly with tool constructs.

The output of MCAP is a set of problem structures (with their resonant environment, system, and expert performance primitives) that can be used to build an instructional curriculum sequence. A problem structure is a complete and detailed task description expressing a performance to be used during instruction, either as an occasion for modeling expert behavior or as a performance challenge to the learner.

The MCAP problem structure is a data structure. A repeating data structure of some kind is common to all analysis methodologies. This is most evident in traditional task analysis in the repeating nature of tasks at different levels of the hierarchy and in cognitive task analysis in the PARI unit (Hall, Gott, & Pokorny, 1995), the regularity of Anderson's rule forms (Anderson, 1993), and the regular analysis structures by the DNA and SMART (Shute, in press) systems. It is likely that the regularity of these analysis units is closely related to a conceptual unit defined by Miller, Galanter, and Pribram (Miller, Galanter, & Pribram, 1960) called the TOTE (Test-Operate-Test-Evaluate) unit.

The MCAP problem structure is expressed as a semantic string—created by merging data fields from the other three analysis views: (1) environment, (2) cause-effect systems, and (3) expert performance. The semantic string expresses a generic problem structure. During instruction a problem structure is given specific instantiating values. The semantic string does not have an absolute structure and can therefore be adapted to the characteristics of tasks related to individual projects and to trajectories of student progress. However, we believe the string to be conditioned by a general pattern of relationships found in everyday event-script or schematic situations (Schank et al., 1994) in which actors act upon patient systems and materials using tools to create artifacts. We believe this dramatic structure to be related to Schank's (Schank & Fano, 1992) list of indices.

A general expression of the semantic string consists of the following:

In <environment> one or more <actor(s)> executes <performance> using <tool> affecting <system process> to produce <artifact> having <qualities>.

This general expression of the semantic string can, in turn, be broken down into more detailed parts corresponding to the detailed definition of the environment, of the cause-effect systems, and of the performance.

The general environment portion of the string can be expressed as follows:

In <location> of <environment> in the presence of <external conditions> in the presence of <tool> in the presence of <information resources> in the presence of <material resources>.

The general system portion of the string can be expressed as follows:

Affecting <system> that exists in <state> manifest through <indicator> and operated using <control>.

The general performance portion of the string can be expressed as follows:

One or more <actor(s)> execute <performance> using <method> with <technique>.

Benefits of the Semantic String

One of the functions of analysis is accountability. Analysis becomes a part of the process of *requirements tracing* (Jarke, 1998) for instructional purposes. Designers must be able to demonstrate that they have achieved some degree of coverage of some body of subject-matter with their instruction.

Accountability requirements have traditionally led to forms of instruction that fill administrative requirements but have little impact on performance. This is especially true when training is regulated and mandated (aviation, nuclear, power distribution, hazardous waste). Accountability in these cases has been equated with verbal coverage, and a formulaic variety of verbal training has become standard in these situations (*Guidelines for Evaluation of Nuclear Facility Training Programs,* 1994).

Instructional objectives are normally used as the accountability tool in forming this type of instruction, and in some cases traditional task analysis methods are used as a means of grounding the objectives in a systematic process to certify soundness and completeness. Accountability in this atmosphere is difficult, and sometimes task analysis principles have to be stretched in order to make the accountability connection.

Acceptance of problem solving as an appropriate form of instruction and assessment makes the accountability problem harder. It creates new problems for accountability, because the basic construct of accountability changes from the verbal check-off to the real and dynamic competency. Instructional designers lack the ability to express dynamic competency and also lack a theory of performance measurement that would generate appropriate performance assessments.

The semantic string mechanism supplies a method for the description of dynamic competency. When the string is instantiated with specific values or with a range of values, it expresses a specific problem or range of problems. Variations of string values make this an expression of a range of performance capability.

Generating Problems and Using Weighting To Focus Problem Sets

Instructional problems are generated computationally using the semantic string by defining a range of values for each field in the string and then systematically substituting values in specific string positions. Generation of problems using the semantic string takes place in two steps: (1) insertion of values from the hierarchically-organized views into the string to create a problem, and (2) selection of specific initial values that instantiate the problem. This results in a geometric proliferation of possible problems, so mechanisms capable of narrowing and focusing problem sets into sequences are important.

This is accomplished by selecting string values depending on the principle the designer is trying to maximize within a problem sequence. A few possible sequence principles are given here as examples:

- *Maximum coverage in limited time*—String values will be selected with the minimum of redundancy. Each problem will contain as many new elements in string positions as possible.

- *Cognitive load management*—String values will be selected in terms of their addition to the current cognitive load. Increases may be due to increased memory requirement, coordination of conflicting sensory demands, integration of parallel decision processes, or a large number of other possibilities. Each string element is judged according to its contribution to load.

- *Integration of complexes of prior learning*—String values are selected as combinations of elements from each of the view hierarchies that practice already mastered areas of the hierarchies in new combinations.

- *Decontextualization of skills*—String values are selected so that they vary systematically, preserving expert performance elements but varying environment and system elements as widely as possible. Core performances are retained in the string but to them are added as wide a variety as possible of non-related performances.

- *Practice to automaticity*—String values are kept as unchanged as possible with the exception of the conditions in the environment, which change in terms of timing factors where possible.

- *Transfer*—String values for expert performance change along a dimension in which performances in the sequence contain similar elements. Environment and system string elements are made to vary widely.

- *Risk awareness*—String values are selected on the basis of weightings attached to performances, system processes, and environmental configurations that have historically posed or have the potential for posing risks.

When string values have been selected, individual problems are instantiated by the designer by specifying data that situates the problem. This data includes:

- *Environment configuration data*—Data that describes the specific environment in which the problem will be presented to the learner.

- *Environment initialization data*—Data that describes variable values of the environment at problem initiation.

- *System configuration data*—Data that describes the configuration of systems that the student will interact with or observe.

- *System initialization data*—Data that describes variable values of the systems at the beginning of the problem.

- *Problem history*—Data that describes the history of events that has brought the problem to its present state.

- *Problem end state data*—Data that describes the states of system and environment at the end of the successfully concluded problem.

Relation to Instructional Objects

Instructional objects, under their several names, are often referred to in the literature as if they were a well-defined, unitary element. However, they must be seen in terms of their place in an architectural hierarchy capable of finding, comparing, and selecting them and then joining them together to perform an orchestrated instructional function that requires more than a single object can accomplish unless it is a self-contained instructional product. An architectural superstructure capable of employing objects in this way is described in the Learning Technology Systems Architecture (LTSA) (Farance & Tonkel, 1999).

This architecture will require a variety of object types, some of them merely content-bearing, but some of them consisting of functional instructional sub-units of many kinds, including in many cases interactive models and related sets of problems defined with respect to the models.

Peters, for instance, describes how ". . . 'knowledge objects' enabled by [an] emergent class of digital libraries will be much more like 'experiences' than they will be like 'things', much more like 'programs' than 'documents,' and readers will have unique experiences with these objects in an even more profound way than is already the case with books, periodicals, etc." (Peters, 1995). This in turn suggests the need for model components that can be brought together in various combinations to create the environments and systems for progressions of problems.

For example, a telephone switch manufacturer, in order to align training objects with training content and to reuse the same objects in multiple training contexts, might create models of three different PBXs (switches) and two different telephone sets, a desk set and a handset, that can be connected in different configurations. The same models could be used for numerous training problems for the installer, the maintainer, and the operator. The independent problem sets (themselves a type of instructional object) would consist of the list of models to be connected together for a particular problem: initial values, terminal (solution) values, and instructional data to be used by independent instructional functionalities (coaches, feedback givers, didactic givers) in conjunction with the problems. The instructional agents, of course, would be a variety of instructional object as well.

MCAP provides a shared methodology basis for deriving suites of model objects interoperable not only with themselves but with instructional agents that share the model-centered instructional viewpoint. The important idea here is not that model-centered principles are right for all occasions but that the creation and use of instructional objects benefits from a process capable of coordinating instructional assumptions with object outlines and connections.

This is the principle we have been exploring with MCAP. We have found it useful to describe a model-centered instructional product architecture that aligns with several layers of design (see Figure 1): instructional models, instructional strategies, instructional problems, instructional message elements, representation, and media-logic. At the same time it allows these levels of design to be integrated into running products, it allows them maximum portability and reusability in a number of modes. Instructional functions can be added independently of model function. The model-centered architecture is illustrated in Figure 6 and includes:

• a problem solving environment that contains everything;
• a problem environment that contains information-bearing locations;
• the paths for navigating between locations;

- cause-effect or event models invisible to the viewer;
- controls and indicators within locations, connected to the models;
- one or more problems to be solved within the problem environment;
- models of expert performance that can be observed;
- resources that supply information for use in problem solution;
- tools that can be used to generate information or to record information; and
- instructional augmentations that offer coaching, feedback, interpretations, explanations, or other helps to problem solving.

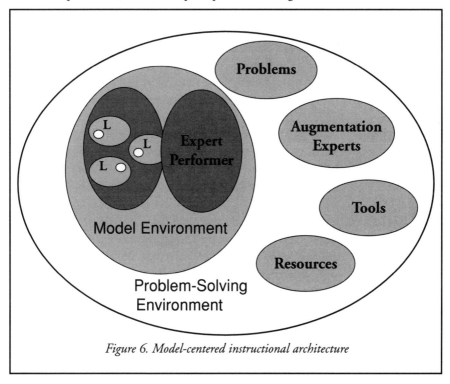

Figure 6. Model-centered instructional architecture

Relation to the Goals of CBI:
Adaptivity, Generativity, and Scalability

Most importantly, linking the origin of instructional objects to the design process—through analysis and design constructs—appears to change the analysis and design process itself in a way that produces primitives that can be used to meet the CBI goals of adaptivity, generativity, and scalability.

Adaptivity is obtained as independent instructional objects are assembled and implemented in response to current learner states. The granularity of adaptivity in object architectures will correspond to the granularity of the objects themselves and the instructional rules that can be generated to control the operations of objects. MCAP is flexible with respect to granularity because it represents elements of environments, systems, and expert performance at high levels of consolidation or at very detailed and fragmented levels. The granularity of object identification can be adjusted to any level between these extremes. This is one of the characteristics that allows MCAP to provide useful analysis and design functionality to both small-scale and low-budget development projects (that will use instructors and overhead projectors) as well as the large-scale, well-financed ones (that may at the high end venture into intelligent tutoring methods).

Generativity is also favored by an analysis that identifies at a high level of granularity the terms that might enter into the instructional dialogue at any level. Generativity is not a single property of computer-based instructional systems but rather refers to the ability of the system to combine any of several instructional constructs with tool and material constructs on the fly: instructional model suites, instructional problems and problem sequences, instructional strategies, instructional messages, instructional representations, and even instructional media-logic. The semantic string method of problem expression—though computationally impractical without adequate data to guide the generation of problems—can, if provided with that data, lead designers to the generation of progressive problem sets and can make possible for computer-based systems the generation of problem sequences.

Scalability involves production of quantity at specified levels of quality within specified time and resource constraints. It also requires an increase in productivity without a proportional increase in production cost. Instructional object technology cannot now provide scalability because the infrastructure of skills, tools, and processes is not available that would support this. Scalability, however, is one of the main arguments provided in promoting instructional object economies (Spohrer, Sumner, & Shum 1998), and adequate technologies for designing and using objects will modify instructional development costs in the same way that roads, gas stations, and mechanic shops modified automobile costs.

Conclusion

Our purpose has been to set instructional objects within a design process context. Standardization efforts related to object properties and indexing will open the floodgates for object manufacture and sharing, but without attention to design process, interoperability among all the necessary varieties of instructional objects and the favorable economics needed to sustain their use will not materialize.

Note

1. This chapter describes research on the instructional design process carried out under the auspices of the Human-system Simulations Center at the Idaho National Engineering and Environmental Laboratory (Department of Energy).

References

Advanced Distance *Learning initiative.* Available: http://www.adlnet.org

Anderson, J. R. (1993). *Rules of the mind.* Hillsdale, NJ: Lawrence Erlbaum Associates.

Atkinson, R. C., & Wilson, H. A. (1969a). *Computer-assisted instruction: A book of readings.* New York: Academic Press.

Atkinson, R. C., & Wilson, H. A. (1969b). Computer-assisted instruction. In R. C. Atkinson & H. A. Wilson, *Computer-assisted instruction: A book of readings.* New York: Academic Press.

Booch, G., Rumbaugh, J., & Jacobsen, I. (1999). *The unified modeling language user guide.* Reading, MA: Addison-Wesley.

Brand, S. (1994). *How buildings learn: What happens after they're built.* New York: Penguin Books.

Burns, H., & Parlett, J. W. (1991). The evolution of intelligent tutoring systems: Dimensions of design. In H. Burns, J. W. Parlett, & C. L. Redfield (Eds.), *Intelligent tutoring systems: Evolutions in design.* Hillsdale, NJ: Lawrence Erlbaum Associates

Burns, H., Parlett, J. W., & Redfield, C. L. (1991). *Intelligent tutoring systems: Evolutions in design.* Hillsdale, NJ: Lawrence Erlbaum Associates

Chi, M., Glaser, R., & Farr, M. (1988). *The nature of expertise.* Hillsdale, NJ: Lawrence Erlbaum Associates.

Clancey, W. J. (1984). Extensions to rules for explanation and tutoring. In B. G. Buchanan & E. H. Shortliffe (Eds.), *Rule-based expert systems: The mycin experiments of the Stanford Heuristic Programming Project.* Reading, MA: Addison-Wesley.

Duffin, J. R., & Gibbons, A. S. (in preparation). *Alignment and decomposition in the design of CBI architectures.*

Edmonds, G. S., Branch, R. C., & Mukherjee, P. (1994). A conceptual framework for comparing instructional design models. *Educational Technology Research and Development, 42*(4), 55–72.

Fairweather, P. G., & Gibbons, A. S. (2000). Distributed learning: Two steps forward, one back? Or one forward, two back? *IEEE Concurrency, 8*(2), 8–9, 79.

Farance, F., & Tonkel, J. (1999). *Learning Technology Systems Architecture (LTSA).* Available: http://edutool.com/ltsa/

Gerard, R. W. (1969). Shaping the mind: Computers in education. In R. C. Atkinson & H. A. Wilson, *Computer-assisted instruction: A book of readings.* New York: Academic Press.

Gibbons, A. S. (1998). *Model-centered instruction.* Paper presented at the Annual Meeting of the American Education Research Association, San Diego, CA.

Gibbons, A. S. (in press). Model-centered instruction. *Journal of Structural Learning and Intelligent Systems.*

Gibbons, A. S., Bunderson, C. V., Olsen, J. B., & Robertson, J. (1995). Work Models: Still Beyond Instructional Objectives. Machine-Mediated Learning, 5(3&4), 221–236.

Gibbons, A. S., & Fairweather, P. G. (1998). *Computer-based instruction: design and development.* Englewood Cliffs, NJ: Educational Technology Publications.

Gibbons, A. S., & Fairweather, P. G. (in press). Computer-based instruction. In S. Tobias & J. D. Fletcher (Eds.), *Training and retraining: A handbook for business, industry, government, and military.* New York: Macmillan Reference.

Gibbons, A. S., Fairweather, P. G., Anderson, T. A., & Merrill, M. D. (1997). Simulation and computer-based instruction: A future view. In C. R. Dills & A. J. Romiszowski (Eds.), *Instructional development paradigms.* Englewood Cliffs, NJ: Educational Technology Publications.

Gibbons, A. S., Lawless, K., Anderson, T. A., & Duffin, J. R. (2000). The Web and model-centered instruction. In B. Khan (Ed.), *Web-based training.* Englewood Cliffs, NJ: Educational Technology Publications.

Gibbons, A. S., Nelson, J., & Richards, R. (2000-a). *Theoretical and practical requirements for a system of pre-design analysis: State of the art of pre-design analysis.* Center for Human-Systems Simulation, Idaho National Engineering and Environmental Laboratory, Idaho Falls, ID.

Gibbons, A. S., Nelson, J., & Richards, R. (2000-b). *Model-centered analysis process (MCAP): A pre-design analysis methodology.* Center for Human-Systems Simulation, Idaho National Engineering and Environmental Laboratory, Idaho Falls, ID.

Gordon, J., & Zemke, R. (2000). The attack on ISD. *Training,* April, 43–53.

Graves, W. H. (1994). Toward a national learning infrastructure. *Educom Review, 29*(2). Available: http://www.educause.edu/pub/er/review/reviewArticles/29232.html

Guidelines for Evaluation of Nuclear Facility Training Programs (DOE-STD-1070-94)(1994). Washington, DC: U.S. Department of Energy.

Hall, E. P., Gott, S. P., & Pokorny, R. A. (1995). *Procedural guide to cognitive task analysis: The PARI methodology* (AL/HR-TR-1995-0108). Brooks, AFB, TX: Armstrong Laboratory, Human Resource Directorate.

Hannafin, M. J., Hannafin, K. M., Land, S. M., & Oliver, K. (1997). Grounded practice and the design of constructivist learning environments. *Educational Technology Research and Development, 45*(3), 101–117.

Hill, T. (1998). *Dimensions of the workforce 2008: Beyond training and education, toward continuous personal development.* Paper presented at Technology Applications in Education Conference, Institute for Defense Analyses, Alexandria, VA, December 9–10.

Jarke, M. (1998). Requirements tracing. *Communications of the ACM, 41*(2).

Kieras, D. E. (1988). What mental models should be taught: Choosing Iinstructional content for complex engineered systems. In J. Psotka & D. L. Massey & S. A. Mutter (Eds.), *Intelligent tutoring systems: Lessons learned* (pp. 85–111).

Lesgold, A. M. (1999). Intelligent learning environments for technical training: Lessons learned. In A. K. Noor (Ed.), *Workshop on advanced training technologies and learning environments.* Hampton, VA: NASA Langley

Merrill, M. D. (1994). *Instructional design theory.* Englewood Cliffs, NJ: Educational Technology Publications.

Merrill, M. D., & the ID$_2$ Research Group. (1996). *Instructional transaction theory: Instructional design based on knowledge objects.* Educational Technology, 36(3), 30–37.

Miller, G. A., Galanter, E., & Pribram, K. H. (1960). *Plans and the structure of behavior.* New York: Henry Holt.

Misa, T. J. (1995). *A nation of steel.* Baltimore, MD: Johns Hopkins University Press.

Montague, W. E. (1988). Promoting cognitive processing and learning by designing the learning environment. In D. Jonassen (Ed.), *Instructional designs for microcomputer courseware.* Hillsdale, NJ: Lawrence Erlbaum Associates.

Noor, A. K. (1999). *Advanced training technologies and learning environments: Proceedings of a workshop sponsored by NASA and the Center for Computational Technology* (University of Virginia). March, NASA/CP-1999-209339.

Peters, P. E. (1995). Digital libraries are much more than digitized collections. *Educom Review, 30*(4), July/August. Available: http://www.educause.edu/pub/er/review/reviewArticles/30411.html

Poulson, M. C., & Richardson, J. J. (1988). *Foundations of intelligent tutoring systems.* Hillsdale, NJ: Lawrence Erlbaum Associates.

Psotka, J., Massey, D. L., & Mutter, S. A. (1988). *Intelligent tutoring systems: Lessons learned.* Hillsdale, NJ: Lawrence Erlbaum Associates.

Reigeluth, C. M. (1999). *Instructional-design theories and models: A new paradigm of instructional theory, Vol. II.* Mahwah, NJ: Lawrence Erlbaum Associates.

Rowland, G. (1993). Designing instructional design. *Educational Technology Research and Development, 41*(1), 79–91.

Schank, R. C., & Fano, A. (1992). *A thematic hierarchy for indexing stories.* Evanston, IL: The Institute for the Learning Sciences, Northwestern University.

Schank, R. C., Kass, A., & Riesbeck, C. K. (Eds.). (1994). *Inside case-based explanation (Vol. 3).* Hillsdale, NJ: Lawrence Erlbaum Associates.

Shute, V. J. (in press). DNA: *Towards an automated knowledge elicitation and organization tool. In S. P. Lajoie (Ed.), Computers as cognitive tools: No more walls* (2nd ed.). Mahwah, NJ: Lawrence Erlbaum Associates.

Silberman, H. F. (1969). Applications of computers in education. In R. C. Atkinson & H. A. Wilson, *Computer-assisted instruction: A book of readings.* New York: Academic Press.

Simon, H. A. (1969) *Sciences of the artificial.* Cambridge, MA: MIT Press.

Spohrer, J. Sumner, T., & Shum, S. B. (1998). Educational authoring tools and the educational object economy: Introduction to thespecial issue from the East/West Group. *Journal of Interactive Media In Education.* Available: http://www-jime.open.ac.uk/98/10/spohrer-98-10-paper.html

Stolurow, L. M. (1969). Some factors in the design of systems for computer-assisted instruction. In R. C. Atkinson & H. A. Wilson, *Computer-assisted instruction: A book of readings.* New York: Academic Press.

Suppes, P. (1969). Computer technology and the future of education. In R. C. Atkinson & H. A. Wilson, *Computer-assisted instruction: A book of readings.* New York: Academic Press.

Wenger, E. (1987). *Artificial intelligence and tutoring systems: Computational and cognitive approaches to the communication of knowledge.* Los Altos, CA: Morgan Kaufmann.

White, B. Y., & Fredricksen, J. (1990). Causal model progressions as a foundation for intelligent learning environments. *Artificial Intelligence, 24,* 99–157.

2.0 Learning Objects and Constructivist Thought

Learning Object Systems as Constructivist Learning Environments: Related Assumptions, Theories, and Applications

Brenda Bannan-Ritland, Nada Dabbagh & Kate Murphy
(George Mason University)

Introduction

Humans are viewed as goal directed agents who actively seek information. They come to formal education [and training] with a range of prior knowledge, skills, beliefs and concepts that significantly influence what they notice about the environment and how they organize and interpret it. This in turn, affects their abilities to remember, reason, solve problems and acquire new knowledge (Bransford, Brown, & Cockling, 1999, p. 10)

Capitalizing on the goal-directed nature of human beings and their prior knowledge for the purposes of enhancing learning has been a continual challenge to educators and those who design and develop instructional technology applications. Learning object systems present yet another technology-based instructional delivery environment with exciting features and attributes that can empower learner-driven experiences and promote cognitive processing if pedagogical considerations are taken into account in their development and evolution. To this point, the majority of literature and applications related to learning object systems have focused primarily on technological attributes, metadata standards, and system specifications issues such as levels of granularity and ensuring interoperability (Wiley, 1998; Singh, 2000). While these are important hurdles to overcome before wide-spread use of these systems can be obtained, it is also crucial at this point to consider the implications of learning object use and implementation in an instructional context prior to full-scale implementation of this technology.

Pioneers in the instructional technology community have begun to grapple with mapping sound instructional principles to the technical attributes of learning object systems for education and training purposes (Merrill, 1999; Interactive Media, 2000). However, many of these efforts have focused on integrating traditional perspectives on learning based in cognitive information processing and instructional systems design. Other efforts have incorporated these perspectives in the use of learning object systems for increased efficiency of the design and development workflow processes. Learning object systems are well suited for these objectives, integrating with ease clearly delineated, traditional taxonomies of learning into these compartmentalized, searchable systems and capitalizing on efficient, reusable content in often arduous instructional design and development tasks. While these efforts demonstrate appropriate consideration of pedagogical principles, to our knowledge, the incorporation of alternative perspectives on learning related to constructivist philosophy have not yet been considered for application to learning object systems.

By their very structure, learning object systems are flexible, dynamic, and highly engaging technology-based environments. These systems have great potential to capitalize on the goal-oriented nature of human learning processes as well as allowing learners to associate instructional content with their prior knowledge and individual experiences as detailed by Bransford and his associates above (1999). To this point, the attributes of the system that would permit learner-driven, constructivist-oriented activities have not yet been fully explored and may reveal significant implications for the development of these systems. This chapter is an attempt to map constructivist principles to learning object systems by considering related assumptions of learning, corresponding theoretical approaches, and instructional applications.

To begin, we review two examples of learning object systems based in similar theoretical approaches: the IDXelerator™ grounded in Instructional Transaction Theory (ITT) and Fountain™ based on instructional systems design and performance support constructs. The IDXelerator™, heavily focused on delivery of instruction, and Fountain™, primarily used for design of instruction, provide examples for considering the possibility of a learning objects system that can be used to induce cognitive processing through learner-driven participation and constructivist principles. We then review different grounding assumptions about how learning occurs and several theoretical perspectives related to constructivist philosophy. Selecting two of these theories, we present in-depth descriptions of instructional applications based in constructivist principles that could inform the development of learning object systems and conclude by presenting projected features of a learning environment based in constructivism. Only through sound pedagogical grounding will learning object systems have the potential to be used as effective learning environments. We hope that this chapter extends the current thinking and development of learning object systems to consider these alternative perspectives and capitalize on them to establish rich environments for both teaching and learning.

Examples of Learning Objects Systems

Merrill's Knowledge Objects and the IDXelerator™

To date, the majority of literature related to applying a specific theoretical framework to learning object architecture has been written by M. David Merrill and his associates at Utah State University. In applying theoretical constructs to learning object systems, Merrill departs somewhat from the analysis and component-oriented instructional strategies of his previous Component Display Theory toward a more integrated, synthesis oriented approach that combines elements of instructional strategies into a more holistic representation of instructional transactions (Merrill, 1999; see http://www.coe.usu.edu/it/id2/ddctoc.htm).

A natural fit to the technical attributes of learning objects, Instructional Transaction Theory (ITT) represents knowledge as objects and related elements or slots of these objects as the components of subject matter content (Merrill, 1999). Inherent in this definition is the perspective that acquiring subject matter content is equivalent to the acquisition of knowledge. ITT then, is a methodology for manipulating these objects and their elements that are represented as specific instructional strategies (see Appendix: Table 2 for a concise review of the attributes of this system). In the explanation of his methodology, Merrill describes a traditional database model of computer-based instruction (CBI) where instructional strategies are embedded in the programming or authoring system code dictated by the designer and cannot be easily re-used without major reconstruction. He contrasts this view of CBI with an instructional system that could potentially permit access to the component parts of content and the dynamic transformation or display of these parts in highly specified configurations.

In his thinking about an instructional system based on ITT, Merrill applies an algorithmic model of computing to instruction. In this view, knowledge is represented by data and instructional strategies are represented as algorithms. These instructional algorithms contain presentation strategies, practice strategies, and learner guidance strategies needed for the learner to achieve the instructional goal. The algorithms dictate various formats representing specific instructional strategies within which a set of knowledge objects can be displayed for the learner.

Merrill details four types of knowledge objects including entities (objects in the world and can include devices, persons, places, symbols), properties (quantitative or qualitative attributes of entities), activities (actions the learner can take to act on objects in the world), and processes (represents events that occur that change properties and are triggered by activities or other processes). The knowledge objects include certain attributes or slots such as name, portrayal (text, audio, video, graphic animation), and description (open compartment that could include function, purpose, and may be defined by a user) and are housed in a knowledge base. Combined, the instructional algorithms prescribe the implementation of an instructional strategy and the interrelationships among the four types of knowledge objects impact the representation or attributes of the object. These system features create the potential for the reference, reuse, and reconfiguration of knowledge objects in the knowledge base into learner-selected instructional strategy representations. Theoretically, the same knowledge objects configured in different ways could be used to construct different types of presentation, practice, or learner guidance strategies.

In addition, relationships between objects can be calculated as well using a defined terminology of additional slots (location, part-of, and has-parts). In this system, the designer needs to take care to accurately describe the object, and the learner needs only to choose the instructional strategy he or she prefers, and the system can then automatically generate a presentation, exploration, simulation, or practice strategy using the same content.

An elaborate instructional system, the power of this proposed technology and the corresponding methodology of ITT is in the generation of a variety of instructional strategy approaches with similar reusable content. Although constrained by system-controlled presentation of content with limited selection of instructional strategies by the learner, the system has marked value for those who may desire an automated approach to designing and delivering instruction. The precision of this architecture in identifying subject matter content is both its strength and weakness. While this type of system provides a solid framework based in cognitive learning theory, it is limited to Instructional Transaction Theory and the translation of instructional strategies or instructional algorithms related to that view.

An existing application that contains attributes of ITT and is used as a learning-oriented instructional development tool is the IDXelerator™ detailed by Merrill and Thompson (in press). The IDXelerator™ contains a library of configured instructional strategies including presentation, practice, learner guidance and knowledge structures directed toward a specific learning goal. Functioning as an enhanced authoring system, the IDXelerator™ allows the designer to select a goal and instructional strategy, and the system then prompts the designer to input appropriate multimedia resources. Providing an instructional shell based on principles of learning, the runtime system is coupled with a popular authoring system called Toolbook™. The IDXelerator™ presents an instructor or designer-driven system that capitalizes on a structured shell of built-in instructional strategies in the hope of producing a higher level of sound design of instructional modules.

Both the knowledge object system proposed by Merrill and the existing IDXelerator™ operate on similar principles based in ITT and structured algorithmic processes. Merrill advocates expanding this system structure or syntax based in cognitive theory to many different content domains including science and mathematics, taking a one-size or structure fits all approach in regard to theoretical grounding. He discourages adaptation of the system by the user by stating that it is better to have an established knowledge syntax *(knowledge object components)* rather than have user-defined knowledge components due to the specific nature of algorithmic computation. From his perspective on and the design of these systems, it makes sense that if users were permitted to define knowledge components or knowledge object attributes, this feature would limit both the capability of the system to access and use learning objects in an effective manner and the generalizability of the instructional strategies. However, there may be alternative ways to incorporate user-defined components and maintain interoperability other than strict construction of limited, specific instructional strategies that need to be explored in order to permit the learner greater participation in the instructional process. Currently, the knowledge object system and the IDXelerator™ based in ITT do present potentially powerful instructional delivery and development systems with well-defined, specific attributes, but these systems do not permit additional learner involvement beyond selection of a pre-configured instructional strategy. The resulting instruction that is delivered to the learner is identical to computer-based instructional systems that do not involve learning objects. The knowledge object systems detailed by Merrill promote great flexibility and involvement by the instructor or designer in selecting the instructional goal strategy, and resources, but comparably little involvement or direction by the learner.

Interactive Media's Fountain™ Learning Database System

Corporations involved in developing technology-based training are tapping into the potential of learning object systems for reasons that include:

- increased efficiency in regard to training development cycle times,
- the potential for increased effectiveness and personalization of training, and
- consistency in design and development tasks.

Another example of a learning objects system that has been developed for internal corporate use is Fountain™, a proprietary system developed and used by Interactive Media Corporation. The Fountain™ system guides the design and development of technology-based training enabled by re-useable learning objects accessed from the system's resource database. Although the current use of Interactive Media's system is not as a learning management tool, the attributes of the system enable the development and delivery of reusable, content-independent strategies that lend themselves to the construction of flexible, modular learning paths that support a variety of learning and performance needs. In addition, this type of system could potentially provide learners the opportunity to generate and contribute resources, just as Interactive Media's instructional designers develop and contribute resources to their database of instructional strategies, resources, and visual interfaces in order to more efficiently produce technology-based technology training.

Interactive Media Corporation has capitalized on learning object architecture to develop a Learning Database^{SM} system called Fountain^{TM} which is a repository of discrete instructional units each comprised of a strategy, instructional content, media elements, and a visual wrapper. Once designed, the objects can be selected and sequenced to address specific performance requirements of corporate employees. In a white paper describing the creation of these objects (Interactive Media Corporation, 2000), Interactive Media has constructed some unique definitions and representations of learning and knowledge objects, and suggests that these elements differ in composition. The architecture of the system presents an open, eclectic approach for including various instructional design constructs and strategies. The structure of Interactive Media's Fountain^{TM} system is heavily based in traditional instructional systems design providing some similarity to Merrill's systems. However, the Fountain^{TM} system is also based in performance support principles which signals somewhat of a departure from the theoretical grounding of other established learning object systems. Fountain^{TM} provides the trainee or learner opportunities for presentation, application, and evaluation of their performance on the job. Strong focus on the learner's performance, in addition to learning objectives and the flexibility of this system to incorporate various instructional strategies presents another approach to the design of learning object systems.

The Fountain^{TM} system houses learning objects that represent short, concise performance-based lessons organized around job tasks and knowledge objects that contain complementary resources providing enabling knowledge in support of the specific job tasks. Learning objects are created by first establishing the identified performance or learning objective central to the target skill (i.e., handling objections to the sale of a product).[1] Then, an appropriate instructional strategy is selected or developed to create templates of interaction related to that strategy (e.g., show an expert modeling a sales conversation, list common objections for various products, provide a simulation in which the learner identifies objections and matches them with appropriate responses, participate in an online collaborative role play, help the learner to write his or her own response to objections). Last, specific content is applied to these instructional strategy templates (e.g., different customer situations or different products). Similar to Merrill's approach, the Fountain^{TM} system promotes generalizability of content-independent instructional strategies, however this system permits the use of many additional types of instructional strategies other than those based in ITT.

A knowledge object contains similar elements and structure including the enabling knowledge or objective (e.g., supporting a sales task), an instructional strategy template (e.g., organization and format of a product reference card), applied content (e.g., information about the specific product), and a visual wrapper. This onion-like layering of performance or enabling objective, instructional strategy, content, and visual interface permits the creation of flexible components that can be reused or adapted in different instructional or training situations.

The knowledge and learning objects are tagged with IMS compliant metadata and cataloged in a Learning Database^SM architecture based on competency models (or key tasks the learner will need to do on-the-job) offering a high level design structure that permits matching objects to particular performance tasks. A customized curriculum can then be assembled with various learning and knowledge objects based on specific factors like job function or business unit. Users can progress through a personalized, prescribed path of learning objects directed toward a specific objective or can access any related knowledge objects during the instruction, or at a later point while on the job in an online performance support system mode. In this way, the system permits both prescribed and flexible use of the objects for learning.

Currently, Interactive Media uses Fountain™ internally to manage the workflow of the design and development of training products. The benefits of this system are increased efficiency of use and consistency of design and development resources that can be molded into different learning objects and reused for multiple training requirements. Interactive Media uses this system to create and house resources representing various design and functionality elements such as interface models, audio, video, graphics components, and instructional strategy applications as well as programming components. Some elements are combined into object "shells" representing a particular performance objective and corresponding appropriate instructional strategies. This attribute of Fountain™ has similarities to Merrill's approach with IDXelerator™ and ITT. Generalized from specific content, these shells can be adapted or reused for different instructional contexts (e.g., using an active listening shell for deployment in courses on interviewing, coaching or problem-solving) easily integrating an alternative interface or different media resources. This same type of generalized structure can be used at a more micro level as well in creating templates based on enabling objectives that represent various types of presentation and evaluation strategies or different ways to engage and involve the target audience.

Because of the flexibility of the system to include various types of instructional strategies, the Fountain™ Learning Database has great potential as a cognitive learning tool. While the more pragmatic goals of reduced design and development cycles are impressive and have significant implications on the instructional design processes involved, the true power of this system may lie in placing the Fountain™ system in the client's hands or incorporating some of the systems' attributes within a learning management system. In the same way, this system could potentially permit the client organization to define, customize, and contribute to training applications according to a set structure, a similar system could permit learners to configure, adapt, and generate learning objects related to a specific learning goal. These flexible system capabilities allow us to glimpse an alternative view of learning object systems as generative, constructivist, dynamic knowledge-building environments used by clients (or learners) rather than an automated instructional delivery system or efficient workflow environment.

The Potential of Learning Object Systems

Both Merrill's knowledge objects approach as well as his IDXelerator™ and Interactive Media's Fountain™ system are outstanding examples of systems that capitalize on classic instructional systems design theory—one system focusing on the delivery of instruction and the other system is primarily used for development work. However, both systems are fairly prescriptive in regard to the outcome of the training or instruction, meaning that the designer, developer, or system identifies and structures the content in a particular sequence for delivery to the learner. These systems present clear objectives, compartmentalized content, and carefully sequenced instructional activities created by the instructor or designer.

We believe that there are alternative theoretical foundations other than a traditional instructional systems design perspective that can be applied to learning object systems based on constructivist philosophy of learning. To the best of our knowledge, a learning object system based in theoretical approaches steeped in constructivism has not yet been developed. Although the learning theories associated with constructivism have very different foundational assumptions than traditional instructional systems design about how we acquire knowledge, the application of related theories and models could provide a new perspective on the development of learning object systems and related instructional tools.

Constructivism is an educational philosophy or perspective that encompasses a wide variety of views, theories, and instructional models. These views seem to converge on at least two principles, according to Duffy and Cunningham (1996): (1) that learning is an active process of constructing rather than acquiring knowledge; and (2) that instruction is a process of supporting construction rather than communicating knowledge. Many constructivists believe that a learner individually interprets their experience, building a unique internal representation of knowledge (Bednar, Cunningham, Duffy, & Perry, 1991). Generally, constructivism holds that most learning domains are ill-defined (complex), that learning outcomes are largely metacognitive in nature, and that learners are required to actively participate in the learning process to construct meaningful knowledge rather than acquire a predetermined set of skills in a pre-specified manner.

In mapping constructivist principles and strategies onto learning object systems, we attempt to project what the attributes of such as system might be. Based on Merrill's and Interactive Media's work in this area, we next explore the potential of learning object systems that could provide a different medium for a constructivist learning environment and incorporate these alternative principles of learning. Ignoring problems of scalability, interoperability, and metadata standards for this discussion, we focused primarily on what the attributes of a system might contain from a pedagogical perspective. Additional dialogue amongst learning object system developers will be needed to ascertain the feasibility of implementing these attributes and the technical specifications involved.

Grounding Assumptions for Learning Object Systems

Learning object systems, like all instructional technology delivery environments, must be rooted in epistemological frameworks to be effective for teaching and learning. Bednar et al.(1991) pointed out the importance of linking theory to practice in the design and development of any instructional system and emphasized that ". . . effective design is possible only if the developer has a reflexive awareness of the theoretical basis underlying the design" (p. 90). In their view, theoretical constructs emerge from our assumptions or perspective on knowledge or how we come to know. The implications of a particular perspective on constructing knowledge are significant in the application of theory and design associated with a specific instructional delivery mechanism.

Hannafin, Hannafin, Land, and Oliver (1997) expand on this by stating that clarifying the foundations and assumptions of different perspectives on learning and aligning theoretical approaches and methods of instruction through grounded design helps to validate instructional applications based in different perspectives. For example, Merrill's work with learning objects has solid reference to Gagné's events of instruction that promotes using appropriate instructional strategies for a particular level of learning and incorporating necessary conditions for learning presentation, practice, and learner guidance (Merrill, 1999). However, what are the epistemological assumptions that underlie Gagné's work? Are there alternative assumptions of learning that could also inform the design of learning objects systems? While it has been stated that there is no value in purporting that one perspective is inherently "better" than the other, there may be great value in linking alternative assumptions to different learning theories, methods and applications that could inform the design and development of learning object systems (Hannafin et al., 1997; Wilson, 1997; Duffy & Cunningham, 1996). In the next section, we review different perspectives on cognition for the purposes of exploring the implications of connecting an alternative set of assumptions and their corresponding theories to learning object systems.

Cognitive Information Processing (CIP)
View of Cognition

Mind as Computer

The assumptions of Gagné's conditions of learning and Merrill's Instructional Transaction Theory related to knowledge objects can be associated with Duffy and Cunningham's (1996) metaphor of the "Mind as Computer" perspective on learning. They state that symbols in the mind are "entirely abstract and independent of any given individual's experience of them; i.e., the operation of the mind is completely independent of the person in whom it is contained" (Duffy & Cunningham, 1996, p. 176).

In this view, the mind manipulates symbols in the same manner that a computer manipulates data. Hence, "the human learner is conceived to be a processor of information in much the same way a computer is" (Driscoll, 1994, p. 68). This analogy has emerged as part of the Cognitive Information Processing (CIP) perspective which has roots in behaviorist and cognitivist views on learning, with behaviorists utilizing the input–output events of a computer system to explain how environmental stimuli become inputs in a learning cycle and behaviors (or responses) become outputs, and cognitivists adding the "black box" as the intervening and impacting variable between input and output to explain the "information processing system" of the learner. In the following section we will refer to the combination of these views as the traditional cognitive view of information processing.

Traditional Cognitive View of Information Processing

Cognitive information processing (CIP) seeks to explain how learning occurs in a multistore, multistage theory of memory (Driscoll, 1994). Implicit in this model is that information undergoes a series of transformations in the mind in a serial manner until it can be permanently stored in long-term memory in packets of knowledge that have a fixed structure. Resulting from this view of CIP is the specification of instructional strategies that assist the learner in processing information in discrete and linear events that align with internal cognitive processes such as selective attention, encoding, retention, and retrieval. "Like the traditional cognitive view, the CIP model portrays the mind as possessing a structure consisting of components for processing information (storing, retrieving, transforming, using) and procedures for using the components." (Phye & Andre, 1986, p. 3). This traditional cognitive view inherently presumes a separation of learning processes and knowledge and implies that instructional strategies are (or should be) independent of the content being taught and that different learning outcomes require different cognitive processes and hence different instructional strategies.

Cognitive Information Processing Assumptions and Learning Objects

Merrill's perspective of a learning objects system and ITT is in our view congruent with the traditional perspective of CIP discussed above. Merrill (1992) capitalizes on the philosophical as well as physical separation of learning processes and content in his approach to learning object systems by stating that the semantics or components of cognitive structures may be unique to an individual but the syntax or structure is not (see Merrill's chapter for further detail regarding knowledge syntax and meta-mental models). Learning objects are containers or compartments for different related elements of knowledge, implying that the content within a given compartment differs but the structure of the knowledge element in a given compartment is the same (Merrill, 1999). This is similar to the view that the mind has a common structure, components, and procedures for learning. Therefore, cognitive information processing (CIP) provides grounding assumptions for Merrill's ITT theory and implementation of a learning objects system. Aligned with the fundamental notions of CIP, in this system knowledge can be represented in a knowledge base external to the learner and, depending on the desired performance (learning goal), a set of instructional transactions is generated to explicitly organize and sequence content in such a manner so as to engage learners in a variety of experiences that facilitate the construction of an organized and elaborated cognitive structure appropriate for the knowledge and skills being taught (Merrill, 1998).

The decontextualized, granular, and reusable nature of learning objects makes it easy and convenient for instructional designers to assemble instructional sequences that are congruent with well-defined, structured learning taxonomies and pedagogical models subscribing to this linear, multistage view of information processing. For example, in a learning objects system an instructional designer could use a preprogrammed instructional strategy like Gagné's events of instruction to assemble an instructional sequence using a searchable database of learning objects. When the user specifies the instructional goal and the learning strategy, the system generates the instructional strategy and the knowledge structure by matching the attributes of the objects to the attributes of the events of instruction. Because of the predetermined syntax of a learning object, different instructional algorithms (transactions) can use the same learning object to teach the same or different subject matter content. This is the underlying principle of ID$_2$ and on which many of Merrill's conceptualized systems like the IDXelerator™ were built (Merrill, in press).

Automaticity and Learning Objects

Separation of content and context, or content and learning process, is a huge benefit to the designer and subject matter expert affording them the automaticity and flexibility of reusing the same learning objects with different instructional strategies to teach the same subject matter or different subject matter content. Development time is considerably reduced and instruction can be assembled and adapted to learners on an as-needed basis by novices and experts alike with predictable success. This offers more from a delivery system perspective but the benefits remain unchanged from a learner perspective. Once the learner selects an instructional strategy, the instruction that is generated is no different than a traditional computer-based instruction delivery system. We liken this approach to placing old wine in new bottles. We need to be careful of using new technologies to implement only thoroughly tested models of teaching, rather than as a catalyst for transforming the learning process by attempting to implement potentially more powerful but not yet fully explored pedagogies (Dede, 1993). Using learning object systems as a more flexible instructional delivery mechanism is one use of these systems; however, when they are used primarily as a delivery or development environment, we ask *"What has changed from a learner perspective?"* In Merrill's or Interactive Media's current use of these systems, learners are still positioned at the receiving end, directed to acquire a predetermined set of skills or knowledge generated by the learning object system or another delivery environment.

We see more potential tangible benefits to the learner if the system is grounded in an alternative cognitive view of information processing that aligns with constructivist philosophy: parallel distributed processing (PDP). This alternative view and related assumptions of how learning occurs present very different theoretical approaches that could be applied to learning object systems and allow the consideration of including the learner as an active partner in the creation, sequencing, and selective use of learning objects.

An Alternative Perspective

Parallel Distributed Processing

An alternative cognitive view of information processing that signals a departure from the cognitive information processing model described above is parallel distributed processing (McClelland, Rumelhart, & Hinton, 1986). PDP perceives long-term memory as a dynamic structure (or network) that represents knowledge in patterns or connections with multiple pathways instead of concept nodes and propositions (Driscoll, 1994). Information processing is understood as a process of activating these patterns, in parallel, to accommodate new information by strengthening the most relevant pattern in the knowledge structure based on the goals of the learner at the time of learning. This perspective of the mind could be thought about as an interconnected web with certain patterns of traveled pathways strengthened and weakened. Knowledge (or cognition) is therefore thought of as 'stretched over' or distributed across the whole network (in this discussion the network is restricted to long-term memory) and not residing in fixed loci (Salomon, 1993). A fundamental distinction between the traditional view of CIP and PDP models of memory is that information processing occurs in parallel instead of a serial manner, activating knowledge patterns simultaneously and continuously adjusting them as a function of new information to resolve cognitive dissonance. In this view cognitive processes (e.g., syntax) and semantics (e.g., content) are not separated but rather distributed over a knowledge network that forms a connectionist model of memory. This model does not, in our view, attempt to describe cognition at a behavioral level since the knowledge network is an interrelated structure of interactions and not a propositional structure. As described by Spiro et al. (1987, p. 181), "highly compartmentalized knowledge representations are replaced with structures characterized by a high degree of interconnectedness." We believe that this nonlinear, fluid and dynamic view of information processing paves the way to the consideration of several constructivist learning theories in which learning objects systems can be grounded. We discuss four of these below.

Cognitive Flexibility Theory

Cognitive Flexibility Theory (CFT) emphasizes the flexible reassembly of preexisting knowledge to fit the needs of a new situation (Spiro et al., 1987). CFT is concerned with "the acquisition and representation of knowledge in a form amenable to flexible use" (Spiro, 1987, p. 64) and is therefore in sharp contrast with the traditional view of CIP in which knowledge is thought of as discrete and static entities to be retrieved intact from memory to demonstrate a learned capability. The essence of CFT is that learners ought to be able to assemble situation-specific knowledge in a domain, and this demands the attuning of special cognitive processing skills. From an instructional perspective, this is achieved by stressing the conceptual interrelatedness of complex content and by providing multiple perspectives of the content so as not to rely on a single schema (Jonassen, 1991).

Situated Cognition

Another theory which treats knowledge as continuously under construction and evolving with each new situation and activity in which the learner is engaged is situated cognition (Browns, Collins, & Duguid, 1989). Rather than acquiring concepts as abstract, self-contained entities, the emphasis is on acquiring useful knowledge through enculturation (understanding how knowledge is used by a group of practitioners or members of a community). Brown et al. (1989) believe that knowledge is similar to a set of tools which can only be fully understood through use. Therefore, the context or the activity which frames knowledge in a particular domain is as important as the content that is learned because it is referenced by that activity.

> Situated cognition argues that learning occurs most effectively in context, and that context becomes an important part of the knowledge base associated with learning. (Jonassen, 1991, p. 11)

This interpretation is consistent with the epistemological assumption of constructivism that "meaning is a function of how the individual creates meaning from his or her experiences" (Jonassen, 1991, p. 10). From a knowledge representation perspective, one can think of cognition in this context as being indexed by the experiences in which the knowledge was produced. Moreover, since multiple experiences are needed to build a situation-sensitive schema, the interconnectedness of these experiences is what forms a knowledge network that is context dependent and progressively under development through activity. Instructional implications of situated cognition include embedding content in real-world tasks, thematic linking across learning domains, and engaging students in authentic activity.

Distributed Cognition

Distributed cognition can be described as an extension of situated cognition based on Salomon's observation that "if cognition is distributed then by necessity it is also situated since the distribution of cognitions greatly depends on situational affordances" (Salomon, 1993, p. 114). This is coupled with the idea that not only do social and other situational factors have an impact on cognitions that occur in one's mind, but that the social processes themselves should be considered as cognitions (Resnick, 1991). Salomon also attributes the exploration of the possibility that "cognitions are situated and distributed rather than decontextualized tools and products of the mind" to the growing acceptance of the constructivist view of human learning (Salomon, 1993, p. xiv). This has prompted a shift in attention to cognitions that are situated, context-dependent, and distributed or stretched over a network that extends beyond the individual. Nardi (1996) notes that distributed cognition is concerned with structure—representations inside and outside the mind—and the transformations these structures go through. Another main emphasis of distributed cognition is on understanding the coordination among individuals and artifacts (how individuals align and share within a distributed process), for example, how two programmers coordinate the task of doing software maintenance among themselves (Flor & Hutchins, 1991).

Distributed cognition does share its roots with other cognitive theories in that it seeks to understand how cognitive systems are organized and takes cognitive processes to be those involved with memory, decision making, reasoning, problem solving, learning, and so on. However, the distinguishing principle between distributed cognition and other cognitive learning theories is that distributed cognition looks for cognitive processes wherever they may happen, on the basis of the functional relationship of elements that participate together in the process.

Generative Learning Theory

Another theoretical model of memory based in neural processing that is applicable to learning object technologies is generative learning theory. Originally conceived under the cognitive information processing paradigm by Wittrock (1974), generative learning theory has recently also been applied in development of multimedia and hypermedia technology-based constructivist learning environments (Cognition and Technology Group at Vanderbilt, 1993; Grabinger, 1996). The focus of the generative learning theory model is that the learner is not a passive recipient of information but an active participant in the instructional experience, constructing knowledge through relating information in the instructional environment to his or her previous experiences and prior knowledge (Grabowski, 1996). Correspondingly, the generative learning process requires the learner to manipulate, interpret, organize, or in some active manner make sense of his or her environment. He or she creates meaning through generative associations between and among elements in the instructional environment and his or her knowledge base.

In constructivist learning environments, generative learning activities may take the form of using technology-based tools for argumentation or reflection in attempting to accommodate various viewpoints with their own (CTGV, 1993). Other types of generative strategies include organization (e.g., summarizing, diagramming), conceptualization (e.g., explaining/clarifying, creating concept maps, identifying important information), integration (e.g., creating relevant examples, relating to prior knowledge, creating analogies and metaphors, synthesizing), and translation (evaluating, questioning, predicting, inferring) (Grabowski, 1996).

In any form of instructional strategy based in this theory, of primary importance is presenting the opportunity to construct new meaning from the learner's interaction with the instructional environment and understanding of specific content. This is an important consideration since generative theory dictates that learning is not limited to the manipulation of existing cognitive structures but can generate new associations for the learner (Grabowski, 1997). Grabinger (1996) points out this distinction by stating:

> The concept of generative learning is an extension of the concept of constructing learning. Students cannot construct their own learning without generating something through active involvement. (p. 675)

Coleman, Perry, and Schwen (1997) contend that constructivists are inclined to involve learners in a generative experience through allocating control of the sequence of instruction to learners. Hannafin (1992) states that generative environments need to task the learner with creating, elaborating or otherwise constructing representations of individual meaning. Technologies such as hypermedia and multimedia have been used to create generative learning opportunities where students create, synthesize, manipulate or debate content. Jonassen, Peck, and Wilson (1999) take this position farther in stating that hypermedia and multimedia should primarily be used for generative processing by the learner in constructing knowledge rather than as a medium to deliver instruction.

Application of Constructivist Theories to Learning Object Systems

The alternative assumptions on knowledge acquisition and theoretical perspectives presented above are heavily related to constructivism and have interesting implications when applied to a learning objects system. Placing the power of this technology in the learners' hands may reveal new attributes of these systems that need to be considered in the standards and metadata discourse. Jonassen and Reeves (1996) distinguish between the use of technology for knowledge construction versus knowledge reproduction in advocating how technological cognitive tools can help learners organize, restructure, and represent knowledge. Reproducing knowledge is more often associated with instructor-led or instructor-designed systems rather than more learner-centered, open-ended participatory, contributive or collaborative, learning environments.

In order to further understand how a learning objects system may be grounded in PDP, constructivism, and associated learning theories, we present a broad view of aligned theories, models, strategies, and corresponding instructional applications that could provide specific constructs and models for integration of these approaches into learning object systems (see Table 1). We select two theories, generative learning theory and cognitive flexibility theory, to explore further using related instructional applications of computer-supported

Table 1: A Broad View of Aligned Theories, Models, Strategies, and Corresponding Instructional Applications

Learning theory	Situated cognition; Distributed cognition	Cognitive Flexibility Theory	Social interaction; Action learning	Social interaction; Activity Theory; Distributed cognition	Generative Learning Theory	Inquiry Theory; Activity Theory
Instructional model	Cognitive apprenticeship; Situated learning	Random Access Instruction	Problem-based learning	Distributed expertise; Knowledge management	Generative teaching model	Situated learning; Experiential learning
Instructional strategy	Coaching; Authentic activity; Modeling; Articulation; Exploration; Scaffolding	Case-based learning; Thematic-based learning; Self-directed learning	Collaboration; Guided inquiry; Authentic activity; Small group instruction; Self-directed learning	Collaborative learning; Learner-centered instruction; Goal-based instruction	Organization; Conceptualization; Integration; Translation	Self-directed learning; Collaborative learning; Authentic activity; Exploration
Instructional application	Apprenticeship; Internship; Story-based instruction; Situated narration	Cognitive Flexibility Hypertext	Problem-centered instruction	Virtual learning communities; Communities of practice	CSILEs; Anchored instruction	Microworlds; Simulations

intentional learning environments and cognitive flexibility hypertexts as models for attributes that could be implemented into learning object systems.

We would like to advocate the application of theories which align with parallel distributed processing and the principles of constructivism to learning object systems. Mapping constructivist theories to this type of delivery system may yield some interesting implications for current features and attributes under consideration by the IMS and corporations involved in developing these systems. The attributes of successful learning environments steeped in constructivist principles could be adapted into learning object systems, providing a basis for the application of an alternative theoretical framework. Next, we discuss two relevant constructivist learning theories and associated technology-based applications; we also attempt to project similar attributes into learning object systems. Our purpose is not to provide an in-depth explanation of all the technical specifications related to these ideas, but to merely explore the possibility of additional features that may present an alternative theoretical framework in addition to encouraging rich learning experiences with learning object systems.

Generative Learning and Learning Object Systems

Learning object systems should be able to be configured as generative learning environments in addition to instructional delivery systems. The overarching flexible, dynamic nature of the medium aligns well with a generative, constructivist pedagogical approach. Permitting the learner as well as the instructor to generatively construct, manipulate, describe, or organize learning objects can enrich the system with additional resources as well as provide a significant learning experience for the user. There is evidence for this perspective in that allowing learners the opportunity to design and link content to show interrelated, complex ideas in building a hypermedia knowledge base, may increase the level of acquired content for students and allow them to demonstrate meaningful content structures (Chuckran, 1992). This study supports the learning benefits of student-produced multimedia or hypermedia as a more powerful learning strategy than the traditional perspective of the student learning from instructor- or designer-produced materials (Jonassen, Peck, & Wilson, 1999).

Capitalizing on these powerful learning techniques within the architecture of a learning object system becomes a more difficult question. However, there are existing features that provide at least a basis for their inclusion. Certainly, the granularity of objects holds promise for a generative learning experience for users of these systems. Wiley (1998) refers to the granularity or fundamentality of learning objects as reducing resources to their most widely usable level of representation that is relevant to the learning task. He proposes a "fundamental" learning object (see Wiley chapter in this volume for taxonomy of learning object types) to represent this high level of granularity and context-independent nature. Isolating or deconstructing resources such as components of text, video, audio to their most fundamental level permits future users to adapt, reconstruct or reconfigure objects into their own meaningful representations rather than merely be delivered a complete instructor representation of content.

Designing content resources that can be "stacked" or layered with various levels of meaning is crucial to supporting an individualization or repurposing of objects by users that constitutes generative use (Wiley, 1998). The flexible use of objects will allow learners to use the various levels of representations of content for creation, elaboration or construction of individual meaning to enhance their learning. Of primary importance is the context in which the learner is engaged and relating the objects in his or her own way for his or her own purpose. Selvin and Shum (2000) relate the use of learning object systems in a collaborative organizational environment as purporting a "memory as a bin" metaphor where the focus of collective cognition is on merely adding to or retrieving existing objects from the "bin." An alternative model that they prefer is based on "memory as reconstruction" where material is not just retrieved from the "bin" but is reconstructed in the context of the individual's understanding and purpose. Selvin and Shum (2000) charge that the next task for collective organizational memory tools is to provide for features that encourage collaborative construction, reconstruction, and negotiation of information. These are powerful constructivist and generative principles that provide an alternative view of the capabilities of learning object systems for learning. This view of learner creation or adaptation of content for the specific context of their learning is similar to the "learners as designers" perspective posited by Jonassen and Reeves (1996):

> Technologies are taken away from designers and handed over to learners to use as media for generatively representing and expressing what they know. Learners, themselves, function as designers using technologies as tools for analyzing the world, accessing information, interpreting and organizing their personal knowledge and representing what they know to others. (p. 694)

Supporting Learners' Generative Creation and Use of Learning Objects

Of course, in permitting learners to organize, restructure, and represent their knowledge by adapting or creating new learning objects, there is a significant need to support them in effectively constructing resources for future use and reusability as well as methods of organization and tagging. Systems that provide design and development support would need to include guidance in the development of granularized objects, creating layered materials and selecting standard meta-tag categories that accurately describe the objects as well as specific guidance in formatting of objects for collaborative construction, reconstruction, and negotiation. This presents a need for a learning management or authoring-like system to guide the creation and adaptation of learning objects. Many corporations are currently implementing learning object systems that provide consistent design and development processes for their instructional design teams. The same type of technology could be used to provide a learning management system that allows users to create original objects and adapt existing ones that then can be integrated and used by others. This opens up learning object systems to learners as well as instructors by establishing an approach more akin to developing a knowledge base or knowledge management system.

Scaffolding Process-Oriented Learning Goals

With learner participation in creating or adapting objects, these systems truly become dynamic and flexible in nature. However, in opening these systems to learners for generative use, instructors still need to create some organization of materials for a true learning experience to occur. As Wilson (1997) points out, constructivist learning activities do not indicate a lack of structure, indeed, some structure and discipline is needed to provide goal-oriented opportunities that allow students to be creative and may actually help students make constructions for learning. Learning environments based in a constructivist framework are more process-oriented rather than content-oriented where learners "are required to examine thinking and learning processes; collect, record and analyze data; formulate and test hypotheses; reflect on previous understandings; and construct their own meaning" in a variety of content areas (Crotty, 1994, p. 31). Constructivist designers attempt to engage learners so that the knowledge they construct is reusable in different situations (Jonassen, Davidson, Collins, Campbell, & Haag, 1995).

An example of a support structure for learning experiences based in constructivist philosophy that can be applied to learning object systems can be found in Computer Supported Intentional Learning Environments or CSILEs (Scardamalia, Bereiter, McClean, Swallow, & Woodruff, 1989).[2] A student-generated communal database, this technology supports intentional learning by providing a system where students can overtly set cognitive goals for themselves and apply effective strategies for the comprehension, self-monitoring, and organization of knowledge independent of content (Scardamalia, Berieter, Brett, Burtis, Calhoun, & Lea, 1992). They accomplish these higher order educational objectives through building a collective database (or knowledge base) of pictures and text that contains information on many different content areas that is available to everyone. The system helps scaffold the organization of the information in many ways, permitting key word searches, providing learners the opportunity to contribute their own information in the form of notes, and presenting various views of content through linking relevant pictures and text notes. Notes constructed by a particular author can be linked to others notes or graphics, providing a mechanism for peer and instructor feedback. Students can also produce a picture or graphic that is linked to a point on another student's graphic permitting the creation of multiple authors or versions of documents and providing the capability to zoom in and out to different levels of detail or content. In addition, students select the "labels" on their authored notes and graphics ensuring that these items can be recalled in multiple contexts.

Similarities between the technical attributes of CSILEs and the features of learning object systems are fairly obvious in the housing of text and graphical items that can be labeled and linked together and searched, for use in multiple ways. Learning object systems are more encompassing, of course, but CSILE presents sound empirical evidence of the educational viability of a closely related micro-level database application. The major distinction, however, between the design of CSILEs and most current learning object systems lies in the facilitation of active rather than passive learning strategies, where students are active agents in constructing their own knowledge (Scardamalia et al., 1992). Guided by the instructor, CSILE focuses on scaffolding processes that involve students in dialogues as well as integrating information from multiple sources, and includes guidelines for formulating and testing student interpretations and beginning theories (Bransford, Brown, & Cocking, 1999).

The CSILE system also focuses on inducing learners' metacognitive processes or strategies that can be applied to any content area. Knowledge is constructed through presenting support mechanisms for process-based (rather than content-based), student-driven, structured tasks (e.g., when students are presented the opportunity to label or select a kind of mental activity they want to engage in like new learning, questions, insights, or problems). These support mechanisms are embedded in the system and function as guidelines or scaffolds in helping the learner overtly state their learning goals, establish their approach for learning, list available content resources, and label their thinking processes. Additional facilities within CSILE that provide metacognitive strategies include features that allow students to raise questions regarding their interests in the subject matter, view or link others' representations of content to their own and compile their inquiries under their individually constructed and established themes and categories (e.g., questions I must answer). Combined, these features and embedded guidelines provide a learner-centered, supportive, generative experience for users in a constructivist learning environment structured to induce learning. CSILE has been used in elementary, secondary, and post-graduate classrooms in a variety of subject areas (Scardamalia & Bereiter, 1993).

Potential of Implementing Generative Activities and Scaffolding of Process-Oriented Learning Goals into Learning Object Systems

Providing learners with metacognitive and other process-based (rather than content-based) support or scaffolds for their learning goals while allowing the generative creation or manipulation of learning objects has great potential to incorporate learner-centered, active, constructivist strategies in a learning objects system. Learners could not only create and tag their own objects but also view, adapt, and manipulate objects created by others (where permitted) in the process of constructing knowledge. Guiding mechanisms or frameworks that prompt a metacognitive or process-based approach similar to CSILE's attributes could be created by instructors and also housed as learning objects. Wiley (see Wiley chapter in this volume for discussion) presents a taxonomy of learning object types that provides determination of levels of context for learning objects delineating a low or high level of reusability of component objects. Guiding framework objects could capitalize on a higher level of reusability by incorporating process-based guidance, rather than being associated with specific content domain. In addition, these framework objects could be linked with others to provide an approach similar to electronic performance support by integrating information, tools, and methodology to support the learner in a particular learning task (Gery, 1991). This approach is very different from Merrill's knowledge object architecture of instructor-defined content that is configured and automatically generated for the learner based on a specific selected instructional strategy.

Just as technical support could be provided for learners to produce their own learning objects according to system specifications, instructional support could also be provided in the form of frameworks to assist learners with their individual learning goals. A framework (Wiley refers to these as "generative-instructional" learning objects in his chapter in this volume) could provide a structure for learners to assemble objects, engage in a goal-oriented process that follows a format based in sound instructional design, and generatively produce a product that can then be added to the system. Theoretically, various types of process-based frameworks could be created with varying structures for many types of instructional strategies based in constructivist philosophy listed by Wilson (1997), including intentional learning environments, storytelling structures, case studies, Socratic dialogue, coaching and scaffolding, learning by design, learning by teaching, and group, cooperative/collaborative learning.

Interactive Media has implemented a similar type of template for their designers to assemble, create, and reuse objects to more efficiently develop training for different clients. The distinction here is that the carefully designed frameworks embedding a specific instructional strategy approach would be used by the learners (not used by instructors or designers for efficient development or automization of instruction) to guide the process of locating, manipulating, and generatively creating material that would lead toward their identified goal. Ideally, this process would also be supported by an instructor who could monitor, make suggestions, and provide feedback on the students' progress. Providing an instructional lens on the potentially vast resources contained in a learning object system through the use of frameworks may help to address the problem of the absence of instructional theory in these systems (Wiley, 1999).

Knowledge-building frameworks akin to a CSILE type of application could be created as learning objects supporting planning, evaluation, and reflective processes when engaged toward purposeful instructional goals. Jonassen, Peck, and Wilson (1999) describe learning processes that are related to constructing a knowledge base including planning the goals, topics, and relationship among topics; accessing, transforming and translating information into knowledge through developing new interpretations and perspectives; evaluating the quality and quantity of the assembled content; permitting feedback and revision of the knowledge base through reorganization and restructuring for more meaningful content. Learning processes such as these could be incorporated into learning objects as Combined Information Objects (CIOs) or "generative-instructional" learning objects at different levels of granularity that provide guidance for learners to generatively contribute to a system that is as much a knowledge base as instructional delivery mechanism.

Cognitive Flexibility Hypertext and Learning Objects Systems

Cognitive Flexibility Theory (CFT) employs a number of instructional prescriptions to address advanced knowledge acquisition and transfer. These include:

- the use of multiple knowledge representations (e.g., multiple themes, analogies, case examples, lines of argument);
- explicitly linking and tailoring concepts to practice and case examples (i.e., situating conceptual knowledge in contexts that are similar to those required for the application of the knowledge);
- incrementally introducing complexity in small, cognitively manageable units;
- stressing the interrelatedness and Web-like nature of knowledge (instead of isolated and compartmentalized knowledge); and
- encouraging the assembly of appropriate knowledge from various conceptual and case resources (rather than the intact retrieval of previously memorized information). (Jacobson & Spiro, 1991, p. 4)

The above instructional features are realized in a Cognitive Flexibility Hypertext (CFH), which is a hypermedia learning environment that allows "multiple juxtapositions of instructional content" through a large and complex conceptual structure (Spiro et al., 1987, p. 65). Implicit in the design of a CFH is a conceptual structure search which allows the learner to "criss-cross" the conceptual landscape by viewing different example cases that show the many uses of the concept under exploration. Cases contain several themes and knowledge is interrelated through the themes that cut across the cases, enabling the learner to focus on the interconnectedness of the knowledge domain in a situated context. This method of representing instructional content through intersecting themes and cases spawns the constructivist principle of knowledge construction, requiring learners to assemble a flexible schema that is situation specific. Browsing through the hypermedia learning environment, learners are exposed to multiple perspectives of the content, and they must analyze the issues by understanding the processes that link the cases to each other. This has implications of high interconnectivity which accounts for flexibility in application (Jonassen, 1992).

This powerful instructional strategy can be more optimally implemented through the use of a learning objects system. Defined as a structural frame or openwork structure, frameworks with a search feature that model the conceptual structure of intersecting themes and cases can be stored as learning objects, preserving the pedagogy underlying a CFH and providing a structure to organize the experience for the learner. In addition, cases, analogies, and themes can also be stored as learning objects with varying degrees of granularity modeling the range and variability of applications of the concept under study. Through contextualized metadata tagging, frameworks can assemble multiple representations of content, based on a learner's selection of a theme or a case, by linking the attributes of the themes to the cases (or vice versa). Implemented as a cognitive flexibility hypertext, the framework becomes a "generic conceptual structure that is particularized not only to the context of a case, but also to the other concepts simultaneously applicable for analyzing the case" (Spiro et al., 1987, p. 70). The interrelated nature of learning object and templates systems is particularly suited for implementing theoretical constructs associated with cognitive flexibility hypertext. As Wiley (1998) suggests "these templates [or frameworks] would help instructors organize and structure the materials according to pedagogically sound constructs."

A Context-Driven Architecture

Embedding the pedagogy of a CFH in a learning objects system provides a context-driven architecture in which the learner selects a context (a theme or a case), and the system populates the framework with conceptually-related themes and cases to provide multiple perspectives of the content.

Learning objects become context-sensitive and are particularized (with meta-data tags) by instances of usage such as a case, an example, a scene, or an occasion of use (Spiro et al., 1987) instead of by type of components of subject matter content as indicated in Merrill's knowledge objects system. Typically, in a learning objects system, representation of learning objects using metadata combined with an interface that has a built-in searching capability offers users the flexibility of synthesizing learning objects resulting in the achievement of an instructional or learning goal. What is generated in this case is a nonlinear, multidimensional representation of content that supports cognitive flexibility instead of a prescribed instructional sequence that satisfies a specific learning goal.

Linking the Features of a CFH to a Learning Objects System

With database-driven Web sites becoming increasingly popular it is certain that the future of hypermedia systems will be powered by such technologies instead of the static, 'hard-coded' HTML documents. Ted Nelson first envisioned the progression of hypermedia systems from a static system to an open and dynamic system by postulating that the operative unit of hypermedia systems will no longer be the 'document' but the 'version' (Wiley, 1998). The 'version' is based on arrangements of small, uneditable media objects called 'Primedia.' By definition, Primedia are reusable objects and therefore can be stored in a database and accessed for multiple uses in multiple contexts. Primedia can range from low to high granularity depending on their relative size as a learning resource, with highly granular resources increasing the efficiency of online instructional support systems due to their greater potential for reusability (Wiley et al., 1999; Quinn, 2000). Wiley (1999) connects the degree of reusability of a learning object to three attributes: fundamentality, discoverablity, and accessibility. What is of concern here from the perspective of mapping the features of a CFH to a learning objects system is fundamentality (or learning object characteristics involving reusability), since these features address the degree of contextualization of a learning object. Wiley's (2000) taxonomy of several types of learning objects that include various characteristics related to reusability, function, number of elements, and context is relevant for application to CFH. As well, in his earlier work regarding reusability of objects, Wiley (1998) distinguishes a Fundamental Information Object (FIO) as independent of context and therefore having the highest degree of reusability. Certainly, an FIO can be combined with other FIOs to produce a Combined Information Object (CIO), resulting in added context but lower granularity. This idea is presented more in-depth in the taxonomy of learning object types that includes descriptions of combined-closed, combined-open, generative-presentation, and generative-instructional learning objects (Wiley, 1998; Wiley, 2000). Of particular significance to the application of cognitive flexibility to learning objects is the CIO, or what is described in more detail by Wiley as the "generative-instructional" learning object that allows for domain-independent presentation and instructional strategies.

In a CFH learning objects system, it is difficult to construct highly granular objects, since the particularization of a learning object is context specific. However, it is possible to look at the instances of usage (cases, themes, scenes, etc.) as having higher granularity than the conceptual framework that links the cases and the themes together. It is also possible to look at introducing cognitive complexity through cases as varying degrees of granularity, starting with "bite-size chunks" or small segments from a larger case without sacrificing the integrity of the topic, and building up to more difficult levels of complexity by introducing the full case (Spiro et al., 1987).

The conceptual structure evident in a CFH provides macro level scaffolding for instructors and learners allowing them to view content through multiple lenses by selecting CIOs (or "generative-instructional" learning objects), such as cases, themes, expert commentaries, and other contextualized learning resources. As a content-independent interface, this framework may have a high degree of reusability; however, it is highly contextual in that it models a process-based approach for learning due to its underlying CFH pedagogy as described above.

Instructor and Learner Use of a CFH in a Learning Objects System

Embedding the pedagogy of a CFH in a learning objects system could provide functionality and flexibility for instructors and instructional designers interested in the design of constructivist learning environments. Instructors for different subject matter content could use the CFH framework to pull in cases and themes related to a particular topic to provide a conceptual representation of the content. In a learning objects system, the ability to represent knowledge using different conceptual structures is truly maximized. With the thematic overlap approach to the exploration of cases, an underlying principle of cognitive flexibility, instructors can populate frameworks with cases from different knowledge domains, enabling links across the curriculum. Since "multiple conceptual representations will be required for each instance of knowledge application" (Spiro et al., 1987), it is important that the system used to generate these configurations of combinations of conceptual structures be extremely flexible, permitting the dynamic rearrangement of usage instances in a nonlinear multidimensional representation. We believe that the architecture of a learning objects system is ideally suited to generate hypermedia learning environments, by virtue of the ease of its use, and the object-oriented approach adopted for storing and reusing objects through metadata tags.

Hypermedia learning environments can provide several levels of scaffolding for learners by specifying the degree of control the learner has in selecting the path of traversing the content. They may vary from rigid prespecification and prestructuring of routines for knowledge use to *immersion in a totally unstructured environment* (Spiro et al., 1987). For novice learners, a suggested navigation path can be essential to the success of the learning environment and the participation of the learner. However as learners progress, they shift from a highly scaffolded navigation mode to a 'free exploration' mode where they independently traverse the themes, increasing their active participation in learning the processes of knowledge assembly (Spiro et al., 1987). A learning objects system could facilitate the process of fading the scaffolding and the rigidity of the hypermedia environment by allowing instructors and designers to dynamically change the structure to suit learner needs. Furthermore, there is the afforded opportunity for learners to customize the structure as they become more familiar with the technology by adding conceptual themes, cases, or case analysis, which can be meta-tagged as learning objects and added to the knowledge database. Equipped with proper tools, learners can also be encouraged to articulate their knowledge by writing commentaries and reflection statements and tagging these as learning objects as well. These processes emphasize learner generation of content that is an underlying principle of constructivist learning.

Conclusion

Attempting to incorporate constructivist principles into learning object systems reveals many considerations for the design of these systems as described above. After reviewing the core assumptions regarding alternative perspectives on cognition, corresponding theoretical perspectives and technology-based constructivist applications, we feel better prepared to further project potential features and attributes that should be considered by developers for implementation into learning object systems. At the very least, we hope this chapter has extended the thinking in regard to these systems as flexible, generative, constructivist learning environments rather than merely efficient instructional or development systems. While all the above instructional approaches are useful in taming a new technology for instruction, we advocate exploring alternative pedagogical assumptions and instructional theories for application into these new systems. This exploration may yield rich learning environments that can present support for powerful, goal-directed, generative experiences for the learner. Placing the power of this technology in the learner's hands may indeed reveal the true potential of this technology for learning. As Scardamalia and her colleagues (1989) have so eloquently stated, ". . . it is not the computer that should be doing the diagnosing, the goal-setting and the planning, it is the student. The computer environment should not be providing the knowledge and intelligence to guide learning, it should be providing the facilitating structure and tools that enable students to make maximum use of their own intelligence and knowledge" (p. 54).

In summary, to incorporate constructivist principles, a learning object system must generally be able to

- support learner-generated artifacts by incorporating learner contributions;
- consist of multiple levels of granularity to afford reusability, flexibility, accessibility and adaptability of learning objects capitalizing on Wiley's (1998) concept of Fundamental Information Object (FIO) or taxonomy of learning object types (Wiley, 2000);
- contain frameworks as learning objects that provide structure for instructional experiences and incorporate a linking system to facilitate their content population.

In the incorporation of generative learning activities, learning object systems need to

- afford discovery, reuse, and manipulation of existing and learner-created objects;
- allow for learner designed and created artifacts that could become learning objects if posted to the system, and permit multiple versions of objects to be incorporated into the system;
- incorporate an archival engine to clear the database of unwanted and outdated contributions;
- allow for learner-produced artifacts to be generated on FIO and CIO levels or according to levels in the taxonomy of learning object types (Wiley, 2000), and tagged according to standards to allow further discovery, retrieval, and manipulation.

Three layers of granularity make the content objects more flexible and supportive of constructivist learning environment activities. In essence, a learning object system based in constructivist pedagogy may potentially operate in this manner:

- Learning objects at the micro-levels (FIO or "fundamental" learning objects) represent content independent of context, and can be used to populate frameworks and learner-generated artifacts. Learning objects could include graphics, video or sound clips, definitions, de-contextualized explanations or lectures, single cases, and problem statements, and so forth.
- Combined information objects (CIOs or "generative-instructional" learning objects) would exist on a micro to macro level continuum from content with minimal added context (e.g., links within a case study to perspectives and themes might include learning goals) to more complete learning activities or

instructional strategies like tutorials, microworlds, simulations, etc. They could populate frameworks and student artifacts, stand alone as learning experiences, or offer just-in-time help or guidance.

• Frameworks represent macro level scaffolding. They are contextualized by the implementation of specific instructional approaches (CSILEs, CFHs, problem-based learning, etc.), and can incorporate other learning objects and various kinds of links. The framework provides the context or structure for the learner and is defined as an object within the database.

Acknowledgments

Appreciation and recognition to Gretchen Porkett, Denise Dorricott, and Interactive Media Corporation for providing examples and insightful comments on this chapter.

Notes

1. Examples used with permission by Interactive Media Corporation.

2. CSILE is now commercially distributed as Knowledge Forum.

Appendix: Table 2
(See pages 90–93.)

Table 2: Comparison of Learning Objects–Based Systems

	Merrill's Knowledge Objects and IDXelerator™	Interactive Media's Learning Database[SM] and Fountain™ Development Tool	Learning Object Database for Constructivist Learning Environments
System Architecture based on . . .	Cognitive Information Processing; Instructional Transaction Theory; Instructional systems design	Cognitive Information Processing; Performance support; Instructional systems design	Parallel Distributed Model of Long Term Memory; Generative Learning Theory; Cognitive Flexibility Theory
View of knowledge & instructional strategies . . .	Algorithmic Model of Instruction, including a view of knowledge as computational algorithms	Competency model that includes a hierarchical view of skills and knowledge organized according to one of many instructional strategy templates. (Strategy templates become learning objects when content is added and media elements are applied.)	Constructivist paradigm asserts knowledge is constructed by the learner; uses open-ended learning environments; learners as designers; learners are active participants in the instructional experience.
Defines objects . . .	Knowledge objects—includes four types: • entities • properties • activities • processes Attributes of knowledge objects are represented by a set of containers or fields (slots) including: • name • portrayal • description	Learning objects—consist of: • core performance or learning objective, • nstructional strategy • content Knowledge objects—include: • central enabling objective that supports learning or performance objectives • instructional strategy • content	Learning objects—consist of: • identifier • data type • description • knowledge object link • generator ID (metadata tag) • content Knowledge objects—consist of: • learning goal • learning environment • links to learning objects • generator ID • content Context wrapper or frame • audience attributes • identifier category • description schema • combination/ aggregation framework • search forms (pull) • object generation forms (put)

	Merrill's Knowledge Objects and IDXelerator™	Interactive Media's Learning Database^{SM} and Fountain™ Development Tool	Learning Object Database for Constructivist Learning Environments
Table 2 (cont., page two of four)			
Objects are housed in . . .	A knowledge base that permits reference, reuse, and reconfiguration of knowledge objects and their attributes into several specific, instructional strategy representations—the same knowledge objects can be configured into different types of instructional strategies for a given content area, including: presentation, practice, and learner guidance.	A learner database that allows for individualized curriculum to be created by combining learning and knowledge objects that represent appropriate instructional strategies based on performance or enabling objectives. Objects and instructional strategies can be adapted based on different content.	An interactive, learner-accessible database that affords learner-generated learning experiences; storage of learner-produced objects; multiple learner manipulation of existing and learner-created objects. Knowledge objects and templates allow combination, manipulation, and reuse of learning objects in various instructional strategies.
Levels of granularity . . .	Represents precise description of both the macro and micro level with types of objects (macro) and specific attributes of objects (micro) integrated within specific instructional algorithms.	Represents a macro level of implementation with objectives, instructional strategies, and content combining to create the object with building blocks of content.	Learning objects exist at fundamental or micro level of granularity to enhance reusability. Knowledge objects may be micro or macro level, depending on contextual references (e.g., may contain an entire hypertext). Guiding templates or instructional frameworks represent macro level scaffolding for learner combination, manipulation, and generation of learning and knowledge objects.
High level instructional components include . . .	• presentation strategies • practice strategies • learner guidance strategies	• presentation of learning activities • application or practic activities • evaluation or testing activities • knowledge objects or enabling knowledge to support the activities	• guiding templates to support learner-generated learning experiences in constructivist learning environments. • means to describe, tag, and store learner-generated knowledge representations • learner portfolio assessment and storage • modeling, scaffolding, coaching available

Table 2 (cont., page three of four)

	Merrill's Knowledge Objects and IDXelerator™	Interactive Media's Learning Database^{SM} and Fountain™ Development Tool	Learning Object Database for Constructivist Learning Environments
Relationship of instructional strategies, objects, and content . . .	Instructional strategies are independent of content, therefore knowledge objects and attributes can consist of components that are not specific to a content area; attributes allow knowledge to be represented across knowledge domains.	Instructional strategies are independent of content, therefore object shells provide a skeleton for instruction without specific content.	Wrappers/guiding templates contain instructional strategies; learning objects are independent of instructional strategies, and knowledge objects may be independent of or contain instructional strategies.
System and objects function . . .	Algorithms dictate various formats for a set of knowledge objects to be displayed and automatically generated.	Designer creation of object shells or instructional strategies that can be applied to create learning and knowledge objects that can be used for multiple areas of content to expedite development.	Learning objects and knowledge objects can be created, aggregated, and manipulated by the learner to support engagement with interactive, personally constructed, generative activities. Learners are guided by instructional strategy templates that implement constructivist strategies such as Cognitive Flexibility Theory.
Flexibility . . .	Highly prescriptive configuration of objects based on Instructional Transaction Theory, limited user input.	Recommended core sequence of objects and strategies; accelerated and remedial paths can be specified; user is able to select both learning and knowledge objects (when permitted). Potentially, an open system for client adaptation and contribution of new objects.	Wrappers/guiding templates exist to allow learner to combine, manipulate, and generate (contribute) content to provide unique and shared resources as a consequence of meaningful learning experiences.

	Merrill's Knowledge Objects and IDXelerator™	Interactive Media's Learning Database^SM and Fountain™ Development Tool	Learning Object Database for Constructivist Learning Environments
Available instructional transactions or applications . . .	Instructional transactions include: • identify • execute • interpret • judge • classify • generalize • decide • transfer • propagate • analogize • substitute • design • discover	Instructional applications include: • modeling • examples • how-to • show me; try it • interactive, sequenced tutorials • case studies • integrated practice, case studies, or simulations • assessment or pre-tests • collaborative activities • step-action tables • job-aids • check your understanding • mastery tests • tools and resources	Context wrapper and templates could include specific guidance based on the following instructional strategies, among others: • case-based learning • problem-based learning • Cognitive Flexibility Hypertexts • Computer Supported Intentional Learning Environments (CSILE) • Situated Learning Environments • learner reflection • portfolio assessment
Learner controlled by . . .	Selection of specific instructional strategy or transaction.	Selection of learning objects in any order (if appropriate) and selection of knowledge objects when needed for support.	Access to levels or layers of information; object manipulation experience and expertise; implement instructor guidance through templates; learner attributes, goals, and creativity.
System controlled by . . .	Once transaction is selected by learner, automatic generation of instruction representing specific, predefined sequence of learning objects. Linking and representing relationships of objects to one another through location and parts-whole relationships.	Sequenced instructional paths are presented to user in hierarchical menu based on performance objectives (but can be selected in any order). Knowledge objects are associated with learning objects to provide additional support for performance tasks.	Learner requests via context wrappers and templates; presented complexity and thoroughness of object tagging schema. Learner ability to use the system. Instructor-controlled access to object layers.

Table 2 (cont., page four of four)

References

Bednar, A. K., Cunningham, D., Duffy, T. M., & Perry, J. D. (1991). Theory into practice: How do we link? In G. J. Anglin (Ed.), *Instructional technology: Past, present and future.* Englewood, CO: Libraries Unlimited.

Bransford, J. D., Brown, A. L., & Cocking, R. (1999). *How people learn: Brain, mind, experience and school.* Washington, DC: National Academy Press.

Brown, J. S., Collins, A., & Duguid, P. (1989). Situated cognition and the culture of learning. *Educational Researcher* (January-February), 32–42.

Chuckran, D. A. (1992). *Effect of student-produced interactive multimedia models on student learning.* Unpublished doctoral dissertation, Boston University.

Cognition Technology Group at Vanderbilt (CTGV), (1993). Designing learning environments that support thinking. In J. Lowyck. D. H. Jonassen & T. M. Duffy (Eds.), *Designing environments for constructive learning.* New York: Springer.

Coleman, S. D., Perry, J. D., & Schwen, T. M. (1997). Constructivist instructional development: Reflecting on practice from an alternative paradigm. In C. R. Dills & A. J. Romiszowski (Eds.), *Instructional development paradigms.* Englewood Cliffs, NJ: Educational Technology Publications.

Collins, A. (1990). Cognitive apprenticeship and instructional technology. In B. F. Jones &. L. Ido (Eds.), *Dimensions of thinking and cognitive instruction* (pp. 121–138). Hillsdale, NJ: Lawrence Erlbaum Associates.

Computer Supported Intentional Learning Environment (CSILE) Group, (1991). *An introduction to CSILE.* Unpublished white paper.

Crotty, T. (1994). *Integrating distance learning activities to enhance teacher education toward the constructivist paradigm of teaching and learning.* Paper presented at the Distance Learning Research Conference, College Station, TX.

Dede, C. (1993). Leadership without followers. In G. L. Kearsly, & W. Lynch (Eds.), *Educational technology perspectives (Vol. 19–28).* Englewood Cliffs, NJ: Educational Technology Publications.

Driscoll, M. P. (1994). *Psychology of learning for instruction.* MA: Allyn and Bacon.

Duffy, T. M., & Cunningham, D. J. (1996). Constructivism: Implications for the design and delivery of instruction. In D. H. Jonassen (Ed.), *Handbook of educational communications and technology* (pp. 170–198). New York: Simon & Schuster/Macmillan.

Flor, N. V., & Hutchins, E. L. (1991). *Analyzing distributed cognition in software teams: A case study of team programming during perfective software mainte-nance.* Paper presented at Empirical Studies of Programmers: Fourth Workshop.

Gery, G. (1991). *Electronic performance support systems: How and why to remake the workplace through strategic application of technology.* Boston: Weingarten.

Grabinger, R. S. (1996). Rich environments for active learning. In D. H. Jonassen (Ed.), *Handbook of research for educational communications and technology.* New York: Simon & Schuster/Macmillan.

Grabowski, B. L. (1996). Generative learning: Past, present & future. In D.H. Jonassen (Ed.), *Handbook of research for educational communications and technology.* New York: Simon & Schuster/Macmillan.

Grabowski, B. L. (1997). Mathemagenic and generative learning theory: A comparison and implications for designers. In C. R. Dills & A.J. Romiszowski (Eds.), *Instructional development paradigms.* Englewood Cliffs, NJ: Educational Technology Publications.

Hannafin, M. J. (1992). Emerging technologies, ISD and learning environments: Critical perspectives. *Educational Technology Research and Development, 40*(1), 49–63.

Hannafin, M. J., Hannafin, K., Land, S. M., & Oliver, K. (1997). Grounded practice and the design of constructivist learning environments. *Educational Technology Research and Development, 45*(3), 101–117.

Hutchins, E., & Hollan, J. (1999). COGSCI: Distributed cognition syllabus. [Retrieved from the World Wide Web.]. Available: http://hci.ucsd.edu/131/syllabus/index.html [1999, 11/14]

Interactive Media Corporation. (2000) *Learning database: An e-learning strategy for performance improvement.* Unpublished manuscript.

Jacobson, M. J., & Spiro, R. J. (1991). *A framework for the contextual analysis of compter-based learning environments.* (Report No. 527). Washington, DC: Office of Educational Research and Improvement (ERIC Document Reproduction Service No. ED 329 938).

Jonassen, D. H. (1991). Objectivism versus constructivism: Do we need a new philosophical paradigm? *Educational Technology Research and Development, 39*(3), 5–14.

Jonassen, D. H. (1992). Cognitive flexibility theory and its implications for designing CBI. In S. Dijkstra, H. P. M. Krammer, & J. J. G. van Merriënboer (Eds.), *Instructional models in computer-based learning environments.* Berlin: Springer-Verlag.

Jonassen, D. H., Davidson, M., Collins, M., Campbell, J., & Haag, B. B. (1995). Constructivism and computer-mediated communication in distance education. *The American Journal of Distance Education, 9*(2), 7–26.

Jonassen, D. H., Peck, K. L., & Wilson, B. G. (1999). *Learning with technology: A constructivist perspective.* Upper Saddle, NJ: Merrill/Prentice Hall.

Jonassen, D. H., & Reeves, T. C. (1996). Learning with technology: Using computers as cognitive tools. In D. H. Jonassen (Ed.), *Handbook of research for educational communications and technology*. New York: Simon & Schuster/ Macmillan.

Koning-Bastiaan. *Connected and scalable: A revolutionary structure for online communities* [online]. Available: http://www.eoe.org.

McClelland, J. L., Rumelhart, D. E., & Hinton, G. E. (1986). The appeal of parallel distributed processing. In D. E. Rumelhart, J. L. McClelland & the PDP Research Group (Eds.), *Parallel distributed processing: Explorations in the microstructure of cognition*. London: MIT Press.

Merrill, M. D. (1992). Constructivism and instructional design. In D. H. Jonassen & T. M. Duffy (Eds.), *Constructivism and the technology of instruction: A conversation*. Hillsdale, NJ: Lawrence Erlbaum Associates.

Merrill, M. D. (1998). Knowledge analysis for effective instruction. *CBT Solutions,* 1–11.

Merrill, M. D. (1999). Instructional transaction theory (ITT): Instructional design based on knowledge objects. In C. M. Reigeluth (Ed.), *Instructional-design theories and models: A new paradigm of instructional theory*. Mahwah, NJ: Lawrence Erlbaum Associates.

Merrill, M. D., & Thompson., B. M. (in press). The IDXelerator: Learning-centered instructional design. In N. G. Nieveen, K. (Ed.), *Design methodology and developmental research in education and training*.

Nardi, B. A. (1996). Studying context: A comparison of activity theory, situated action models, and distributed cognition. In B. A. Nardi (Ed.), *Context and consciousness: Activity theory and human-computer interaction*. Cambridge: MIT Press.

Phye, G. D., & Andre, T. (1986). *Cognitive classroom learning*. Orlando: Academic Press.

Resnick, Lauren B. (1991). Shared cognition: Thinking as social practice. In Lauren B. Resnick, John M. Levine, & Stephanie D. Teasley (Eds.), *Perspectives on socially shared cognition* (pp. 1–20). Washington, DC: American Psychological Association

Quinn, C. (2000). Learning objects and instruction components. *Educational Technology & Society, 3*(2).

Salomon, G. (1993). *Distributed cognitions: Psychological and educational considerations*. New York: Cambridge University Press.

Scardamalia, M., & Berieter, C. (1993). Technologies for knowledge-building discourse. *Communications of the ACM, 36*(5), 37–41.

Scardamalia, M., Berieter, C., Brett, C., Burtis, P. J., Calhoun, C., & Lea, N. S. (1992). Educational applications of a networked communal database. *Interactive Learning Environments, 2*(1), 45–71.

Scardamalia, M., Berieter, C., McClean, R. S., Woodruff, E. (1989). Computer supported intentional learning environments. *Journal of Educational Computing Research, 5,* 51–68.

Selvin, A. M., & Shum, S. J. B. (2000, July 16–19 2000). *Rapid knowledge construction: A case study in corporate contingency planning using collaborative hypermedia.* Paper presented at the KMAC 2000: Knowledge Management Beyond the Hype, Birmingham, UK.

Singh, H. (2000). *Achieving interoperability in e-learning.* Available: http://www.learningcircuits.org/mar2000/singh.html [2000, March]

Spiro, R. J., Feltovich, P. J., Jacobson, M. J., & Coulson, R. L. (1987). Cognitive flexibility, constructivism, and hypertext: Random access instruction for advanced knowledge acquisition in ill-structured domains. In T. M. Duffy & D. H. Jonassen (Eds.), *Constructivism and the technology of instruction: A conversation.* Englewood Cliffs, NJ: Lawrence Erlbaum Associates.

Wiley, D. A. (1998). *Effective and efficient education.* Available: http://wiley.byu.edu/dle/wiley/e3/

Wiley, D. A. (1999a). *Learning objects: Finding and incorporating digital resources into online instruction.* Paper presented at the Association for Educational Communications & Technology, Long Beach, CA.

Wiley, D. A. (1999b). *The post-Lego™ learning object.* Available: http://wiley.byu.edu/post-lego/

Wiley, D. A. (2000). Learning object design and sequencing theory. Unpublished doctoral dissertation, Brigham Young University. Available: http://davidwiley.com/papers/dissertation/dissertation.pdf

Wiley, D. A. (2002). Connecting learning objects to instructional design theory: A definition, metaphor, and taxonomy. In D. A. Wiley, (Ed.), *Instructional Use of Learning Objects.* Bloomington, IN: Agency for Instructional Technology and Association of Educational Communications and Technology.

Wiley, D. A., South, J. B., Bassett, J. Nelson, L. M., Seawright, L., Peterson, T., & Monson, D. W. (1999). Three common properties of efficient online instructional support systems. *ALN Magazine, 3*(2) [online]. Available: http://www.aln.org/alnweb/magazine/Vol3_issue2/wiley.htm

Wilson, B. G. (1997). Reflections on constructivism and instructional design. In C. R. R. Dills, A.J. (Ed.), *Instructional development paradigms.* Englewood Cliffs, NJ: Educational Technology Publications.

Wittrock, M. C. (1974). Learning as a generative process. *Educational Psychologist, 11*(2), 87–95.

Designing Resource-Based Learning and Performance Support Systems

Michael J. Hannafin & Janette R. Hill
(University of Georgia) &
James E. McCarthy (Sonalysts, Inc.)

Introduction

The transition of the education and training communities to paperless, digital work and learning environments has important implications. Principal among these issues is whether traditional approaches will simply be adapted, or if new approaches—involving varied cognitive demands, systems design, and focus—will evolve. Conventional approaches have long-standing education and training traditions, but they have come under criticism with the transition to digital approaches. These often involve the re-production of media and approaches that have been developed previously, tending to increase dramatically both the cost and the time required to develop training and education products and services. The focus of traditional approaches on the teaching and learning of isolated knowledge and skills has also been questioned. Simply re-hosting existing education and training approaches using digital media may optimize neither human nor technology's capabilities.

Two promising developments have emerged: (1) Electronic Performance Support Systems (EPSS) design technology, and (2) resource-based approaches to media production and access. Using knowledge object technology, multimedia resources can be tagged and re-used to support a wide range of education and training (as well as workplace) needs. EPSS technology has likewise emerged to address a range of both performance and learning demands. The link between these developments, however, is relatively new. The purposes of this chapter are to frame the learning-performance issues associated with EPSS use, to introduce EPSS design and implementation issues, to describe the relevance of resource-based approaches to EPSS design, and to present an EPSS project involving the application of knowledge object/resource-based approaches.

The Emergence of
Electronic Performance Support Systems

Simply stated, performance support systems help users do or accomplish things as they attempt to perform (Dorsey, Goodrum, & Schwen, 1993); EPSSs do so using computational technologies (Hoschka, 1996). An EPSS is a system of task-integrated online job aids, support tools, and information systems that assist users with workplace performance (IETI, 1995; Stevens & Stevens, 1996). While some have expressed the need for caution (e.g., Clark, 1992), EPSS technology has gained broad acceptance in the education and training communities (see, for example, Banerji, 1999; Gery, 1991, 1995; Hannafin, 1996; Huber, Lippincott, McMahon, & Witt, 1999; Raybould, 1995). Interest in EPSS technology has been evident in professional organizations, corporate training and education environments, and academic R&D settings (Carr, 1992).

EPSS focus represents a shift from acquiring knowledge to performing tasks (Collis & Verwijs, 1995; Gustafson, Reeves, & Smith, 1995). While there remains an important role for traditional education and training, the shift to user-centered, performance-based models is both inevitable and imminent (Hannafin, 1993, 1995). The delivery model has shifted from courses that teach decontextualized knowledge and skill to modules that support performance involving relevant knowledge and skill. This shift has affected all forms of education and training (IETI, 1995).

EPSS design practices represent a convergence among several related fields and specialties, including human performance technology, computer-supported collaborative work, technical communications, electronic publishing, instructional design, and workplace training (McGraw, 1994; Sherry & Wilson, 1996; Witt & Wager, 1994). According to Foshay and Moller (1992), research in the field of human performance technology must draw from a range of theoretical perspectives including behavioral, cognitive, and organizational psychology, as well as communications and general systems theory. Thus while the foundations for EPSS design are found across disciplines, they are organized and refined in none.

According to Gloria Gery (1995), two simple goals define what *any* EPSS should provide: (1) software to integrate knowledge, data, and tools required to help a performer succeed at a task, and (2) task structuring that guides performers to create deliverables. In a sense, EPSS technology is not so much a unitary design concept, with fixed features and components, as it is a perspective on designing systems that support learning and/or performing. This, however, can prove elusive and deceptively complex. A recent volume describing the development of EPSS and other tools to support instructional design (van den Akker, Branch, Gustafson, Nieveen, & Plomp, 1999) highlights the advances realized in the 1990s as well as needed research and development.

The Emergence of Resource-Based Approaches

One area in particular need of development for EPSS technology is the integration and use of resources. Resources have always been integral to training. Resource-based approaches extend the traditional use of available information and media by reusing and manipulating them to accommodate specific situational requirements. In EPSSs, resources are individual media (text, video, pictures, graphics, etc.) that have the *potential* to support performance. Resources are organized sets of data combined by an expert or specialist to convey a message, thus providing information related to a specific topic and/or task (Clark, 1998).

The pre-digital era constrained the creation and distribution of resources. Existing resources, primarily static in nature, were created to address specific situational needs and used largely intact. The need and demand for the flexible use of resources grows as the creation of digital resources continues to evolve. At the same time, developments in knowledge object technology and standards for classifying digital media (e.g., metadata), are transforming the very nature of media. Increasingly, individuals must find and adapt resources to meet training and learning needs unlike those for which the resource was initially created.

Resource-based approaches offer the potential for establishing situational relevance in a flexible development/delivery environment. They involve the identification and re-use (or adaptation) of existing resources to support varied, rather than only specific, training and learning needs. (See Hill and Hannafin [2000] for a more in-depth discussion of resource-based learning environments [RBLEs].) Resource-based approaches support efforts to adapt information to meet particular training needs. The meaning of a given resource is continually redefined by situating it in different contexts. Resources are considered to be epistemologically neutral, or can be made so, enabling their adaptation to varied directed or learner-centered environments. Various tools and pedagogical techniques assist the learner in tasks ranging from those embedded in the environment to those elicited by the learner or trainer. The tools and techniques (electronic to human-based; directed to open-ended) are viewed as partners in the process, supporting the learner and trainer in their work (Beswick, 1990; Freire, 1993). Such approaches utilize a variety of resources, including print (e.g., manuals, magazines), nonprint (video, audio, computer-based instruction), and human (e.g., trainer, librarian) resources to accomplish goals and specific performance outcomes.

Resource-Based EPSSs: An Integrated Perspective

In this section, we examine the potential of combining resource-based approaches with EPSSs to address the growing demand for just-in-time, individualized training built upon reusable digital resources. (See Table 1 for a summary of the main characteristics and examples as demonstrated in the Tactical Readiness Instruction, Authoring, and Delivery [TRIAD] system.)

Components

Resource-based EPSSs combine four core design components: resources, contexts, tools, and scaffolds. The ways in which the varied elements within the components are combined will vary depending upon the goals, context, and participants. A brief examination of each of the components will help in developing a greater understanding of the complexity of the environments.

Resources. Resources are the core information represented in resource-based EPSSs. They come in a variety of formats, ranging from electronic to print to nonprint to human. Resources take two predominant forms: static and dynamic. Static resources are immutable. They represent a fixed recording of ideas, facts, and beliefs at a specific point in time (e.g., textbooks, magazines). Dynamic resources, on the other hand, undergo frequent, sometimes continual change. Many Web-based resources, for example, are revised continuously, ranging from hourly updates (e.g., temperature databases at the National Weather Service), to several times a day (e.g., *New York Times* online). Dynamic resources provide a tool for providing up-to-the-minute information.

Both static and dynamic resources are tagged with specific information (e.g., details on the content, goals the resource relates to, etc.). The tagging enables the designer and developer to search an object library, find resources that match specific content and/or performance criteria, and access the best resources for a given learning or performance context. Growth in resource-based approaches has been evident across both corporate and government sectors. Motorola (1998), for example, is currently involved in a company-wide effort to create an object-based learning library. This electronic library will be filled with hundreds of learning objects: granules of expert/specialist knowledge. These objects will be made accessible to a wide-audience within an organization (Clark, 1998), enabling trainers to create instruction by combing various objects (i.e., resources). Similarly, the U.S. Department of Defense's Advance Distributed Learning (ADL) initiative employs a similar concept, sharable content objects (SCOs) to enable the sharing of the SCOs between and across a variety of users and contexts (Brower, 1999).

Performance contexts. Contexts are the settings, real and virtual, in which learning and/or performing circumstances are framed. Contexts, characterized by situations and goals, can be externally directed or learner generated.

Table 1. Characteristics of a Resource-Based EPSS

Feature	Description	Instantiation in TRIAD
Resources ***Information objects represented in the system***		
Static	Stable objects	Training manuals, reports, videos
Dynamic	Changing objects	Knowledge objects
Contexts ***Where/how performance is situated***		
Induced	Real or virtual	Does not apply
User-defined	Individual determines what problem and/or need to address	Does not apply
Imposed	External agent	Tacit defined externally; author developed TACMEMO; readers/users implement
Tools ***Enablers for locating, accessing, and manipulating resources***		
Searching	Find	Controlled author/user access to user different document section(s)
Processing	Gather and structure	Notes; bookmarks (specific to tactic requirements
Manipulation	Test and refine	Practice and assessment
Communication	Share information	Feedback; performance evaluation
Scaffolding ***Guides for the process***		
Conceptual	Identify relationships	Alternative explanations; "fit" between given tactic and related fleet operations
Metacognitive	Identify what you know	Background procedures minimize cognitive demands
Procedural	Navigation and logistics	Help system and tool tips; controlled access via table of contents
Strategic	Alternative perspectives/ approaches	Varied forms of support provided to author in the form of guidance, examples, sample TACMEMOs, etc.

Externally directed approaches are used to support learning and/or perform-ance per requirements external to the user (Haycock, 1991). An external agent (e.g., trainer, instructional designer) typically establishes the venue (real or vir-tual), sets the pace and sequence of resource use, facilitates interactions and activities (e.g., use of the library), and establishes goals for the learner to achieve. In learner-generated approaches, the individual defines the perform-ance goal based on unique needs, which in turn influences decisions related to where to seek resources (i.e., library, archives, the Web), what is needed, and when the need has been satisfied. Guidance may be sought from an external source (e.g., trainer, community expert), but assistance is initiated at the indi-vidual's discretion.

Tools. Tools are critical to locating, accessing, and manipulating the needed resources, as well as interpreting and evaluating the usefulness of the resources. Tools enable users to organize and present their understanding in var-ious ways (Jonassen & Reeves, 1996). Searching, processing, manipulation, and communication tools are among those commonly used.

Searching tools range from sophisticated search services with special-ized search capabilities (e.g., individual user profiles) to simplistic electronic library catalogs providing author, title, and subject searching for everyone. Web search engines (e.g., Yahoo, InfoSeek, AskJeeves), for example, extend capabil-ities and the breadth of resources that can be retrieved in a single search.

Processing tools enable the learner to gather and structure information or data. They support the collecting, organizing, integrating and generating of information. These tools enable a user to formalize relationships within and between ideas and, in some instances, between documents and management tools.

Manipulation tools, which vary in their sophistication and complexity, provide the ability to test and act upon ideas. Although relatively simplistic, spreadsheets are often used as examples of exceptionally powerful manipulation tools (see, for example, Grabe & Grabe [1998] or Jonassen & Reeves [1996] for an overview of spreadsheet applications). Users can engage in "what-if" activi-ties, as well as proposing and testing alternative solutions (Ramondetta, 1992).

Communication tools, both asynchronous and synchronous, enable the sharing of information in a variety of forms including text, voice, and video. A variety of communication tools have been used for enhancing face-to-face class-es as well as distance-delivered courses (see, for example, Dehoney & Reeves [1999], Francis [1997], Gamas & Nordquist [1997], Laffey, Tupper, Musser, & Wedman [1998], Witmer [1998]). The tools support a variety of activities: one-on-one interactions between trainer and trainee, small-group interactions, expert counseling, and presentations. Communication tools can also assist in community building (Palloff & Pratt, 1999; Parson, 1997; Weedman, 1999).

In these resource-based environments, individuals use e-mail to communicate with the trainer and listservs to participate in small-group projects; they view PowerPoint® presentations that are "Web-ized," and they engage in synchronous chat sessions, where weekly dialogues address various issues related to the course (Hill, 2000).

Scaffolding. Scaffolds act as assistants in the process, guiding users as they engage in learning and/or performance activities. Scaffolds come in varied forms, including conceptual, metacognitive, procedural, and strategic. *Conceptual* scaffolds assist the users in deciding what to consider, guiding and supporting them in recognizing relationships (Anderson-Inman & Zeitz, 1993). Used in real-time interactions or as reflective tools, conceptual scaffolds can be trainer- or user-generated, ranging from PowerPoint® presentations created by the trainer to an individual learner's cognitive map, showing links among various concepts.

Metacognitive scaffolds assist learners in assessing what they know, ranging from subtle reminders to reflect on the goal or problem, to directed decision-making in complex, ill-defined problems. Metacognitive support assists users by reducing cognitive load, enabling them to successfully engage in more complex processes such as critical thinking and reflection (Chang & Rice, 1993).

Procedural scaffolds assist the user in navigating and otherwise using the system. Site maps ranging from simplistic textual organizational charts to complex graphical representations, for example, can be useful guides for the learner attempting to use a particular system (Grabe & Grabe, 1998). *Strategic* supports offer the learner alternative ways to approach a task. Strategic support may come from an expert external to the system or may be embedded within a specific application or resource. As an intellectual partner, strategic supports can assist by off-loading tasks to the system, allowing learners to focus on other areas as the system shares the cognitive burden of the task (Pea, 1985).

TRIAD: A Case Study

A system currently under development provides an interesting example of resource-based EPSS in application. The Tactical Readiness Instruction, Authoring, and Delivery (TRIAD) project is developing a set of authoring and delivery tools that will enhance the quality of tactical guidance disseminated through the U.S. Navy.

Background & Purpose

Decision-makers within the U.S. Navy are faced with increasingly complicated and stressful tactical environments. These environments are characterized by situational uncertainty, time compression, and capable adversaries. To cope with such environments, today's decision-makers must have absolute command of a vast and varied knowledge base. Decision-makers must be familiar with situational cues, their ship and fleet capabilities and limitations (as well as those of potential adversaries), and tactics at his or her disposal (as well as those that potential adversaries might employ).

Some of this knowledge comes from formal training. However, the bulk of it is developed through experience and personal study of tactical publications (including Tactical Memoranda [TACMEMOs]) and combat system doctrine (Cannon-Bowers, 1995; Cannon-Bowers et al., 1994). The TRIAD project is a PC-based system being designed and developed to improve TACMEMO readership. TRIAD will provide authors with an integrated tool set to enable them to create tactical documentation (i.e., TACMEMOs) using a variety of multimedia presentation techniques, and to create associated interactive multimedia instruction (IMI) to support the documented tactic/doctrine. In turn, readers will receive a multimedia tactical documentation "product set" that supports tactic/doctrine presentation and briefing, instruction, quick reference, and facilitation of electronic feedback regarding tactic/doctrine evaluation. In the following sections, we emphasize TRIAD's role in facilitating the authoring of efficient and effective TACMEMOs.

Development Context

TACMEMO development begins with the identification of a tactical deficiency and development of a tactical solution that addresses that deficiency. The resultant tactic is disseminated to Fleet units via a TACMEMO. TACMEMOs are experimental tactics written by project officers. Project officers are provided with structural guidance[1] (i.e., the sections that a TACMEMO should include, and the order of those sections). However, despite the potential importance of the tactic for specifying offensive or defensive options and actions, they are provided with little or no guidance as to how to author a document that effectively and efficiently communicates it.

Once written, TACMEMOs are read by personnel ranging from flag-level commanders (i.e., Admirals) through junior enlisted personnel. At every level, readers must balance the need to read and understand new TACMEMOs against the press of their competing responsibilities. Their task is made more difficult by documents whose formats are not consistent with the reader's needs. As evidence, we recently queried a group of readers on their use of TACMEMOs. Within this group, TACMEMOs are used extensively as reference documents and are rarely studied. Only one participant indicated that he often read the body of the TACMEMO. Most indicated that they did so only on occasion; the remainder indicated they read the body of the TACMEMO rarely, if ever. By contrast, a large majority of participants indicated that they consulted TACMEMOs during operations.

Author Interview Process

After a tactic has been defined, the author uses TRIAD to create a product set. The process consists of three stages: interview, edit, and review. During the interview stage, the author creates and/or imports existing resources regarding the tactic in response to TRIAD-supplied interview questions. For example, the author might be asked to define the tactic (text), describe the tactic using an illustration (graphics), generate a scenario that supports practice (simulation), and/or import a video that shows tactic evaluation results. A given resource may be used in multiple portions of a given TACMEMO, and may be used or re-used for non-TRIAD purposes as well. As the interview progresses, TRIAD adds the information provided by the author to its database and tags each resource accordingly.

Using the information gained from the interview, TRIAD generates a draft TACMEMO product set consisting of the following integrated components: Base Document, Tactic Training Component, Quick Reference Guide (QRG), Feedback, and Brief. The Base Document contains the core TACMEMO content and procedures. The Tactic Training component addresses training requirements keyed to specific tactics knowledge and skills identified in a given Base Document. The QRG is an online job aid designed to distill the most essential aspects of the tactic for ready reference and to enable the user to link to associated Base Document and Tactic Training sections of the TACMEMO. Feedback, of a formative nature related to the tactic's usefulness, is elicited from users and recorded electronically. Finally, TRIAD generates a PowerPoint® presentation "brief" containing the primary information contained in the tactic. The brief can be edited and otherwise modified to provide greater or lesser breadth and depth, per audience needs.

The process continues with a guided elaboration and augmentation of the draft product set. The process consists of three iterative strategies, confirming, elaborating, and fine-tuning, designed to help authors refine and augment content. Confirmation assists authors in validating content accuracy and completeness as well as confirming TRIAD-generated structures and sequences. Confirmation is critical because it safeguards the accuracy of both the content and structure of TRIAD-generated documents. Elaboration helps authors to extend, amplify, and otherwise augment TRIAD documents. Authors elaborate and detail descriptions and supporting examples, especially those considered critical to the user's knowing and implementing the tactic. Fine-tuning enables the author to clarify information, directions, instruction, and presentation. At this step, the author amplifies key information, reducing or eliminating ambiguity and unclear or nonessential information.

Although the process will be largely transparent to the author, the authoring process will create a set of knowledge objects and organize them into the product set to be delivered to readers. The process begins through progressive decomposition of the product set's content. That is, the author is first asked to specify broad categories of information that the product set will address (e.g., Threats, Weapon Systems, Tactical Employment) and to specify one of these categories as the main thrust of the product set. For example, a given product set may focus on how to use a certain weapon to defeat a certain threat. In this case, the Tactical Employment, Weapon, and Threat categories would all be uses, but the Tactical Employment category would be marked as being the central theme or frame.

After specifying the broad categories of concern, the author breaks each category into smaller and smaller units (see Figure 1). For each category, the author is asked to specify which of a set of possible anchors are important to the product set. For example, within the Threat category, the possible anchors include Type, Mission, Design Characteristics, Identifying Characteristics, etc. This process continues as the author determines which aspects of the anchors themselves to discuss. For example, within the Identifying Characteristic anchor, the author could choose to discuss Identifying Features and/or Indicators via Equipment.

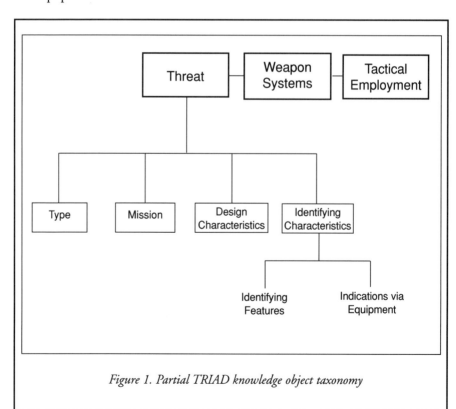

Figure 1. Partial TRIAD knowledge object taxonomy

The interview process continues by further decomposing the material to be presented (e.g., creating sub-sections for the base document or learning objectives for the tactic training component) and by eliciting content associated with a particular element (e.g., creating a description of a piece of equipment or a particular practice exercise). Content is added to the skeleton created through decomposition in two ways. First, TRIAD provides tools that will allow authors to create novel content. Perhaps more importantly, TRIAD also provides a utility with which authors will be able to search a library of knowledge objects and identify those that can be imported and used within the current knowledge set. This use of existing content will serve to add consistency to the information that is provided to the fleet. It will also make the quality of the delivered material more consistent and reduce the cost of producing product sets.

Once the interview is completed and the draft product set generated, the edit stage commences. Here, the author is again presented with the draft product set and can choose to edit any or all of the product set components. The author can add new media and edit existing media (text, graphics, animation, simulation, etc.). The author can import related media from the local TRIAD database, or from a remote database, into a product template and then edit as desired.

The review stage commences after all TACMEMO product set components have been developed. The TRIAD system will integrate the components into a review document with all associated markings. This review version can be distributed via multiple means (paper, local area network (LAN), wide area network (WAN), disk, etc.). Reviewers will be able to comment within the document and return these comments to the author. Comments received electronically will be stored in the TRIAD database for use by the TACMEMO author to revise components as required. The capability to merge comments into the document will be provided. As in the edit stage, the author can create/import new media and edit existing media (text, graphics, animation, simulation, etc.) in response to review comments.

This process of assembling the product set components into a review document, distributing the document for review, incorporating review comments, and reassembling the product set can repeat as necessary until a final product set is approved. Upon completion of the review process, TRIAD will assemble the TACMEMO product set for final packaging and subsequent distribution to readers (compact disk/digital videodisk (CD/DVD) or LAN/WAN). TRIAD will support document version control throughout this process.

TRIAD as a Resource-Based EPSS

In a sense, the TRIAD authoring environment is a resource-based EPSS for producing EPSSs. That is, the authoring environment must support authors as they attempt to produce a TACMEMO "product set" that supports the performance of field users (readers). It is useful, therefore, to consider TRIAD as a family of EPSSs, some designed to aid the author's performance and others to support readers' performance. In the following, we illustrate some of the characteristics and design decisions discussed previously in this chapter.

Resource Usage

TACMEMO development provides fertile ground for resource-based approaches. Often, several TACMEMOs describe the same weapons, systems, concepts, etc. in different contexts. Many of the resources relevant to associated tactics (e.g., training manuals, reports, graphics, videos) have been developed for other purposes and can be readily accessed. Resource-based approaches allow such media to be developed once and used many times, improving efficiency and consistency across TACMEMOs.

TRIAD is inherently resource-based in its instantiation of knowledge object technology. Knowledge objects (sometimes referred to as learning objects or sharable courseware objects) can be thought of as boxes with labels outside but sealed contents within. The label reveals the contents of the box. Knowledge object boxes may themselves contain multiple objects. As such, the knowledge objects provide an elegant way to store and organize the contents of our TRIAD product sets. The labels, known as the object's metadata, help in the organization function and make it possible to look for and re-use a knowledge object that contains desired content (the object's data).

TRIAD knowledge objects are constructed through a process of decomposition and population. The decomposition process breaks down large, complex tasks into distinct requirements, and results in a given number of empty "boxes" or knowledge objects. The population process essentially rebuilds the decomposed parts into connected wholes by filling the empty boxes with new or recycled media that are situationally relevant to the TACMEMO.

Additional insights on the use of knowledge objects within TRIAD can be gained if one views from a different perspective. Rather than considering how they are created, we could think of them in terms of the resultant products. From this perspective, one can see that the product set as a whole can be considered a large knowledge object. That is, the authoring process creates many *individual* knowledge objects that are, in turn packaged into one large knowledge object (see Figure 2). The various components of the product set can then be seen as sub-sets of the grand knowledge object (boxes within

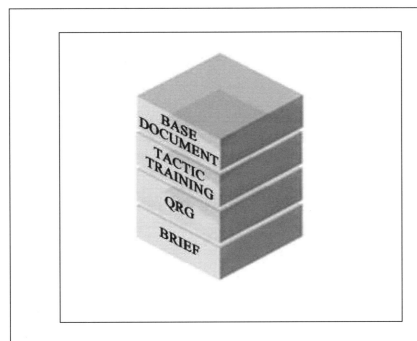

Figure 2. Knowledge object packaging process

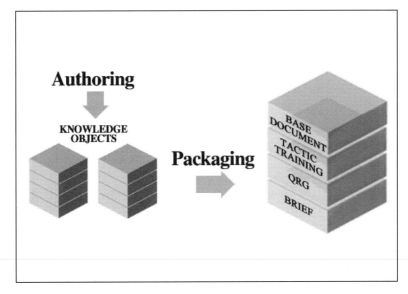

Figure 3. Individual knowledge object

boxes). The base document contains the encyclopedic representation of the tactic at hand. The tactic training component addresses a subset of the content covered by the base document, the QRG continues the refinement by addressing a subset of the content covered in tactic training, and the brief contains content that can be used to explain the tactic to others.

From this perspective, a single knowledge object can be envisioned as a single vertical slice through the product set as a whole. The object's representation would be dependent on the viewing context. Consider a particular slice through the product set shown in Figure 3. The knowledge object represented by that slice might include data associated with the base document, tactic training component, QRG, and brief. However, only portions of the knowledge object would be rendered at any given time. The rendition of the knowledge object within the base document component would be quite different than that seen in the instructional module or the QRG.

The resource-based approach also provides maintenance advantages. As information changes (e.g., about the capabilities of some weapon system), the knowledge objects that use that information must be changed. However, it is not necessary to change every document that describes that system. By fixing the shared resource, the documents are automatically updated when they are redistributed.

Contexts

Within TRIAD, context is usually negotiated. Superiors establish contexts either implicitly (we are moving to this theatre of operations) or explicitly (prepare a brief that summarized all the tactical information/guidance pertaining to this threat). However, the individual user generally has wide discretion in how he/she uses the available resources and tools. Further, individual users will generally attend to and process information quite differently as a function of their current responsibilities. TRIAD provides the resources and tools, and the users use them to meet their real-time performance requirements.

Tools

TRIAD's tools support those functions determined to be most important in its eventual implementation contexts. *Searching* happens at two levels within TRIAD. At one level, users can search for product sets that contain terms of interest to them. This search results in two lists: product sets for which the term could be considered a main idea or keyword and product sets that use the term in a less significant, more embedded way. The second level of search occurs *within* a given product set. Once again, users can search for key terms. Rather than merely providing a list of "hits," TRIAD annotates a table of contents to reflect sections that contain the term. The user can then jump to likely sections and find the search term highlighted. At both levels, TRIAD attempts to place search results in context to help users focus their efforts and build a mental model of the content of interest.

Processing tools within TRIAD include notes, bookmarks, highlighting. These tools allow users to "mark-up" product sets to reflect their current interests. As their focus changes, the annotations can be modified or deleted. On a grander scale, the PowerPoint®-hosted brief provides a powerful processing tool. Using PowerPoint®, and the one or more default presentations, the user can gather and manipulate information to serve immediate needs. The primary *manipulation* tools within TRIAD are the practice and assessment areas within the tactic training component. These areas allow users to test their understanding of the content and provide guiding feedback to help them improve performance.

The most obvious *communication* tool is the feedback component. The forms in this component allow a command to provide insights to the tactic developer. These insights are used to improve subsequent versions of the tactic or to discontinue its use. In a more subtle way, the presentation can be considered a communication tool, both for the original author and for the local personnel responsible for explaining the tactic to others. Finally, in special cases, the processing tools discussed earlier can be used as communication tools. Generally, other users can not see a given user's annotations. However, if a user has special privileges and chooses to do so, that user can choose to enter public notes, bookmarks, or highlights. These public annotations can help a leader communicate his/her perspective on a tactic to the rest of his/her team and thereby improve coordination and performance.

Scaffolding

Scaffolding assists individuals as they engage various activities. For example, conceptual scaffolding assists the learner in defining what to consider. Within TRIAD, the searching mechanisms described earlier also function as conceptual scaffolds by directing the user's attention to product sets and sections that are likely to contain the most relevant information. At a macroscopic level, the majority of conceptual scaffolding actually takes place during authoring. By enforcing a performance-focus during authoring, TRIAD ensures that the base document, tactic training component, QRG, and brief indicate to the user the key concepts within a given product set.

Metacognitive scaffolding is provided through the practice and assessment area in the tactic training component. These sections provide a definitive indication of what each user knows. Rather than just providing an indication of correctness, these spaces try to capture "teachable moments" and deliver guiding feedback to users. *Procedural scaffolding* is provided through a task-oriented help system and results-oriented tool tips. Rather than defining buttons and functions, TRIAD's help system and pop-up tips describe how to complete tasks and explain the consequence of using a control. The TRIAD navigational construct is another procedural scaffold. Depending on user actions, this construct provides a table of contents, an index, or a list of the active bookmarks.

Issues in Design, Development, and Implementation

Establishing a necessary relationship between learning and performing is a significant undertaking (Laurel, 1990; Raybould, 1990, 1995). Debate has surfaced as to which—performance or learning—is subordinate to the other: Is learning fundamentally prerequisite to performing or can performing become the impetus for learning (see, for example, Laffey, 1995; Rosenberg, 1995)? These are key issues for resource-based EPSSs. TRIAD reflects particular assumptions and decisions related to both the links between learning and performing and the manner in which its features are being designed. In the following section, we introduce several issues and describe how TRIAD addressed each.

Is Learning Prerequisite to, Incidental to, or the Product of Performance?

Learning as prerequisite to performance. Traditional learning and cognition theories and research posit hierarchical dependencies among knowledge and skill (see, for example, the analysis provided Hannafin & Rieber, 1989). Accordingly, many instructional systems design (ISD) approaches were honed through the basics-first, bottom-up teaching-learning approaches to military education and training refined by Gagné. Presumably, fundamental elements of complex intellectual skills and procedures must be learned in order to execute (and understand) the more advanced intellectual skills and procedures. These intellectual skills are considered the building blocks of complex reasoning and problem solving. To the extent more advanced procedures can be implemented without requisite knowledge and skill, the skill is generally thought to have been simply rote memorized (intellectual, procedural) and implemented under algorithm-like conditions rather than being a product of reasoned judgment and understanding.

Learning as incidental to performance. A second class of learning involves the acquisition of knowledge and/or skills that are not explicitly taught. Learning may be considered incidental to versus mandatory for performing (or vice versa). How much and what kinds of incidental learning result from guided performing and how much learning *must* result from extended EPSS support? To the extent learning benefits accrue incidentally, but such knowledge or skill is not deemed essential, it may represent "value-added" from the EPSS.

Salomon (1990) suggested that technology experiences may yield a cognitive residue as a consequence of tool engagement; that is, learning may be a by-product of EPSS engagement. If so, the simple use of the tool may promote incidental understanding of underlying concepts, or establish an organizer that helps to anticipate, select, and relate the knowledge. Bell and Winn (2000) suggest that well-crafted technologies make individuals smarter and more productive, and that such effects are often more durable than traditional teaching-training approaches. Sherry and Wilson (1996) describe EPSS scaffolds through which users become increasingly capable though online support, and eventually acquire the knowledge and skill needed to perform, independent of support tools.

While attractive in principal, this is neither acceptable nor sufficient in many cases. There is little evidence that either EPSS designers or the corporate/ organization users of such systems recognize that systems promote incidental rather than intentional learning. Typically, management presumes that learning has occurred to ensure that employees will function independently. And rarely do such systems promote enough incidental learning to ensure independent performance. Learning is tacitly assumed to be the product of EPSS use, but the systems fail to cultivate the required learning.

Learning as required of performance. Generally, models of EPSS facilitated performance assume that basic underlying knowledge and skills are acquired through performance; some embed features to increase the probability that this acquisition will occur. The EPSS immerses the user in actual task performance wherein knowledge and skills are anchored. Successful execution of required performances presumably enables the bootstrapping of related knowledge and skill while providing rich contextual referents for encoding and subsequent retrieval.

Unlike incidental learning where knowledge and skill are value-added, self-sufficiency requires the independent ability to perform without the aid of the system. That is, EPSSs are presumed to generate residual effects. EPSS will be available initially and faded or eliminated subsequently; users will become increasingly self-reliant as they perform more effectively and acquire the underlying knowledge and skill. Indeed, under these assumptions, the user must learn sufficiently to perform without EPSS scaffolding.

These views are consistent with the conceptual bootstrapping tenets of situated cognition theory. But how (or do) individuals learn through technology tools designed to promote performance? We cannot assume that individuals understand simply because they perform with the support of an EPSS. To the extent knowledge and skill *must be engendered* by the EPSS, the success or failure of the system needs to be weighed against both criteria. Typically, both are assumed; rarely have they been simultaneously verified or validated. Nor have the features of EPSS systems that contribute to learning versus performing been well articulated.

Is there antagonism between learning and performing? Antagonism can exist between learning and performance. It is not clear which and when EPSS features facilitate learning or performing at the expense of one another. For example, some programs provide general supports (e.g., online documents, help), but fail to support either learning or performing very well. Large volumes of poorly focused material (e.g., manuals, reference guides, forms, etc.) are made available online, but little corresponding guidance is offered to scaffold their use. As a result, the EPSS is often more cumbersome, complex, and difficult to implement than the nonelectronic versions they were designed to replace. EPSSs fail because the designers naively assume that simply providing online resources facilitates learning and/or performance. Instead, it complicates navigation and the user's ability to establish relationships and sequence information.

A key set of issues concerns how judgments related to knowing, understanding and performing become operational in EPSS systems. Depending on the features and focus, EPSSs may promote the learning of enabling knowledge and/or skills as situations dictate (Laffey, 1995). They may augment understanding associated with particular knowledge or actions, or supplant certain cognitive functions deemed either too mundane to warrant training or too complex to attempt to teach (Gery, 1995). The latter is often the case where performance contexts require little-used, exceedingly detailed or highly idiosyncratic knowledge or skill sets. They are considered key to specific situations but of very little utility beyond them (such as in tax preparation programs such as TurboTax).

TRIAD's focus. We have already noted that learning is not an explicit goal for TRIAD authors. That is, we expect our authors to produce quality products; it is not necessary that they learn the principles on which those products are based. Nonetheless, it is intellectually interesting to consider if, and how, authors will learn from their performance.

Learning may be considered *incidental to* versus *mandatory for* the performance. If any learning is to take place among TRIAD authors, it is almost certain to be incidental. However, TRIAD poses another interesting question: Does the learning result from the performance itself or from witnessing the product of performance? That is, if our authors learn, will it be because they were stepped through a systematic design process or because they have been shown the results of such a process and now aspire to produce something similar on their own?

At this point, answering this question is an exercise in speculation. However, our current belief is that the work sample will contribute more to the author's growth (if any) than the experience. Because the instructional design principles are hidden within implicit templates, which are further hidden behind interviews (to aid usability), the process itself is unlikely to be manifestly instructive. However, in an area where there is a dearth of good examples, viewing a well-constructed product set may well improve transfer performance.

Scaffolding vs. Planned vs. Learned Dependence

Some EPSSs makes no pretense that they "teach" or performers "learn." Their goals are simply to automate task functions by supplanting the cognitive processes that underlie a performance. There is no expectation that tasks ultimately will be performed independently. Continued reliance is planned and by design.

Frequently, however, the expectations or requirements involve increasingly self-reliant performers. Support systems are expected to influence learning (and user performance) without sustained reliance on the EPSS; users become increasingly self-sufficient by learning from their EPSS (Stevens & Stevens, 1996). According to Sherry and Wilson (1996), "[groups] that utilize online . . . systems may find that performance is improved, expertise is developed earlier, and the scaffolding or 'training wheels' of the EPSS can be removed or ignored whenever learners feel that their performance has become viable on its own." For many, both learning and independent performance are not merely goals; they are presumed.

Interestingly, this does not occur routinely. Often, systems promote performance at the expense of learning; that is, they fail to develop the understanding needed to perform without the support system. This can be manifested in several ways. Rather than fading performance scaffolds, they remain available continuously, reducing the requirement to perform independently. Alternatively, some EPSS both scaffold the performance and teach the knowledge and skills embodied in the performance, but do so ineffectively. Finally, some systems presume that the knowledge and skill embodied in a performance are acquired naturally by virtue of performing effectively. In some cases, this occurs; in others, it does not. To the extent the cognitive processing and restructuring attendant to performance are required or desired, we must identify EPSS structures and features that promote both learning *and* performance.

TRIAD's focus. As noted earlier, one of the first decisions that the TRIAD development team had to confront was the learning vs. performance goal requirements. In addition to helping the author produce high-quality product sets, should TRIAD increase the authors' knowledge of instructional design, technical writing, performance support, etc.? Indeed, previous work in this area has spanned the range of possibilities on this question. For example, Tennyson (1993; Elmore & Tennyson, 1995) explicitly set about to develop an EPSS that would enable authors to gain more instructional design insight as it attempted to support their fledgling instructional design efforts. That is, it attempted to embody the approach mentioned earlier as scaffolding. In describing his work, Tennyson (1993) noted, "Although ISD Expert cannot be considered a means for teaching ISD, the very nature of the system's philosophy, which assumes that authors will gain knowledge with experience, will result in continuing improvements in ISD applications."

In a later description, Elmore and Tennyson (1995) describe the Integrated Courseware Engineering System (ICES). They postulate the ICES would operate in three modes: Tutor, Coach, and Consultant. The tutor mode would be more prescriptive and function over a narrower range of problems. However, as the author gained experience (and, presumably, competence), the system would act more like a coach, and then a consultant. Within these modes, more experienced authors would exercise more direction over the design process and the system would only step in to offer advice and assistance with rare or unique instructional design problems.

An alternative approach is offered by Merrill (1993; Cline & Merrill, 1995). Merrill's goal is to increase instructional design efficiency, not to increase the instructional design competence of a group of users. To enable subject-matter experts and other instructional design novices to efficiently create high-quality instruction, Merrill developed the ID Expert. ID Expert uses Merrill's notion of instructional transactions[2] to create templates (transaction shells) that can be populated with domain knowledge: "Instructional transactions implicitly provide instructional design principles for the content being presented due to their inherent structure to teach different types of knowledge" (Cline & Merrill, 1995). Within Merrill's approach, independent author performance is never a goal.

The TRIAD approach is more akin to Merrill's approach than Tennyson's. This was a pragmatic design decision based on the nature of the user population. TACMEMOs are written by middle grade officers with operational experience relative to the assigned tactical project warfare area. These individuals possess a minimum of a bachelor's degree and at least some computer skills. Some, but not all, individuals may have instructional skills if previously assigned to a training or instructor billet. Project officers are temporarily assigned to TACMEMO development commands. When their tour of duty is up, they will move on to other duties. While with the development command, a given project officer is likely to develop only one or two TACMEMOs. Within this framework, we must assume dependence and build a system that appropriately structures the author's performance.

Within TRIAD, the majority of development will occur through the use of implicit templates. That is, the templates are used to guide an interview with the author and to organize the resultant content. This approach has the benefits of Merrill's template approach, while masking much of the complexity from the author. It ensures a high level of compliance with theoretically sound instructional design principles without requiring the author to master those principles.

Bootstrapping Knowledge with Performance

Generally, EPSS performance is contextually rooted in real world versus classroom settings. Performance is scaffolded via online support tools ranging from explicit direction through explanations of the knowledge and skill required of the task. Knowledge and skills are not taught with the goal of subsequent transfer to work tasks; they are anchored within the performance itself. They are not isolated from the contexts in which they have meaning for a given task; rather, they are embedded naturally (Stevens & Stevens, 1996).

It is important to note that cognitive skills *may be* acquired by performing EPSS-facilitated tasks. Smith and Unger (1997) described "conceptual bootstrapping" where new interpretations and understandings derive from experiences garnered from learning in realistic contexts; that is, understanding is deepened through the strong contextual referents associated with performing "real" tasks. For EPSSs, this could be an important windfall, since by design they situate cognition authentically.

Though intuitive and widely assumed, in practice the presumed learning assumption has rarely been scrutinized. Indeed, the reverse may occur. Some have voiced concern that the narrowness of many EPSSs may obscure the relevance and potential further applicability of knowledge and skills. Rather than employing the rich context to make apparent the knowledge and skill relevance, EPSSs may focus so intently on "doing" that users invest few or no cognitive resources to understand (Gavora & Hannafin, 1995). Instead of deepening understanding by bootstrapping knowledge and skills, such systems signal that understanding is not important, and users invest cognitive resources accordingly (cf. Hannafin et al., 1996).

It is apparent that EPSS features can influence user perception of both the importance of anchored knowledge and skills as well as the success or failure of performance itself. The same features have the potential to amplify or minimize the perceived importance of such knowledge to the user. It is not clear whether cognitive bootstrapping is feasible in the design of EPSSs that *must* promote performance.

TRIAD's focus. TRIAD provides one example of a system that must promote performance. As noted earlier the TRIAD team knowingly decided not to bootstrap authoring knowledge with performance. Rather, since authors have little need for long-term understanding of instructional design principles, these principles are "hidden" behind an interface designed to support efficient production.

On the other hand, long-term knowledge is a requirement for TRIAD readers. Here, bootstrapping by performance is not only possible but essential. To accomplish this goal, TRIAD provides ample opportunities for readers to apply their knowledge in realistic situations. These practice and assessment activities are an important additional to current TACMEMOs.

Knowledge as "Tool"? The Transfer Paradox

We know far more than we understand; indeed, there is no compelling reason to understand fully many of the things we know. Such information has been described as "inert." Inert knowledge has little utility for subsequent learning or performing as it is often learned for very specific purposes. For many, a great deal of formal education involves the acquisition of inert knowledge in order to meet specific test requirements or remember particular information. While such learning may be an especially noble goal for either student or teacher, the consequences are generally limited to the individual's personal and academic learning endeavors.

In other cases, however, there is a clear requirement that knowledge and skill will be transferred to progressively more complex learning and/or performing tasks. Sometimes transfer expectations are well known and discrete, such the adaptation of tactics to new weapons systems whose structures and features mirror earlier systems. For the application of prerequisite knowledge and skill in well-defined domains, the results are encouraging. "Low-road" tasks involve routine application of knowledge and skill under relatively straightforward circumstances. Near transfer tends to be relatively successful using traditional bottom-up, hierarchical approaches (Hooper & Hannafin, 1991).

At other times, the transfer requirements are important but not explicit or known initially. Many important tasks are complex by their nature. Compelling evidence suggests that transfer of knowledge or skill to qualitatively different problems, contexts, or domains is inconsistent at best and problematic at worst (e.g., Greeno, Smith, & Moore, 1993). Traditional bottom-up approaches are largely ineffective for performances requiring critical judgments—those where effective performance is most important and valued (Hannafin, 1992). "High road" tasks, where reasoning and cognitive complexity demands require the greatest interpretation, evaluation, and judgment, are both critical to situational problem solving and much more difficult to promote. Knowledge, skill, and situativity are more conditionally linked in complex tasks, making the selection and deployment of specific actions difficult to anticipate in advance, much less to teach or train.

Technology-enhanced EPSSs may offer an alternative. Pea (1985) suggested that technology both causes individuals to reorganize mental processes to accommodate variations as well as allowing users to alter the tasks themselves in an attempt to engage concepts more deeply. Transfer metaphors and models may be reconceptualized by approaches that do not segregate knowledge and skill from context. Both the learning presumed shaped by education and training approaches, requiring initial acquisition and subsequent application, as well as the mental processes engendered by technology facilitation, may promote knowledge, skill, and performance that is fundamentally more contextually sensitive and transferable. To the extent both learning and performance are valued, EPSSs may provide a different type of learning activity, one characterized more by manipulation than accumulation, and more by construction than compilation.

Despite the dominance of traditional teaching-learning models in military education and training, transfer to workplace settings has proven elusive. The metaphor of knowledge as tool has become increasingly popular in depicting the utility (or lack thereof) of knowledge. Knowledge as tool involves the ability to retrieve relevant background and skills, to analyze their relevance to given circumstances, to transform knowledge with the introduction of new information, and to deploy it successfully in learning and/or performing settings (Jonassen & Reeves, 1996). It requires organization, integration, and understanding beyond simple knowing.

TRIAD's focus. To a large extent, far transfer is not an issue within TRIAD. Generally, TACMEMOs are written to address specific issues; their contents pertain to a given issue and transfer beyond that issue is seldom required. However, it is vitally important that TRIAD support near transfer. That is, when a situation arises, the reader must recognize that it falls within the class addressed by a given TACMEMO and respond accordingly. To support this form of situated recall, the TRIAD interview has been informed by contemporary conceptions of situation assessment and decision making (e.g., Zsambok & Klein, 1997).

Complexity and Usability Tradeoffs

EPSS systems have evolved into larger and more complex environments. They offer a myriad of online resource options (e.g., layers of menus and options) as well as layered advice and task structures. Laffey (1995) outlined dynamic EPSS system features that marry the best of technological capabilities with the automatic building of tools, artifacts, and strategies. He suggests that dynamic, intelligent design features can create a robust EPSS providing just-in-time support and guidance in contextually rich environments. While authorities describe the current trends in design that have influenced EPSS evolution, little attention has been given to prescribing such design features or how to combine them to meet learning and performance expectations.

Usability has proven another barrier to effective EPSS design and use. While EPSSs can be highly effective as a means of providing users timely and relevant information, it is often no simple task to use one. Users tend to defer to their peers for support, and are often unwilling to make use of the online help facilities that the programs themselves offer. Others have reached similar conclusions across corporate as well as traditional school settings. EPSSs will not be used at all, much less effectively, if the features are not readily understood or do not address key cognitive as well as procedural performance demands.

TRIAD's focus. A second EPSS design dimension described earlier was the tension between providing extremely capable, but complex EPSSs on one hand, and simpler, but more usable, systems on the other. With this in mind, TRIAD developers have chosen to emphasize usability. Again, several reasons can be cited. TRIAD would dramatically change the way TACMEMO authors did business; for many, this alone would be difficult for them to accept. If TRIAD was difficult to use, the quality of the potential product set would be immaterial; authors would simply not use the tool and would not produce product sets. As a result, the potential would never be realized. However, if the initial product was easy to use and thus demonstrated its value, the authoring community would "pull" for expanded capabilities. Therefore, we are initially producing a simpler product. As it proves successful, there will be ample opportunity to expand its capabilities.

In addition to weighting the design decision towards usability, the TRIAD development team adopted a user-centered development approach. This included an early needs analysis to ensure that the developed functionality was useful, as well as on-going formative evaluations to ensure that it is usable. A spiral design approach ensures that as opportunities for improvement are identified, resources will exist to capitalize on them.

Dedicated v. Flexible Tools

The increase in just-in-time support and contextual relevance has blurred many traditional distinctions between classroom and field-centered training and education. Considerable interest has been expressed in optimizing the flexibility and utility of systems traditionally designed to support multiple functions. In principal, EPSSs are ideally suited to support on-demand performance in authentic work contexts. Technology instigates the elusive "teachable moment"—situations optimal to understanding, while extending the "zone of proximal development"—wherein the capacity to understand is supported beyond the individual's independent capabilities (Salomon, Globerson, & Guterman, 1989; Salomon, Perkins, & Guterman, 1991). EPSSs situate users in the "performable" moment, involving authentic problems and tasks; technology scaffolds and facilitates performance while potentially, but not necessarily, deepening understanding. The hope is to extend the design technology to address learning and performance under controlled training and education contexts. This could provide significant versatility and power to EPSS designs.

In contrast, some EPSSs are so narrowly defined that exceedingly limited information and functions are made available. This may result in users needing to access external resources for task completion or making poorly informed decisions without the benefit of needed online support or job aids. Neither performance nor learning has been supported; indeed each has been complicated.

TRIAD's focus. The TRIAD delivery environment must support a range of performances, including third-party explanations of the tactic. That is, often one individual aboard a ship or other command is asked to "brief" the TACMEMO to others. Briefing the tactic is one of the most common tasks for our users. It is also one of the most important; the brief may be the only exposure many of their shipmates have to the tactic. Unfortunately, it is also one of the most error-prone tasks. The briefers must communicate the tactic to others, but they often lack needed background in instructional design and communication. Moreover, unlike the authors, the briefers often may not even be experts in the tactic.

Clearly, explaining the tactic is a different task than performing the tactic. As such, TRIAD provides different tools to support performance. Within TRIAD, we provide a well-constructed, performance-oriented brief that briefers can use as-is or tailor to fit their immediate situation. By providing a solid foundation to the training session, we increase the likelihood that the third-party brief is true to the original TACMEMO.

Closing Comments

Many education, training, and support functions have, or will soon be, been transformed by resource-based, knowledge object technologies. In a sense, even the phrase "learning object" unduly limits the potential utility of a resource, since it suggests that re-use aspects will be learning-focused. This may or may not prove to be true; certainly, in TRIAD's case, it is not. TRIAD's conceptualization of knowledge objects is more inclusive and cross-functional, linking families of resources both within and beyond a given system. At its topmost level, knowledge object technology makes possible the most open of open system design. Will we capitalize on such openness or attempt to cordon off segments and claim them as our own?

It remains to be seen whether or not we ultimately open rather than segregate teaching-learning-training uses of digital resources. The ISD field has a rather dim recent history in its reluctance to pursue or embrace approaches energized outside the walls of its traditional nuclear community. Knowledge object technology, however, portends change of a very different kind; it is a pragmatic imperative rooted in neither philosophical underpinnings nor epistemological beliefs about the nature of understanding. It seems inevitable that systems designed to optimize the value of any given resource between and among use functions will continue to emerge—with or without the leadership (or compliance) of the traditional instructional design field. The decision is ours—individually and collectively.

Acknowledgements

The authors can be reached at: *Michael J. Hannafin, University of Georgia, 611 Adeerhold Hall, Athens, GA 30602 (706/542-3157, FAX: 706/542-4321, hannafin@coe.uga.edu); Janet R. Hill, University of Georgia, 604 Aderhold Hall, Athens, GA 30602 (706/542-3810, FAX: 706/542-4032, janette@coe.uga. edu); and James E. McCarthy, Sonalysts, Inc., 215 Parkway North, Waterford, CT 06385 (800/526-8091, Ext. 443, FAX: 860/447-8883, mccarthy@sonalysts.com).*

Notes

1. Often, even this minimal guidance is violated.

2. An instructional transaction is a "complete sequence of presentations and reactions necessary for the student to acquire a specific type of instructional goal" (Cline & Merrill, 1995).

References

Anderson-Inman, L., & Zeitz, L. (1993). Computer-based concept mapping: Active studying for active learners. *The Computing Teacher, 21*(1), 6–11.

Banerji, A. (1999). Performance support in perspective. *Performance Improvement Journal, 38*(7), 6–9.

Bell, P., & Winn, W. (2000). Distributed cognitions, by nature and by design. In D. Jonassen & S. Land (Eds.), *Theoretical foundations of learning environments.* Mahwah, NJ: Lawrence Erlbaum Associates.

Beswick, N. (1990). *Resource-base learning.* London: Heinemann.

Brower, J. M. (1999). Military tunes to virtual classroom. *National Defense, 84*(552), 65–67.

Cannon-Bowers, J. A. (1995). *Application of multimedia technology to training for knowledge-rich systems.* Technical Development Plan. Program Element PE0603733N.

Cannon-Bowers, J. A., Salas, E., Duncan, P., & Halley, E. J. (1994) *Application of multimedia technology to training for knowledge-rich systems.* Paper presented at 13th Interservice/Industry Training Systems and Education Conference. Orlando, FL.

Carr, C. (1992). Performance support systems: The next step? *Performance & Instruction, 31*(2), 23–26.

Chang, S. J., & Rice, R. E. (1993). Browsing: A multidimensional framework. *Annual Review of Information Science and Technology,* (28), 231–76.

Clark, R. C. (1992). EPSS—Look before you leap: Some cautions about applications of electronic performance support systems. *Performance & Instruction, 31*(5), 22–25.

Clark, R. C. (1998). Recycling knowledge with learning objects. *Training & Development, 52*(10), 60–63.

Cline, R. W., & Merrill, M. D. (1995). Automated instructional design via instructional transactions. In R. D. Tennyson & A. E. Barron (Eds.), *Automating instructional design: Computer-based development and delivery tools.* Berlin/Heidelberg: Springer-Verlag

Collis, B. A., & Verwijs, C. (1995). A human approach to electronic performance and learning support systems: Hybrid EPSSs. *Educational Technology, 35*(1), 5–21.

Dehoney, J., & Reeves, T. C. (1999). Instructional and social dimensions of class Web pages. *Journal of Computing in Higher Education, 10*(2), 19–41.

Dorsey, L. T., Goodrum, D. A., & Schwen, T. M. (1993). Just-in-time knowledge performance support: A test of concept. *Educational Technology, 33*(11), 21–29.

Elmore, R. L., & Tennyson, R. D. (1995). Psychological foundations for automated instructional design. In R. D. Tennyson & A. E. Barron (Eds.), *Automating instructional design: Computer-based development and delivery tools.* Berlin/Heidelberg: Springer-Verlag

Foshay, W. R., & Moller, L. (1992). Advancing the field through research. In H. D. Stolovitch & E. J. Keeps (Eds.), *Handbook of human performance technology: A comprehensive guide for analyzing and solving performance problems in organizations* (pp. 701–714). San Francisco: Jossey-Bass.

Francis, J. W. (1997, December/January). Technology enhanced research in the science classroom: Student track down proteins through the Internet maze. *JCST,* 192–196.

Freire, P. (1993). *Pedagogy of the oppressed: New revised 20th anniversary edition.* New York: Continuum.

Gamas, W., & Nordquist, N. (1997). *Expanding learning opportunities through online technology. NASSP Bulletin, 8*(592), 16–22.

Gavora, M., & Hannafin, M.J. (1995). Perspectives on the design of human-computer interactions: Issues and implications. *Instructional Science, 22*, 445–477.

Gery, G. (1991). *Electronic performance support systems: How and why to remake the workplace through the strategic application of technology.* Tolland, MA: Gery Performance Press.

Gery, G. (1995). Attributes and behavior of performance-centered systems. *Performance Improvement Quarterly, 8*(1), 47–93.

Grabe, M., & Grabe, C. (1998). *Integrating technology for meaningful learning* (2nd ed.). Boston: Houghton Mifflin.

Greeno, J., Smith, D., & Moore, J. (1993). Transfer of situated learning. In D. Detterman & R. Sternberg (Eds.), *Transfer on trial: Intelligence, cognition, and instruction.* Norwood, NJ: Ablex.

Gustafson, K. L., Reeves, T. C., & Smith, M. L. (1995). Evaluation of an EPSS for instructional design in corporate training centers. In M. Muldner, (Ed.). *Training in business and industry* (pp. 53–67). Enschede, The Netherlands: University of Twente Press.

Hannafin, M. J. (1992). Emerging technologies, ISD, and learning environments: Critical perspectives. *Educational Technology Research and Development, 40*(1), 49–63.

Hannafin, M. J. (1993). *The cognitive implications of computer-based learning environments.* Report prepared for USAF AL/HRTC, United States Air Force Office of Scientific Research, Bolling AFB.

Hannafin, M. J. (1995). Open-ended learning environments: Foundations, assumptions, and implications for automated design. In R. Tennyson (Ed.), *Perspectives on automating instructional design* (pp.101–129). New York: Springer-Verlag.

Hannafin, M. J. (1996-October). *Technology and the design of interactive performance support systems: Perspectives, issues, and implications.* Presented at the International Conference on Educational Technology, Beijing, China.

Hannafin, M. J., Hannafin, K. M., Hooper, S. R., Rieber, L. P., & Kini, A. (1996). Research on and research with emerging technologies. In D. Jonassen (Ed.), *Handbook of research in educational communication and technology* (pp. 378–402). New York: Macmillan.

Hannafin, M. J., & Rieber, L. P. (1989). Psychological foundations of instructional design for emerging computer-based instructional technologies: Parts I & II. *Educational Technology Research and Development, 37,* 91–114.

Haycock, C. A. (1991). Resource-based learning: A shift in the roles of teacher, learner. *NAASP Bulletin, 75*(535), 15–22.

Hill, J. R. (2000). Web-based instruction: Prospects and challenges. In R. M. Branch & M. A. Fitzgerald (Eds.), *Educational Media and Technology Yearbook* (25), 141–155.

Hill, J., & Hannafin, M. J. (2000). *Teaching and learning in digital environments: The resurgence of resource-based learning.* Submitted for publication.

Hooper, S., & Hannafin, M. J. (1991). Psychological perspectives on emerging instructional technologies: A critical analysis. *Educational Psychologist, 26,* 69–95.

Hoschka, P. (Ed.). (1996). *Computers as assistants: A new generation of support systems.* Mahwah, NJ: Lawrence Erlbaum Associates.

Huber, B., Lippincott, J., McMahon, C., & Witt, C. (1999). Teaming up for performance support: A model of roles, skills, and competencies. *Performance Improvement Journal, 38*(7), 10–15.

IETI. (1995). Special issue on electronic performance support systems. *Innovations in Educational and Training International, 32*(1).

Jonassen, D., & Reeves, T. (1996). Learning *with* technology: Using computers as cognitive tools. In D. H. Jonassen (Ed.), *Handbook of research for educational communications and technology* (pp. 693–719). New York: Macmillan.

Ladd, C. (1993). Should performance support be in your computer? *Training & Development, 43*(8), 23–26.

Laffey, J. (1995). Dynamism in electronic performance support systems. *Performance Improvement Quarterly, 8*(1), 31–46.

Laffey, J., Tupper, T., Musser, D., & Wedman, J. (1998). A computer-mediated support system for project-based learning. *Educational Technology Research & Development, 46*(1), 73–86.

Laurel, B. (Ed.). (1990). *The art of human-computer interface design.* New York: Addison-Wesley.

McGraw, K. (1994). Performance support systems: Integrating AI, hypermedia, and CBT to enhance user performance. *Journal of Artificial Intelligence in Education, 5*(1), 3–26.

Merrill, M. D. (1993). An integrated model for automating instructional design and delivery. In J. M. Spector, M. C. Polson, & D. J. Muraida (Eds.), *Automating instructional design: Concepts and issues.* Englewood Cliffs, NJ: Educational Technology Publications.

Motorola University (1998). Motorola's learning objects initiative. *Training & Development, 52*(11), 69–73.

Palloff, R. M., & Pratt, K. (1999). *Building learning communities in cyberspace : Effective strategies for the online classroom.* San Francisco: Jossey-Bass.

Parson, P. T. (1997). Electronic mail: Creating a community of learners. *Journal of Adolescent & Adult Literacy, 40*(7), 560–565.

Pea, R. (1985). Beyond amplification: Using the computer to reorganize mental functioning. *Educational Psychologist, 20*(4), 167–182.

Perez, R. S., & Emery, C. D. (1995). Designer thinking: How novices and experts think about instructional design. *Performance Improvement Quarterly, 8*(3), 80–95.

Ramondetta, J. (1992, April/May). Using computers: Learning from classroom trash. *Learning, 20*(8), 59.

Raybould, B. (1990). Solving human performance problems with computers. A case study: Building and electronic performance support system. *Performance & Instruction.* Washington, DC: National Society for Performance & Instruction.

Raybould, B. (1995). Performance support engineering: An emerging development methodology for enabling organizational learning. *Performance Improvement Quarterly, 8*(1), 7–22. Available: http://www.cet.fsu.edu/SY2000/PIQ/Raybould.html

Rosenberg, M. J. (1995). Performance technology, performance support, and the future of training: A commentary. *Performance Improvement Quarterly, 8*(1), 94–99.

Salomon, G. (1990). Cognitive effects with and of computer technology. *Communication Research, 17*(1), 26–45.

Salomon, G., Globerson, T., & Guterman, E. (1989). The computer as a zone of proximal development: Internalizing reading-related metacognitions from a reading partner. *Journal of Educational Psychology, 81*(4), 620–627.

Salomon, G., Perkins, D., & Guterman, E. (1991). Partners in cognition: Extending human intelligence with intelligent technologies. *Educational Researcher, 4,* 2–8.

Sherry, L., & Wilson B. (1996). Supporting human performance across disciplines: A converging of roles and tools. *Performance Improvement Quarterly, 9*(4), 19–36. Available: http://www.cudenver.edu/public/education/sherry/pubs/pss.html

Smith, C., & Unger, C. (1997). Conceptual bootstrapping. *The Journal of the Learning Sciences, 6*(2), 143–182.

Stevens, G. H., & Stevens, E. F. (1996). *Designing electronic performance support tools: Improving workplace performance with hypertext, hypermedia, and multimedia.* Englewood Cliffs, NJ: Educational Technology Publications.

Tennyson, R. D. (1993). A framework for automating instructional design. In J. M. Spector, M. C. Polson, & D. J. Muraida (Eds.), *Automating instructional design: Concepts and issues.* Englewood Cliffs, NJ: Educational Technology Publications.

van den Akker, J., Branch, R., Gustafson, K., Nieveen, N., & Plomp. T. (Eds.). (1999). *Design approaches and tools in education and training.* Dordrecht, The Netherlands: Kluwer Academic Publishers.

Weedman, J. (1999). Conversation and community: The potential of electronic conferences for creating intellectual proximity in distributed learning environments. *Journal of the American Society for Information Science, 50*(10), 907–928.

Witmer, D. F. (1998). Introduction to computer-mediated communication: A master syllabus for teaching communication technology. *Communication Education, 47,* 162–173.

Witt, C. L., & Wager, W. (1994). A comparison of instructional systems design and electronic performance support systems design. *Educational Technology, 34*(7), 20–24.

Zsambok, C. E., & Klein, G. (1997). *Naturalistic decision making.* Mahwah, NJ: Lawrence Erlbaum Associates.

Learning Objects to Support Inquiry-Based, Online Learning

Chandra Hawley Orrill
(Ohio University)

Introduction

The current move toward reusable, easy to build tools for supporting information acquisition in learning environments (Downes, 2000; Merrill & ID$_2$ Research Group, 1998; Myers, 1999) is an important one for further consideration. While there are undoubtedly advantages to the development of these learning objects, we have, as a field, overlooked the most important aspect of the tools—how they support student learning. The discussion on learning objects thus far has focused largely on their design and technical development (e.g., LTSC, 2000). The purpose of this chapter is to describe one potential use of learning objects—as support tools in a project-based action learning environment. This environment depends on student immersion in real-world problems with scaffoldings of various kinds to support their inquiry (Jonassen, 1999). Further, and perhaps most critically, it includes social interaction among peers (e.g., Duffy & Cunningham, 1996; Jonassen, 1999; Savery & Duffy, 1995).

> The process of using technology to improve learning is never solely a technical matter, concerned only with properties of hardware and software. Like a textbook or any other cultural object, technology resources for education—whether a software science simulation or an interactive reading exercise—function in a social environment, mediated by learning conversations with peers and teachers. (Bransford, Brown, & Cocking, 1999, p. 218)

As conceptualized by the ID$_2$ group (e.g., Merrill, 1999; Merrill & ID$_2$ Research Group, 1998; Merrill, Jones, & Li, 1996), learning objects offer ease of development, a high degree of interchangeability, and a higher degree of individualized learning than traditional group-focused instructional interventions. However, these objects grow out of and exemplify a strong information processing foundation (Driscoll, 1994). After all, used as stand-alone teaching agents, they rely exclusively on the notion that information—which, in this belief system, is synonymous with "knowledge" (Mayer, 1999)—is a commodity that can be transferred from the computer to the student. Once the student has seen the information and studied the information, she will be able to pass the test on that information. And, presumably, once the student has processed the information, she will be able to use it as part of a larger knowledge base.

In the current conception, there is also a strong leaning toward the notion that people should learn small amounts of discrete information at one time and slowly build a network of these information chunks. For instance, an object may teach a single process or idea. Once that content is mastered, the student will move on to the next process or idea. Each object is discrete and separate from the next. In the end, however, the student is expected to tie these discrete pieces together in order to understand larger ideas. In this additive approach to education, it would be assumed that if a learner were to study maps of each region of the world independently, that learner would eventually be able to create a representation of the entire world.

Finally, there is a strong emphasis in the common conception of learning objects on the traditional "presentation, practice, feedback" model that is regarded as an exceptional tool in helping to deliver information to students. That is, the learning object presents the information, provides the student with an infinite amount of practice, and provides a test that allows the computer to provide feedback. This harkens back to the view that because computers are infinitely patient, the student is free to work on the material for as long as necessary, and, if she fails to master the content, she will be able to revisit the learning object. Of course, it does not embrace, or even acknowledge, the notion that the information may be more readily learned if learners have access to it in multiple presentation modes.

Learning objects built on this information delivery model fail to provide solutions for many current learning environments. The current movement in education today calls for students to develop *information age skills* rather than build content bases (e.g., Boyer Commission, 1998; Brown, 2000; Mayer, 1999; U.S. Dept. of Labor, 1991). That is, businesses are looking for students who have critical thinking and problem solving skills, communication skills, and know how to be professionals in their fields rather than simply knowing about the field itself. In short, businesses are looking for people who have learned how to learn. In response to these calls, and in response to our increasing understanding of learning and instruction, there are many varieties of inquiry-based, constructivist learning environments being developed. For example, problem-based learning (e.g., Savery & Duffy, 1995) and goal-based scenarios (e.g., Schank, Berman, & Macpherson, 1999) are becoming increasingly common in higher education, K–12 classrooms, and corporate training.

Many of these more authentic approaches to education suffer from some of the same problems as traditional approaches. In constructivist environments as in others, students need access to good content, ways of measuring their understanding, and the ability to have multiple exposure opportunities when confronted with new information. Because of these needs, learning objects seem to provide an excellent support tool in these inquiry-based learning environments. However, using learning objects in constructivist ways requires some rethinking of the objects and careful consideration of their use.

The purpose of this chapter is to explore the implications of using learning objects to support a constructivist learning environment. To illustrate our ideas, a description of the MBA Without Boundaries program (MBAWB) project involving the development of a library of learning objects to support a project-based, inquiry learning environment is included. This environment, the MBAWB, is a mostly Web-based, cohort model for earning an MBA degree at Ohio University (http://mbawb.cob.ohiou.edu/brief.html). This two-year program uses a combination of complex, authentic problems and face-to-face residencies to help its students develop all of the content, process, and leadership skills and knowledge they need. It addresses the needs of highly motivated people who cannot attend a traditional, face-to-face program.

While the MBAWB offers a strong program that has had a high level of success, there are still areas for improvement. One area of improvement centers on information sources. At the beginning of the MBAWB, students purchase a set of books that provide a foundation in all the areas in which they will be working. In addition to these books, students are strongly encouraged to use the Internet as a key resource. However, there has been no effective way for students to share what they find within their own cohort—or with other cohorts. This has led to frustration as students wade through the Internet quagmire looking for critical information, project after project. This also leads to heavier demands being placed on the faculty as students become frustrated by the difficulty they are having in locating appropriate information. In an effort to ease strain on faculty and provide a viable library, the MBAWB faculty is creating a set of learning objects to support students as they work through their projects.

Learning Objects in the
Constructivist Learning Environment

Much ado has been made of constructivism over the past two decades. In fact, it has become such a popular buzzword, that many people are adopting it to describe anything that involves students working together or working on projects. Unfortunately, this sells constructivism as a theory far short. The fundamental belief of constructivism should be kept at the heart of any design effort of a constructivist learning environment. That belief is that knowledge is constructed—it is not a transferable commodity, rather it is developed within each individual based on her experiences and understandings of the world around her (Bruner, 1990; Driscoll, 1994; Duffy & Cunningham, 1996; Jonassen, 1999; Savery & Duffy, 1995). While it is undeniable that multiple people can have similar understandings, each walks away from a learning situation with a somewhat different understanding of what they have learned and how it can be used.

In action, a constructivist environment supports the development of understanding in a number of ways. The environment should be based around an authentic problem that provides a motivating context for learning (Jonassen, 1999; Savery & Duffy, 1995; Schank et al., 1999). These problems should be open-ended, allowing students to tackle situations in authentic ways to solve a problem with no one right answer. The constructivist learning environment should allow for social negotiation so students can test their understandings against others' and readily share information (Jonassen, 1999; Lave & Wenger, 1991; Savery & Duffy, 1995; Vygotsky, 1978). Finally, the environment should be designed to help students construct knowledge. This is supported by social negotiation and through context, but also depends on modeling and scaffolding to help students become successful learners (APA, 1997; Jonassen, 1999) as well as opportunities for reflection in and on action (APA, 1997; Schon, 1987).

Cognitive Apprenticeship

Under the epistemological umbrella of constructivism, we find a number of theories and approaches that become relevant to our discussion of learning objects for the MBAWB. One key element of our specific context is the need for authentic learning. Both the cognitive apprenticeship (Brown, 2000; Brown, Collins, & Duguid, 1989) and the situated learning (Lave & Wenger, 1991) movements have brought the notion of learning *in situ* into public discussion. Both movements have asserted that in order to develop professionals in a field, we must provide our learners with an opportunity to develop as professionals. Too often, education focuses on learning *about* a profession rather than learning to be a professional. "Many of the activities students undertake are simply not the activities of practitioners and would not make sense or be endorsed by cultures to which they are attributed" (Brown et al., 1989, p. 34). Particularly in the case of a professional school, such as a school of business, there is no higher goal than producing professionals; therefore, the educational experience of the students should be designed to move in that direction.

In order to help our students become professionals in the field, we must focus on creating cognitive apprenticeships for them—that is, creating learning environments that let students construct understandings of the world through *doing* (Brown, 2000; Brown et al., 1989; Duffy & Cunningham, 1996). This is a move away from the emphasis on developing *knowing* that typically prevails in educational settings (Brown et al., 1989). It should be noted, however, that this *doing* is at a cognitive level, not a behavioral one (Mayer, 1999) and that one of the underlying assumptions of this kind of learning by doing assumes that "[w]hen students learn how, they inevitably learn content knowledge in the service of accomplishing their task" (Schank et al., 1999, p. 165). Students need to engage in authentic activities—real-world problems and situations that they might face in their workplaces. They need to deal with real activities in which professionals in their field engage. And they need to have opportunities to develop the processes and thinking of a professional through increasingly complex situations. These learning opportunities need to be scaffolded in a way that allows learners to move from lower-stakes circumstances to higher stakes as they learn (Lave & Wenger, 1991). Without a rich, holistic learning environment the learner's experience is impoverished, disconnected, and somewhat random. The learner needs to have a rich context—such as a real-world, ill-structured problem. This context needs to be provided in a way that allows the learner to work within her zone of proximal development (Vygotsky, 1978).

The cognitive-apprenticeship notion of learning to use tools (including cognitive tools) in the ways that professionals really use them becomes even more critical to the learning experience when the learners are already professionals in their fields. The learners already know something about how the field works and how some of the tools might be used. Further, they are busy being practitioners in their field. These two factors—a working knowledge of the field and busy-ness—lead them to have little tolerance for an "ivory tower" approach to education. They want authentic learning that allows them to immediately apply their academic work to their professional lives. We see this in our MBAWB students as well as in other students who are full-time professionals, such as the author's graduate students who are full-time teachers.

Open-Ended Learning Environments

The context is a critical element in this discussion. Our challenge in "teaching" students is not to identify key information they need to know and sequence it for delivery. Instead, our challenge is to provide an environment that is rich with learning experiences and resources. These environments should be learner-centered in that the students are responsible for determining what is important in the problem they are solving (Savery & Duffy, 1995). Further, they need to be open learning environments (OLEs) (Hannafin, Land, & Oliver, 1999; Hill & Land, 1998) that support students in developing their own understandings of that which they have decided is important. Rather than allowing instruction that simplifies "detection and mastery of key concepts by isolating and instructing to-be-learned knowledge and skill" (Hannafin et al., 1999, p. 119), OLEs require that complex problems be used that link concepts and content to real situations where the "need to know" is naturally generated. These are environments in which instruction is more than a transaction of information from the machine to the student (Merrill & ID_2 Research Group, 1998).

Merrill has argued that all content must eventually be decontextualized in order to be generalized from one instance to another (Merrill, 1992). As might be expected from this, the ID_2 group's learning objects can cover a variety of materials in discrete units much the same way an encyclopedia might. However, this argument is absolutely reversed from the constructivist ideal (Bednar, Cunningham, Duffy, & Perry, 1992; Duffy & Cunningham, 1996) and from the perspective of "legitimate peripheral participation" (Lave & Wenger, 1991). In the MBAWB approach, we have adopted the perspective that students should learn everything in context because the more similar the learning environment is to the "real world" the students will face after their learning experience, the more easily they will be able to adapt what they have learned to that environment (Savery & Duffy, 1995). We have combined this with the scaffolding notions that suggest allowing students to work in more and more complex situations which require revisiting their existing knowledge as they construct new understandings.

The essential nature of a learning context is the underlying premise to the entire MBAWB program (Stinson & Milter, 1996) and an idea that drives our learning objects. We do not expect that students will ever access the learning object library unless they have questions—either related to their MBAWB projects or their jobs. The context gives them a reason to visit the objects and provides something for them to anchor the information in the learning objects to.

Within the OLE, learning objects act in two key ways: as resources and as scaffolding. As resources, they are designed specifically to enable students easy access to information in a just-in-time fashion. If a course problem requires a student to do a needs analysis or learn about a certain accounting technique, there needs to be information readily available to students on those topics. In this way, the learning objects help support the students in becoming *bricoleurs*—that is, becoming the users of tools to build things that are important to them (Brown, 2000). Their job is to decide which tools will work to build their desired product.

Second, learning objects provide a certain degree of scaffolding for the student. In this case, it is the way we use the objects that provides the scaffolding. First, they offer conceptual scaffolding (Hannafin et al., 1999) in that we are creating the objects to help students focus on concepts key to their understanding. The MBAWB learning objects team envisions that learners will start at a broader level and work more deeply—uncovering more detail and more complex ideas as they go through the library of objects.

Learning objects also offer strategic scaffolding. They will be offering a variety of approaches to the concept to support the learners in developing a deeper understanding of the object's content (Hannafin et al., 1999). The learner will first see a brief overview of the specific topic of an object, and then she will be able to access more detailed information. There will be advice from experts contained in each object as well as complex cases ("war stories" and "case studies") that demonstrate practical application to the learner. Further, there will be links to more information, to related objects, and to other key information.

Finally, there is potential in our learning objects for metacognitive scaffolding through reflection in the assessment area. Because our primary concern is with students determining whether they understand the content, whether the content is what they need, and what they still need to know to answer their larger question, the purpose of our "tests" is quite different from that of traditional ones. We have the freedom—and, in fact, the imperative—to use innovative strategies in the test section that allow students to evaluate their own thinking, to reflect on where they are, and to evaluate their mental models for inconsistencies. In this way, we are allowing students to "test their mettle" before "going public" to their team with their ideas (Schwartz, Lin, Brophy, & Bransford, 1999).

Social Negotiation

Key to any constructivist environment and particularly important to both the OLE approach and cognitive apprenticeship model is an implicit valuing of the communities of practice that are developed as part of the learning process. To the MBAWB team, learning is a process of social negotiation—what we learn is shaped by those around us and, in fact, meaning is determined not only by each individual but also by the culture within which the individual is acting (Duffy & Cunningham, 1996; Lave & Wenger, 1991). Without context, information is quite meaningless. For example, one of the author's education graduate students reported that on a standardized test she had to give her first graders, a question asked the student to select the picture that showed a road leading into a city. The students in the class all chose the two-lane road—after all, the highway leading to their rural town was two lanes wide. However, the test writers had determined that the "correct" answer was the four-lane road, using a different context from that of the students. The answer they were asking for had no relevance in the students' lives. Social understanding and context are inseparable and inescapable.

Each student in an OLE setting such as ours participates in at least one community of practice—the community formed by the students in the class and the instructor. In the MBAWB, and in an increasing number of educational experiences, the students participate in at least two communities of practice simultaneously. They are active in the community of learners through an asynchronous conferencing system, e-mail, and other communications tools while simultaneously being full participants in the community of practice at their workplace. This learning ecology (Brown, 2000) not only strengthens the knowledge base of the individuals involved, but also fosters "cross-pollination" between the multiple communities represented in each cohort. In the learning community of practice, we see both talking *within* and talking *about* the profession, both authentic activities critical to learning (Lave & Wenger, 1991). It is the talking *about* activity that learning objects hope to inform. The intention is that the explicit knowledge developed through work with the objects will inform the tacit knowledge base of the student and that the student's tacit knowledge will contribute to the communities of practice of which the student is a part (Brown, 2000).

Learning Objects as Knowledge Objects

Outside the world of learning objects, the phrase "knowledge objects" has been used to describe "tight integration of the understandings [students] develop" (Entwistle & Marton, 1994, p. 166). In their study they were considering how we deal with new information in creating meaning. Their study indicated, in fact, that we might need to develop *understanding* of a subject or discipline before we can learn facts—the students need some sort of prior understanding to anchor the facts to before they are meaningful. These understandings, and the facts students link to them, are the knowledge objects. This notion, actually, more closely matches our conceptual framework than the learning objects notions put forth by Merrill's ID_2 group (Merrill, 1999; Merrill & ID_2 Research Group, 1998; Merrill, Jones, & Li, 1996).

One key way that this desire to build learning objects that represent knowledge objects manifests itself is in our design process. We are essentially creating a concept map of the entire program and providing learning objects for each of the items in the concept map. In fact, at the learning object level, we have asked the faculty to create visual concept maps that break down their own "knowledge objects" in their area of expertise in order to provide an idea of what pieces of their knowledge fit together to create the objects. Further, this gives each learning object a place within the larger map that represents the body of information an MBA needs to be comfortable with. By using the concept mapping technique, we are also able to consider whether there is a need for learning objects that break down an idea further.

Our ultimate desire is that students will use our learning objects to form their own bodies of understanding. Because of our fundamental belief that there is no single "correct" body of understanding, we are not attempting to create *the* MBA concept map. Instead, we are recognizing that the faculty will be providing a body of information in the objects that will be used within an overarching context that drives students' need to know the information. The students will take that information, put it into their own contexts, work with it in their own community of practice, and leave with a different body of knowledge than each individual faculty member might have. That is exactly our goal. Because this is our goal, students will not have access to much of the concept map. The one element they will benefit from is links to learning objects that have been designated by faculty as being closely related to the object they are currently working on. However, there will be no attempt to incorporate the entire concept map for the library into the learning objects or the navigation structures.

Building Learning Objects for the MBAWB

The MBAWB has turned to learning objects as an enhancement to the learning environment currently offered. The Web-based learning objects library will be provided to the students as another body of material to support their work on the real-world problems that remain at the center of all learning. This library will focus on the foundational information that remains virtually unchanged over time (such as "what is an income statement?"). Students will still be expected to seek out and use other Internet-based resources for the more dynamic information—we expect that our students will develop business research skills and develop the ability to work in ill-structured inquiry environments as part of their program. As with the other resources in the program, the learning objects will be used by the students on an as-needed basis. However, we do not anticipate that students will see learning objects as optional—we expect that they will come to rely on the learning objects library as a primary source of information.

Our view of learning objects fits Wiley's definition, *"any digital resource that can be reused to support learning"* (Wiley, 2000, p. 23). Our objects are certainly designed to support learning. More specifically, we are supporting learning in an inquiry-based environment by providing necessary materials in an easy-to-access format. The learning objects are meant to be reusable. Most immediately, they will be reused project after project for the duration of each MBA cohort. The MBAWB leadership also anticipates the potential use of subsets of the objects in other courses—particularly at the undergraduate level—and the use of the learning object library by alumni who are professionals in the field. And, by necessity, the MBAWB learning objects are digital. In fact, because of the distributed nature of the program and our desire for easy maintenance, our learning objects are exclusively Web-based.

Our objects, however, differ in some critical ways from the conventional definitions of learning objects. One fundamental difference is the size of the object. Each of our learning objects is the sum of a number of smaller pieces. The MBAWB learning objects will usually include introductory text, video, case studies, war stories, a further reading list, and a self-test. There are no purposely accessible smaller components, although we acknowledge that students might use the "Save as . . ." option to save these smaller pieces, and the objects are not generated by dynamically combining a number of smaller elements based on metadata tags. This is quite different from the view of objects as being able to be instantly generated from small components (LTSC, 2000). The MBAWB approach is attempting to address the issues of reusability and repurposability (Wiley, 1999) by thinking of the learning objects only in our specific context. We recognize that we are limiting the reusability of the primary building blocks of the learning objects by linking them so tightly to each other. However, we are providing more integrated information within each object, thereby allowing students to more readily see whether an object meets their current needs and how it meets those needs. This, of course, ties back to the larger learning context and our fundamental beliefs about the roles of the learning objects in scaffolding learning and supporting information access needs of students in OLEs.

Another critical difference between the MBAWB use of learning objects and other ideas about them is our conception of their ultimate purpose. Our goal and design approach is to create a set of approximately 500 objects that will represent a body of information known by an expert in business. These objects will not replace the learning context; rather they will be a supporting part of it. They depend heavily upon the problem and on the social context, including support and questioning from the faculty, to be effective. We are not attempting to create a point-and-click MBA program.

As described in Downes (2000), we envision the objects existing within a database. We will be using his notion of separating the content from the "look" of the page. We anticipate using XML or some other standard to dynamically generate the visible objects from the data in the database. We will be storing the information in a presentation-independent form in the database and will use templates to generate the presentation form. By using this approach, we will be able to create a template for easy upgrading and maintenance of the objects as well as providing a means for controlling how students enter each object. Further, by using a database, it will be easy to modify portions of the objects as necessary without the need to edit multiple HTML pages. While our learning objects contain multiple components, rather than individual building blocks, we see using the same kinds of metadata and structuring as helping us to generate the objects rapidly—an undeniable benefit of the learning object idea.

To us, the user's entry point to each learning object is critical in helping to prevent navigational disorientation. We plan to create a system that allows students to always access the summary page for the learning object before accessing any further content. This has two important advantages. First, by providing the concept brief, we provide an opportunity for students to quickly determine whether this object contains the information they need. Second, when a student moves from one object to another, it will be immediately apparent because the first page will always be the concept brief.

Pieces of the Objects

As previously discussed, the MBAWB learning objects will contain a variety of materials arranged in a standard way. Each object will consist of a number of parts: a glossary entry, concept brief, content overview, readings, examples, problems/cases, war stories, "self-test," and bibliography. By including such a variety of materials, we attempt to provide multiple representations of the information so that learners can develop more holistic and transferable understandings of the objects.

Technically the learning objects will fall under Wiley's (2000) "combined-open" classification. There will be a number of discrete items pulled together into a packet of Web pages. However, they will functionally be more like the "combined-closed" objects because each packet of learning objects will be presented to the user as a single unit. We will provide no overt ability for the students to access individual pieces of the larger objects. Each of these packets will be comprised of pieces its author has chosen to put together. The objects will not be dynamically generated from the metadata tags as some learning objects might be. Further, the self-tests will be specific to the object as a whole and will help the learner consider her own understanding of the concept covered by the object. While we are limiting reusability because the objects are more detailed than a collection of pictures, for example, we are developing the objects to contain more contextual information to help users. Each of the pieces, with the exception of the glossary entry, will be accessible from anywhere within an object. The glossary entry will serve as one navigational strategy for getting the students to the information they need. They will have access to a complete glossary of terms with brief definitions. The student can use this to select a concept or process they want more information on.

The objects will always open to the concept brief page that will include a summary of information about the concept or process that is the focus of the learning object. It will most closely parallel an encyclopedia entry on the topic. The length will be one or two paragraphs. The student can, from this page, decide where to go within the object to support her own learning best. The choices from this page—and all the other pages within the object—will be to go to the content overview, problems or cases, war stories, or self-test.

The content overview section will include a full description of the content of the object written by an expert in the content area—either a professor or a businessperson. This section will include five to ten pages of text describing the process or concept. Our goal is to provide the content in a way that allows students to see how it is applicable to the business world. Thus, the examples will reside in this section of the object. The content overview will also be the gateway to the additional readings that are available about the topic. These readings may include publicly accessible online materials as well as materials the MBAWB has obtained copyright permissions to use in this closed system. The goal is to provide as much information as possible to students without requiring them to scour the Internet. The bibliography will also be accessible from the content overview section. It will point students to other resources—both in print and on the Internet—that might be helpful to them in developing their understanding.

The examples, as part of the content overview, may be realistic microcases of the process or concept at work. They will not necessarily be based on real situations and may not be as complex and rich as a case would be. They are intended to provide an alternate way to demonstrate what the content overview is talking about. Examples may also include tools or screenshots of tools that are used by practitioners so students can see what those are and how they work.

The problems or cases may consist of text, audio, and/or video. They will include examples of the concept or process at work in a real business situation. The cases will be complex and include rich detail about when and how to use the information from the learning object. The problems and cases, as well as some of the examples, will provide some of the variety necessary to help students transfer the content to other situations (Bransford et al., 1999).

The war stories are designed to give a real account of what happened in an implementation of the process or concept. These video and audio clips will include discussion of the things that went well and what kinds of things can go wrong. They will feature practitioners in various business settings. The goal of these pieces is to help students see a richer picture and to help them understand how the content or process fits into a larger context.

Finally, the self-test will provide an opportunity for students to measure their own understanding of the content of the learning object. The students may revisit the test/reflective activity as many times as they want. The test will not involve any interaction with the facilitators. The tests will either be reflective in nature—asking students to consider their understandings on new cases, or they may use computer-scored multiple choice items in cases where that is appropriate. In all cases, the tests will either be self-scoring or provide model answers with elaboration so that the students can measure their own understanding and benefit from seeing how an expert thinks through the same situation.

Navigating in and between Objects

In all of these sections, there will be common within-object navigation. The student will be able to use point-and-click steering to move from one section of the object to the next. There will not be a way to use a search engine to go directly to a particular part of the object. Instead, there will always be a "front door." In this way, we aim to reduce the risk of students becoming lost in the learning objects library (Fleming, 1998; Nielsen, 2000). While we recognize that some people might see this structure as limiting the learning object potential by not allowing pieces to be interchangeable, we see this structure as being superior in helping students work with considerable information by always having a beginning for the objects and always having the same basic pieces within the objects.

One of our greatest concerns and interests with learning objects is supporting the students in moving through them effectively. Unlike the ID_2 learning objects, the MBAWB learning objects cannot be sequenced because we cannot expect that students will move through the information in a particular order. In fact, expecting them to do that would harm the learning environment because it would remove ownership of the problem from the students (McCombs & Whisler, 1997; Savery & Duffy, 1995). If we cannot support student movement between and within the objects based on their evolving needs and understandings, the objects will not be serving the scaffolding functions they are intended to serve.

In our ideal implementation, students will have full access to the complete library of objects from their first day in the MBAWB program. There are a number of implications of this. First, the MBAWB students exhibit diverse levels of skill in both navigating the Internet and in their content knowledge. This means that we will need to offer a variety of options, such as browsing and searching, so that we can support both expert and novice searchers and learners. Novice learners in any area not only do not know much, but also are not able to express what they need to know (Hill, 1999). We will need to provide an easy way for them to get what they need. The glossary is our primary means for doing this. It provides the novice users with the opportunity to use browsing methods—following point-and-click paths—rather than forcing them to search for something that they may not even be able to adequately define using search terms. The glossary attempts to support the novice by providing little pieces of information about each entry to help learners identify whether an object is appropriate or not appropriate to them.

As further support to novices, we may package learning objects into certain groups to help prevent students from getting lost in the information. This packaging could be automated by using keywords or it may come from the faculty specifically pointing out a small subset of learning objects that support students in getting started with their projects. Further, by identifying a starter set, we would help the students move toward asking the question *"Is what I have found sufficient? Am I ready to end the search?"* (Hill, 1999).

Likewise, we know that by the end of the program our students are more expert in both their search capabilities—because they will have done some Internet searching as part of the MBAWB program—and their content knowledge. They will be more likely to know how to express what they do not know. And, they will be more capable of assessing the value of the information they have found. Unlike novices who tend to browse the Internet, experts focus on deliberate searches (Hill, 1999). In order to address the needs of these users, we will provide a strong search capability centered on keywords. This means that while they can only access a given learning object from its "front door," students will have some ability to search on the subcomponents of the learning objects. Therefore, if they were searching for a particular keyword that appeared in a "war story," they would be able to find the object that contained that keyword. To further help them find their specific component of the object, the search engine will offer specific information about the exact piece the keyword relates to.

The between-objects navigation will also include the ability to move between related objects. This list of related learning objects will be generated based on the concept maps completed by the faculty showing their thoughts on how information fits together. The related objects will also be determined, to an extent, by the projects. We intend to take the project contexts within which the students work into account in our programming. However, we do not intend to imply particular relationships in our learning objects library. While we can identify pieces that seem to be tied together, we do not want to infer that those relationships are static or the only relationships possible. Because of this, the concept map relations will never be made apparent to the students.

Conclusions

While, in the end, the tools may look similar, the cognitivist and constructivist uses of learning objects are undeniably different. They are meant to serve different purposes—both practically and philosophically. They do have some very important similarities, however. Both situations provide learning objects that are transferable to new situations and can be put together in a variety of ways to achieve a variety of goals. The intent in both cases is the same—to provide information to students that capitalizes on the multimedia capabilities of computers in an affordable, time-sensitive way. Both strive to be easy enough to work with so that the instructor/facilitator can easily create new objects. And both use the same kinds of structuring.

While we are only in the beginning phases of developing these objects, they have forced us to consider what we value most in the learning process and how the objects fit that picture. Perhaps the most striking and important difference between the MBAWB learning objects and those of Merrill's ID$_2$ group and others is the dependence of the MBAWB objects on the greater context. Because they are a part of an open learning environment (Hannafin et al., 1999), the use of learning objects relies on context, social negotiation, self-directed learning, and reflective practice in order to be effective. This is in stark contrast to Merill's objects which neglect the critical nature of the larger context (Merrill, 1992).

Further, the constructivist objects do not seek to replace the teacher or even act as information transmittal tools. Instead, they are presented as pieces of knowledge that students can easily access and draw from to enhance their understanding of the business world. This is not a transactional process. It is our commitment to the notion that learning is a process of constructing meaning rather than a process of acquiring information that drives our efforts in these learning objects.

Acknowledgements

The author would like to thank John Stinson, the head of the MBAWB Learning Objects Project, for his contribution to the thinking presented in this paper and for letting her become an active participant in the development of the learning objects library. She would also like to thank Jason Orrill for his comments on earlier drafts of this chapter.

References

APA (American Psychological Association). (1997). *Learner-centered psychological principles.* Washington, DC: American Psychological Associations' Board of Educational Affairs.

Bednar, A. K., Cunningham, D., Duffy, T. M., & Perry, J. D. (1992). Theory into practice. In T. M. Duffy & D. H. Jonassen (Eds.), *Constructivism and the technology of instruction* (pp. 17–34). Hillsdale, NJ: Lawrence Erlbaum Associates.

Boyer Commission on Education Undergraduates in the Research University. (1998). *Reinventing undergraduate education: A blueprint for America's research universities.* Stony Brook, NY: Author.

Bransford, J. D., Brown, A. L., & Cocking, R. R. (1999). *How people learn: Brain, mind, experience, and school.* Washington, DC: National Academy Press.

Brown, J. S. (2000). Growing up digital: How the Web changes work, education, and the ways people learn. *Change, 32*(2), 10–20.

Brown, J. S., Collins, A., & Duguid, P. (1989). Situated cognition and the culture of learning. *Educational Researcher, 18*(1), 32–42.

Bruner, J. (1990). *Acts of meaning.* Boston: Harvard University Press.

Downes, S. (2000, May 23, 2000). *Learning objects* [essay]. Available: http://www.atl.ualberta.ca/downes/naweb/Learning_Objects.htm (2000, May)

Driscoll, M. P. (1994). *Psychology of learning for instruction.* Boston: Allyn and Bacon.

Duffy, T. M., & Cunningham, D. J. (1996). Constructivism: Implications for the design and delivery of instruction. In D. H. Jonassen (Ed.), *Handbook of research for educational communications and technology* (pp. 170–198). New York: Simon & Schuster/Macmillan.

Entwistle, N., & Marton, F. (1994). Knowledge objects: Understandings constituted through intensive academic study. *The British Journal of Educational Psychology, 64*(1), 161–178.

Fleming, J. (1998). *Web navigation: Designing the user experience.* Sebastopol, CA: O'Reilly & Associates.

Hannafin, M., Land, S., & Oliver, K. (1999). Open learning environments: Foundations, methods & models. In C. M. Reigeluth (Ed.), *Instructional-design theories and models: A new paradigm of instructional theory* (Vol. II, pp. 115–140). Mahwah, NJ: Lawrence Erlbaum Associates.

Hill, J. R. (1999). A conceptual framework for understanding information seeking in open-ended information systems. *Educational Technology Research and Development, 41*(1), 5–27.

Hill, J. R., & Land, S. M. (1998, February 18–22). *Open-ended learning environment: A theoretical framework and model for design.* Paper presented at the Convention of the Association for Educational Communications and Technology, St. Louis, MO.

Jonassen, D. (1999). Designing constructivist learning environments. In C. M. Reigeluth (Ed.), *Instructional design theories and models: A new paradigm of instructional technology* (Vol. II, pp. 215–239). Mahwah, NJ: Lawrence Erlbaum Associates.

LTSC (Learning Technology Standards Committee). (March 2000). *Standards for learning object metadata.* Web site, IEEE. Available: http://ltsc.ieee.org/doc/wg12/LOMv4.1.htm (2000, July)

Lave, J., & Wenger, E. (1991). *Situated learning: Legitimate peripheral participation.* New York: Cambridge University Press.

Mayer, R. H. (1999). Designing instruction for constructivist learning. In C. M. Reigeluth (Ed.), *Instructional design theories and models: A new paradigm of instructional technology* (Vol. II, pp. 141–160). Mahwah, NJ: Lawrence Erlbaum Associates.

McCombs, B. L., & Whisler, J. S. (1997). *The learner-centered classroom and school: Strategies for increasing student motivation and achievement.* San Francisco: Jossey-Bass.

Merrill, M. D. (1992). Constructivism and instructional design. In T. M. Duffy & D. H. Jonassen (Eds.), *Constructivism and the technology of instruction* (pp. 99–114). Hillsdale, NJ: Lawrence Erlbaum Associates.

Merrill, M. D. (1999). Instructional transaction theory. In C. Reigeluth (Ed.), *Instructional-design theories and models: A new paradigm of instructional technology* (Vol. II, pp. 397–424). Mahwah, NJ: Lawrence Erlbaum Associates.

Merrill, M. D., & ID_2 Research Group. (1998). ID expert: A second generation instructional development system. *Instructional Sciences, 26*(3–4), 243–262.

Merrill, M. D., Jones, M. K., & Li, Z. (1996). Instructional transaction theory: Instructional design based on knowledge objects. *Educational Technology, 36*(3), 30–37.

Myers, K. L. (1999). Is there a place for instructional design in the information age? *Educational Technology, 39*(6), 50–53.

Nielsen, J. (2000). *Designing Web usability: The practice of simplicity.* Indianapolis, IN: New Riders.

Savery, J. R., & Duffy, T. M. (1995). Problem based learning: An instructional model and its constructivist framework. In B. G. Wilson (Ed.), *Constructivist learning environments: Case studies in instructional design* (pp. 135–148). Englewood Cliffs, NJ: Educational Technology Publications.

Schank, R. C., Berman, T. R., & Macpherson, K. A. (1999). Learning by doing. In C. M. Reigeluth (Ed.), *Instructional design theories and models: A new paradigm of instructional technology* (Vol. II, pp. 161–182). Mahwah, NJ: Lawrence Erlbaum Associates.

Schon, D. A. (1987). *Educating the reflective practitioner: Toward a new design for teaching and learning in the professions.* San Fancisco: Jossey-Bass.

Schwartz, D. L., Lin, X., Brophy, S., & Bransford, J. D. (1999). Toward the development of flexibly adaptive instructional designs. In C. M. Reigeluth (Ed.), *Instructional-design theories and models: A new paradigm of instructional theory* (Vol. II, pp. 183–213). Mahwah, NJ: Lawrence Erlbaum Associates.

Stinson, J. E., & Milter, R. G. (1996). Problem-based learning in business education: Curriculum design and implementation issues. *New Directions for Teaching and Learning, 68,* 33–42.

U.S. Department of Labor (1991). *What work requires of schools.* Washington, DC: The Secretary's Commission on Achieving Necessary Skills.

Vygotsky, L. S. (1978). *Mind in society: The development of higher psychological processes.* Cambridge, MA: Harvard University Press.

Wiley, D. A. (1999). *Learning objects and the new CAI: So what do I do with a learning object?* [essay]. Available: http://wiley.byu.edu (2000, July)

Wiley, D. A. (2000). *Learning object design and sequencing theory.* Unpublished Doctoral Dissertation, Brigham Young University, Provo, UT. Available: http://davidwiley.com/papers/dissertation/dissertation.pdf

3.0 Learning Objects and People

Designing Learning Objects to Personalize Learning

Margaret Martinez

If a student does not want to learn, she will not;
Regardless of the quality of the instruction offered her.
If a student wants to learn, she will find a way;
Regardless of the quality of the instruction offered her.

Introduction

The Web offers the perfect technology and environment for individualized learning because learners can be uniquely identified, content can be specifically personalized, and learner progress can be monitored, supported, and assessed. Technologically and technically, researchers are making progress toward realizing the personalized learning dream with adaptive learning object technology. However, two important considerations are being ignored or overlooked in accomplishing the personalization dream. One missing consideration concerns a whole-person understanding about key psychological sources that influence how individuals want and intend to learn online. Conventional, primarily cognitive solutions (which focus on how learners process, build, and store knowledge) offer a restricted view of how people learn and too often lead to unstable or ineffective online learning solutions. A more whole-person perspective includes emotions and intentions as critical factors in the learning process. Also missing is the integration of instructional purpose, values, and strategies into the design, development, and presentation of content (objects). Up to now, developments have focused on technology rather than more important learner-centric issues.

To address these critical issues, this chapter introduces learning orientations. Learning orientations use the whole-person perspective (as an alternative to cognitive-rich theories) and recognize the impact of emotions and intentions on learning. Learning orientations offer strategies and guidelines for designing, developing, and using objects for personalized learning. To describe this perspective, this chapter will examine (a) the often overlooked dominant impact of emotions and intentions on learning; (b) critical human relationships between learning environments, key psychological factors (e.g., conative, affective, social, and cognitive) that influence learning; and (c) design guidelines for supportive learning solutions and environments that adapt to how people learn best. These insights suggest multiple ways to design objects that address how individuals learn, perform, and achieve differently.

This chapter is aimed at readers wanting new design perspectives for building objects that personalize instruction in adaptive learning environments. The purpose is to suggest that traditional approaches based on classroom practices are not always suitable for online learning. Missing from conventional approaches is the consideration of two important issues. The first is a comprehensive understanding about individual learning differences. Second is the close integration of instructional value into the design of learning objects.

As we build and present objects for successful personalized learning, some designers are finding that conventional, primarily cognitive perspectives are flawed by a heavy emphasis on how individuals think (cognitive processes). These perspectives particularly lack adequate consideration of how people want or intend to learn online. Moreover, these explanations overlook the dominant impact of emotions, intentions, and social factors on learning. It is not enough to assume that if products are instructionally sound (from a cognitive perspective) and technologically sophisticated, that they will be widely adopted and uniformly appreciated, managed, and utilized. The typical lack of attention to emotions, intentions, and social factors, and over-reliance on technology often result in instructional products that are not actually useful. For clarity, the author will call content objects *learning objects* only if the objects are used for instructional purposes, meaning that learning objects are content objects meaningfully presented to accomplish specific objectives related to learning. Additionally, they are designed using a conceptual framework embedded with instructional theory, strategies, and methodology. Otherwise, objects will be referred to as content objects.

The Whole-Person Perspective

The overall failure of many online instructional projects (e.g., low completion rates) highlights the important limitations of the typical cognitive approach. Web courses that lack adequate support for how people learn differently (from a whole-person perspective) end up being more informational than instructional. It is especially important to remember that in traditional settings instructors have been in the classroom managing emotions, intentions, and social and cognitive issues on an individual or group basis (some more effectively than others). Until the advent of online learning and rapidly changing requirements, it was seemingly enough to deliver primarily cognitive instructional solutions and rely on the instructor to deliver the personal approach. The reality is that many online learners (after years of instructor-managed learning) are simply not adequately prepared for self-managed online learning. Too many lack the self-motivation, intentions, independence, learning efficacy, or learning management skills to stay online learning continually and successfully. In a recent NCREL paper, Valdez and colleagues (2000) noted:

Berryman and others criticize American education for fostering inert knowledge, or "passive learning, that has been identified as structured upon behavioral principles" (Berryman, 1993; Besser, 1993; Popkewitz & Shutkin, 1993). Berryman (1993) defines passive learning thus:

> Passive learning means that learners do not interact with problems and content and thus do not receive the experiential feedback so key to learning. Students need chances to engage in choice, judgment, control processes, and problem formulation; they need chances to make mistakes. (p. 375)

Berryman and others attribute passive learning practices to the system of industrial management in which each person's task is laid out carefully by the administrative powers. Each worker is told not only what to do but how to do it. Berryman claims that this industrial management style of education "places control over learning in the teacher's, not the learner's hands."

In order to design objects successfully, it will be necessary to account for the many factors that impede or facilitate learning. Secondly, it will be necessary to identify and match the theories, conceptual frameworks, processes, relationships, methodologies, treatments, and environments that best influence more successful learning for different types of learners. Incorporating these factors into object design is essential to the creation of instructionally sound learning solutions.

What theories, strategies, and methodologies support sophisticated online learning needs? Snow and Farr (1987) suggested that sound learning theories require a whole-person view that integrates cognitive, conative, and affective aspects, "otherwise, explanations about learning differences will be ambiguous and isolated from reality" (p. 1). According to Snow (1989), the best instruction involves individualized treatments that differ in structure and completeness and high or low general ability measures. Highly structured treatments (e.g., high external control, explicit sequences and components) seem to help students with low ability but hinder those with high abilities (relative to low structure treatments). Bereiter and Scardamalia (1989) also suggested that learners in supportive environments have high levels of self-efficacy and self-motivation and use learning as a primary transformative force. Despite an increased interest in emotions, intentions, and personalized learning in the past two decades, most of today's researchers recognize cognitive factors as the dominant influence on learning and other key factors are relegated to a secondary role. This research typically alludes to or at best discusses aspects of conation and affect. Nevertheless, these personalized learning approaches remain largely dependent on dominant cognitive formulations.

Personalization

The Web offers an excellent environment for personalized learning, especially using objects. Personalized learning needs to use strategies that can address individual needs and promote individual success. It must also use technology to change the individual objects presented to each learner based on their individual needs. Personalization may take many forms as it adapts content, practice, feedback, or navigation to match individual progress and performance. For example, two individuals using the same instruction simultaneously may see two completely different sets of learning objects. The greatest benefit of learning personalization is the system's ability to make complex instruction easier by presenting only the specific information that a particular learner wants or needs in the appropriate manner and at the appropriate time. Another wonderful benefit of personalization is that each time you personalize, you learn and store a little more about a learner's unique set of needs.

Personalization Types

There are many ways to personalize learning. Nevertheless, like the terms "learning styles" and "motivation," personalization is another ill-defined term. In order to be more specific, personalization is described here with five levels of increasing sophistication, each level describing a specific personalization strategy. From the simplest to most complex, the five strategies are: (a) name-recognized; (b) self-described; (c) segmented; (d) cognitive-based; and (e) whole-person-based. Each type has a specific purpose, influence, and resulting impact. These strategies can work separately but to be most effective they should work together to create a comprehensive or hybrid learning experience.

Name-recognized personalization. Name-recognized personalization is simple and easy to implement. This strategy is useful and powerful because most people value being acknowledged as an individual. For example, the learner's name can appear in the instruction, or previous activities or accomplishments that have been collected and stored can later be presented when appropriate.

Self-described personalization. Self-described personalization enables learners (using questionnaires, surveys, registration forms, and comments) to describe preferences and common attributes. For example, learners may take a pre-course quiz to identify existing skills, preferences, or past experiences. Afterwards, options and instructional experiences appear, based on the learner-provided answers.

Segmented personalization. Segmented personalization uses demographics, common attributes, or surveys to group or segment learning populations into smaller, identifiable, and manageable groups. For example, learners who share a common job title or class, or who work in a certain department, would receive content based on prescriptive rules that would support the learning and performance requirements for their segmented group.

Cognitive-based personalization. Cognitive-based personalization uses information about cognitive processes, strategies, and ability to deliver content specifically targeted to specific types (defined cognitively) of learners. For example, learners may choose to use an audio option because they prefer hearing text rather than reading it. Or, a learner may prefer the presentation of content in a linear fashion, rather than an unsequenced presentation with hyperlinks. This type of personalization operates on more complex algorithms than the previous types and is able to factor more learner attributes into each interaction. This strategy works by collecting data, monitoring learning activity, comparing activity with other learner behavior, and predicting what the user would like to do or see next.

Whole-person personalization. Whole-person personalization uses learning orientations. This strategy supports the complex set of deep-seated psychological sources (in addition to the conventional cognitive-based prescriptions) impacting differences in learning and performance. This personalization strategy makes predictions about delivering content from a whole-person perspective. It not only delivers content to help learners achieve learning objectives but it also attempts to improve overall learning ability and enhance online learning relationships. As the individual learns, the system also learns as it collects data, tracks progress, and compares responses and common patterns to improve responses (i.e., it becomes more precise over time). In its most sophisticated form, whole-person personalization requires real-time personalization using inferential technology to modify responses to a learner based on a dynamic learner model that is changing throughout the learning experience, when it occurs, just as it occurs.

Learning Orientations Theory

This chapter introduces *learning orientations* for personalized learning. The purpose is to provide the theoretical basis for personalizing learning based on a whole-person perspective that recognizes the dominant influence of emotions and intentions on learning. Cognitive factors play a secondary role, albeit still important role. Learning orientations suggest that as individuals have different learning experiences, and as they mature as learners, they gradually become more confident, sophisticated, and adept at understanding and managing an increasingly complex interplay of personally relevant affective, conative, social, and cognitive learning factors. Thus, the significant contrast in how individuals approach learning, their "learning orientation," lies in the unique, personal way that they understand, assess, and manage learning to achieve or accomplish goals. For example, an understanding of the extent and depth of fundamental desires, values, and beliefs about why, when, and how to use learning and how it can accomplish personal goals or change events is fundamental to understanding how successfully an individual wants or intends to experience learning. Likewise, the degree to which designers understand learning orientations is the degree to which they can design objects for personalized learning.

Learning Orientations

Learning orientations: (1) highlight the influence of emotions, intentions, social, and cognitive factors on learning (how the brain supports learning); (2) identify and address the higher-order psychological dimension that can differentiate learning audiences; and (3) guide analysis, design, development, and evaluation of learning objects and environments. Learning orientations describe an individual's complex intrinsic managing and use of key psychological factors (to varying degrees) as they approach and experience learning. Learning orientations are not learning styles. The key distinction is that whereas learning styles recognize the dominant influence of cognitive factors (and demote other factors to a secondary or no role), learning orientations recognize the dominant influence of emotions and intentions. This perspective reflects recent neurological research that provides evidence for the dominant influence of the brain's emotional center (Ledoux, 1996) on learning and memory. Highlighting the importance of intentions, Woodward (1998) also provides evidence describing the important use of goal orientation (intentions) for learning and development from an early age.

In Figure 1, the learning orientation construct describes three key learner-difference factors: (a) conative and affective learning focus, (b) committed strategic planning and learning effort, and (c) learning independence or autonomy. *Conative and Affective Learning Focus* describes the individual's will, commitment, intent, drive, or passion for improving, transforming, setting and achieving goals, and meeting challenges. *Strategic Planning and Committed Learning Effort* refers to the degree that learners plan and commit deliberate, strategic planning and effort to accomplish learning. *Learning Independence or Autonomy* refers to the individual's desire and ability to take responsibility, make choices, and control, self-assess, self-motivate, and manage or improve their learning. As shown in Figure 1, a number of factors (left column) play a role in determining an individual's orientation to learn. What is most notable about this model is the suggestion that emotions and intentions, not cognitive ability or technological superiority of an innovation, play the key role in determining learning success.

Learning orientations present a comprehensive, human view that can be used as a framework for examining the dynamic flow (stimuli that activate emotions and stimulate responses for learning) between (a) deep-seated psychological learning factors (conative, affective, social, and cognitive); (b) past and future learning experiences; (c) choices and responses to treatments; and (d) learning and performance outcomes.

The interplay between the deep-seated psychological sources of emotional reactions, learning differences, responses, and outcomes suggests that a complex conceptual structure exists with a qualitative order of influence. A clear definition of brain activity supporting this conceptual structure would explain or predict how learning orientation strongly influences outcomes in differentiated

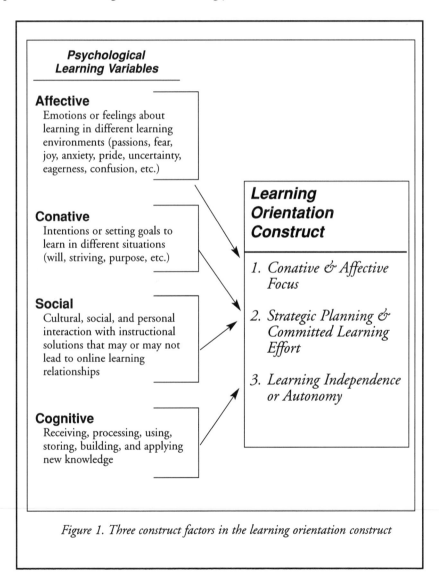

Figure 1. Three construct factors in the learning orientation construct

learning audiences. Figure 1 suggests that emotions and intentions (at the top of the hierarchy) stimulate responses that cultivate and manage subordinate differences in learning, such as preferences, styles, and abilities. In turn, emotional responses influence our cognitive assessments, choices, and use of cognitive strategies and skills.

Learning Orientations Model

The learning orientations model (Table 1) describes four categories that broadly represent the existing diversity of learning orientations, enables us to explain key sources of learning differences, and describes specific strategies to mass customize learning (in terms of instruction, assessment, and environments): *Transforming, Performing, Conforming,* and *Resistant Learners.*

Transforming learners are generally highly motivated, passionate, highly committed learners. They place great importance on learning and use it as an important intrinsic resource to bring about and manage change (innovate). They rely on their visionary, creative, holistic thinking, sophisticated learning, problem solving, and strategic planning ability, and capacity to commit great effort and endure stressful challenges. They use independence, personal strengths, persistence, constant desire for challenges and exploration, high standards, learning efficacy, risk-taking, and positive expectations to self-motivate and self-direct learning successfully. However, these learners may become demotivated and bored, frustrated, or even resistant in environments or conditions that mismatch their assertive, exploratory, self-directed learning needs.

Contrasts: In contrast to other learning orientations, *transforming learners* know that they can plan and strategically commit great effort to accomplish important, long-term, transformational goals. They seldom solely rely on deadlines, structured environments, short-term projects, normative performance standards, expected social or instructional compliance, extrinsic rewards, or others for learning efficacy or self-motivation. Instead they rely on themselves or prefer mentoring relationships to learn and use learning as a valuable resource to innovate or transform.

Performing learners are generally self-motivated in learning situations (task-oriented, project-oriented, hands-on applications) that interest them. Otherwise, they seek extrinsic rewards for accomplishing objectives that appear to have less value and perhaps require more effort then they are initially willing to commit. They may clearly acknowledge meeting only the stated objectives, getting the grade, streamlining learning efforts, and avoiding exploratory steps beyond the requirements of the situation and learning task, commiserate with their degree of interest in the stated goal. They take some control and responsibility for their learning but often rely on others for motivation, goal setting, coaching, schedules, and direction. However, they may self-motivate and

Table 1. Four Learning Orientation Profiles

Orientation	Conative/Affective Aspects	Strategic Planning & Committed Learning Effort	Learning Autonomy
Transforming Learners (Innovators)	Focus strong passions and intentions on learning. Are assertive, expert, highly self-motivated learners. Use exploratory learning to transform to high, personal standards.	Set and accomplish personal short- and long-term challenging goals that may not align with goals set by others; maximize effort to reach personal goals. Commit great effort to discover, elaborate, and build new knowledge and meaning.	Assume learning responsibility and self-manage goals, learning, progress, and outcomes. Experience frustration if restricted or given little learning learning autonomy.
Performing Learners (Implementers)	Focus emotions/intentions on learning selectively or situationally. Self-motivated learners when the content appeals. Meet above-average group standards only when the topic appeals.	Set and achieve short-term, task oriented goals that meet average-to-high standards; situationally minimize efforts and standards to reach assigned or negotiated standards. Selectively commit measured effort to assimilate and use relevant knowledge and meaning.	Situationally assume learning responsibility in areas of interest, but willingly give up control in areas of less interest. Prefer coaching and interaction for achieving goals.
Conforming Learners (Sustainers)	Focus intentions and emotions cautiously and routinely as directed. Low-risk, modestly effective, extrinsically motivated learners. Use learning to conform to easily achieved group standards.	Follow and try to accomplish simple task-oriented goals assigned and guided by others, try to please and conform; maximize efforts in supportive environments with safe standards. Commit careful, measured effort to accept and reproduce knowledge to meet external requirements.	Assume little responsibility, manage learning as little as possible, comply, want continual guidance, and expect reinforcement for achieving short-term goals.
Resistant Learners (Resistance)	Focus on not cooperating; perceive needs in other directions. Are actively or passively resistant. Avoid using learning to achieve academic goals assigned by others.	Consider lower standards, fewer academic goals conflicting personal goals, or no goals; maximize or minimize efforts to resist assigned or expected goals either assertively or passively. Chronically avoid learning (apathetic, frustrated, discouraged, or "disobedient").	Assume responsibility for not meeting goals set by others, and set personal goals that avoid meeting formal learning requirements or expectations.

Situational Performance or Resistance: *Learners may situationally improve performance, or resist in response to positive or negative learning conditions or situations.*

exert greater effort and excellence in situations that greatly interest or benefit them. They most often are detailed-oriented, lower risk, skilled learners
that systematically and capably get the project done as they achieve average
to above average learning objectives and tasks, according to their own personal goals. These learners lose motivation or may even get angry if too
much effort is required and the rewards are not enough to compensate the
perceived effort.

Contrasts: In contrast to transforming learners, *performing learners* are
short-term, detail, task-oriented learners (less holistic or big-picture thinkers).
They take fewer risks with challenging or difficult goals, commit less effort,
focus on grades and rewards, and will cheerfully achieve less whenever standards are set below their capabilities. They are most comfortable with interper-
sonal, coaching relationships, and rely on or like external support, resources,
and interaction to accomplish a task. In contrast to conforming learners, these
learners have more sophisticated skills, commit greater effort to achieve higher
standard goals, and prefer more sophisticated learning and performance environments with entertaining interaction that creates progressive effort, interest,
competition, fun, and attainable goals.

Conforming learners are generally more compliant and will passively
accept knowledge, store it, and reproduce it to conform, to complete routine or
assigned tasks (if they can), and to please others. They prefer learning in groups
with explicit guidance and feedback. These learners do not typically: think holis-
tically, critically, or analytically; synthesize feedback; solve complex problems;
monitor and review progress independently; or accomplish challenging goals.
They are typically less skilled, uncomfortable with decision-making, and may
have little desire to control or manage their learning, take risks, or initiate change
in their jobs or environment. Learning in open learning environments, which
focuses on high learner control, discovery or exploratory learning, complex problem solving, challenging goals, and inferential direction, may frustrate, demoral-
ize, or demotivate these learners. They need scaffolded, structured solutions,
guiding direction, simple problems, linear sequencing, and explicit feedback.

Contrasts: In contrast to other learning orientations, *conforming learners*
learn best in well-structured, directive environments using explicit, step-by-step
procedures. Unlike transforming and performing learners, who have stronger,
more positive beliefs about learning, and greater learning efficacy, conforming
learners believe that learning is most useful when it helps them avoid risk and
meet the basic requirements in their job. They are comfortable with minimum
effort on simple goals that others set for them and help them achieve.

Resistant learners lack a fundamental belief that academic learning and
achievement can help them achieve personal goals or initiate positive change. Too
often they have suffered repeated, long-term frustration from inappropriate

learning situations. A series of unskilled, imperceptive instructors, unfortunate learning experiences, or missed opportunities have deterred resistant learners from enjoying and using learning to progress or improve. These learners do not believe in or use formal education or academic institutions as positive or enjoyable resources in their life.

Resistant learners are resistant for many reasons. Ironically, some resistant learners may actually be eager learners on their own outside of formal learning institutions. For example, they may be frustrated transforming learners who aggressively resisted the strictures of too structured or restrictive goals and environments, and chose to learn on their own, quite successfully. These learners may have learned to dislike school but they may also have learned how to succeed using their own strategies outside of school.

Contrasts: In contrast to other learning orientations, *resistant learners* focus their energy on resistance within the formal system, whether it is passive or aggressive. Their need to progress or improve lies in directions other than the established norm. Some will progress on their own, others will fall along the way.

Learning orientations are generalizable to all learning situations and are not domain or environment specific. However, despite a general learning orientation, individuals may situationally manage approaches to learning differently (not change learning orientation) in response to a topic, delivery method, environment, condition, or teacher. For example, a transforming learner may prefer learning more cautiously with less learner control if the topic is unfamiliar or complicated. However, once they reach their comfort level they might gradually push themselves to greater independence (a more typical approach). Although learners' reactions and processes naturally vary depending on the learning task and situation, a conforming learner is unlikely to become a performing learner (change learning orientation) very quickly or at all. To change learning orientation is to change the deep-seated psychological sources that influence learning. For example, a conforming learner who intentionally experiences more risk, independence, holistic thinking, and complex problem-solving may over time push themselves into a performing orientation. These considerations about how individuals approach learning differently raise important issues about presenting objects in environments that identify and match these individuals' situational approaches.

Another important consideration is that learning orientations are not arranged in a value hierarchy with transforming learners valued highest at the top. Each learning orientation has strengths and possible areas for intentional improvement. For example, a transforming learner, who wants to learn more intentionally, may focus sometimes on less passion and exploration and attend to short-term details and task-completion. In contrast, a performing learner may want to focus on more holistic, long-term thinking.

Designing Learning Objects for
Personalized Learning

Unfortunately, current design efforts for learning objects have avoided critical instructional design issues, probably because standards, strategies, and guidelines for personalized learning are still fuzzy concepts for some. As a result, the need for an instructional framework showing how to present learning objects to achieve instructional objectives is being ignored or overlooked. This situation is comparable to building a house without a blueprint. Two questions have to be asked. How can learning objects be presented in an instructionally sound manner if the presentation is not guided by the appropriate planning, learning, and instructional information? More importantly, how can one conceivably design and develop learning objects without the larger picture of how they should be instructionally used or presented? Wiley (1999) argues that "while current leading object metadata is capable of facilitating reuse and repurposability at the level of instructional clip art, its poverty of instructional design information suggests that it is incapable of achieving the more worthy goal of automating the construction and delivery of individualized, instructionally meaningful material from individual learning objects. That is to say, it currently seems to be incapable of supporting automated instructional development" (p. 9). Wiley (1999) suggested that many alternatives are possible, positing that "an instructional architecture, or instructional event model, can provide detailed specifications for the type and amount of context to build within a learning object" (p. 7). He provides Gagné's framework as a simplest case:

> One example [instructional event model] is Gagné's Nine Events of Instruction. If developers were to adopt this model up front, learning objects could be built to fulfill the specific requirements of each step in the instructional process. Then, any learning object which meets the requirement "stimulate recall of prerequisite knowledge for music theory instruction" can be substituted in the place of any other, provided that certain assumptions are met. (p. xx)

Designing
Personalized Learning Environments

In the fifties, Cronbach (1957) challenged the field to find "for each individual the treatment to which he can most easily adapt" (p. 681). He suggested that consideration of the treatments and individual together would determine the best payoff because we "can expect some attributes of person to have strong interactions with treatment variables. These attributes have far greater practical importance than the attributes which have little or no interaction" (p. 681).

Assembling learning objects to create supportive, personalized learning environments is an additional challenge. To be effective, learning objects should be designed to exist in environments that address the unique sources of learning differences and influence success. More specifically, they should emulate the instructor's experienced, intuitive ability to recognize and respond to how individuals learn differently and creatively foster interest, value, enjoyable, and more successful, independent learning. If we are to meet Cronbach's challenge for better learning environments, then we need to learn how to present objects that provide "for each individual the treatment [personalized environment] which he can most easily adapt" for the best payoff. Below are simple guidelines for presenting learning objects to create personalized learning environments for three learning orientations:

For transforming learners, design discovery-oriented, unsequenced, and mentoring environments. These environments are for learners who want to be passionate, assertive, and challenged by complex problem solving, and who are able to self-motivate, self-manage, and self-monitor learning and progress to attain high-standard, long-term goals.

For performing learners, design task- or project-oriented, competitive, and interactive (hands-on) environments. These environments should use coaching, practice, and feedback to encourage and support self-motivation, task solving, self-monitoring progress, and task sequencing, while minimizing the need for extra effort, risk, and difficult standards.

For conforming learners, design simple, scaffolded, structured, facilitated, low-risk environments that use explicit, careful guidance to help individuals learn comfortably in an easy, step-wise fashion.

These descriptions foster comfortable, fun environments that support broad variability in learning from a whole-person perspective, not simply in cognitive terms. They consider how emotions and intentions influence learning and thinking processes. For example, in conforming environments, conforming learners can comfortably manage low risk, linear, and facilitated activities as they achieve carefully sequenced goals and increasing accomplishment. In contrast, the transforming environment would be overwhelming and frustrating for conforming learners. Emotions and intentions are powerful influences that guide how successfully individuals intend to learn. Presenting learning objects to create personalized learning environments that match learning orientation is a step in meeting the challenges that now confront global education and training.

Metadata Standards for
Learning Objects

Learning objects are indeed a good idea, but as long as they lack instructional value, we will be unable to use them effectively. From a practical and technical perspective, common metadata standards define what data needs to be collected and stored to provide descriptive information about a content object. The result is a content object metadata specification (e.g., showing title, author, and description for each object). Metadata standards theoretically should also enable the appropriate use of a content object as a learning object. In this case, the purpose is to enable learners to use one or more learning objects to achieve one or more instructional objectives.

The metadata on a library catalog card provides information commonly used for finding a book or other media form, but has little instructional information concerning the reader's instructional use of the item. If our sole purpose is to provide metadata for describing content objects, the descriptive information commonly included by most standards today is sufficient. However, learning objects have important embedded instructional objectives and, if we are not providing instructional information in metadata, all we have is a content object. If we ignore key instructional issues, how can we successfully use learning objects for learning?

Many groups are working together to define common international standards that the world can adopt for describing learning objects that can be interoperable, reusable, repurposable, and effectively managed and presented. Their common interest is to find a minimum set of metadata standards that will support the worldwide deployment of learning objects for multiple purposes. Just a few of the groups participating in these worldwide standards-making efforts through the IEEE Learning Technology Standards Committee (LTSC, 2000) are:

- Alliance of Remote Instructional Authoring and Distribution Networks for Europe (ARIADNE, 2000)
- Instructional Management Systems (IMS, 2000) Project
- Dublin Core Education Working Group (DC-Ed, 2000)
- Advanced Distributed Learning Initiative (ADL, 2000)

Nonetheless, the current lack of attention to instructional factors and the over reliance on technical or technological issues may result in development of learning objects that are not widely used even though the products may be technically sophisticated. More than likely, if international metadata standards do not include data instructional and learning information, we may see the rapid rise of incompatible extensions to the metadata. In order to increase the usability of learning objects, it will be necessary to expand the consideration of higher-level instructional requirements and account for the many factors that impede or facilitate learning.

Extending his simplest case, Wiley (1999) suggested two extensions to learning object metadata that could address this issue. These extensions address the two critical instructional issues that have been addressed in this chapter. He proposes the introduction of one field that identifies the instructional framework or architecture to which the learning object was designed. He proposes a second field that conveys individual-difference information. The following sample metadata is simple and could easily "facilitate an immediately (technologically) implementable method" of delivering personalized instruction (Wiley, 1999, p. 10).

Educational. Instructional Architecture = Gagné9

Educational. Individual Difference.Orientation = Transforming

Both examples are an attempt to address the critical (higher-level) instructional issues that are being overlooked. In the first example, Wiley (1999) describes instructional architecture, as a common "model that provides for all the events of the instructional process" (p. 10). He uses Gagné's Nine Events of Instruction to illustrate a very simple model. If developers were to adopt a basic model, "learning objects could be built to fulfill the specific requirements of each step in the instructional process" (Wiley, 1999, p. 10). Obviously, establishing a common reference model is difficult, but not impossible. Even if we could agree on two or three models, this is vastly better then totally ignoring the overall instructional purpose of a learning object.

Above, the second example describes a simple method to introduce learning orientations as metadata. The purpose of this metadata element is to alternate the presentation of learning objects to match learning differences from the whole-person perspective. In other words, this tag would serve as an executive control and might deliver interactivity differently to different learning orientations.

Design Strategies and Guidelines

Several guidelines are included in Table 2 to address possible instructional considerations. These descriptions (organized by three learning orientations) are intended as general design guidance for presenting learning objects. They consider key issues that influence online learning and provide information for accommodating the differences. Their overall purpose is to match the orientation to foster self-motivation, interest, interaction, and more successful, independent learning. These same descriptions are also useful for creating a set of evaluation criteria against which learning objects may be evaluated.

Table 2. Strategies and Guidelines for Three Learning Orientations

Learning Issues	Transforming Learners	Performing Learners	Conforming Learners
General Relationship	Prefer loosely structured, mentoring relationships that promote challenging goals, discovery, and self-managed learning.	Prefer semi-complex, semi-structured, coaching relationships that stimulate personal value and provide creative interaction (hands-on).	Prefer safe, structured, guiding relationships that help them avoid mistakes and achieve easy learning goals in a simple fashion.
Goal-Setting and Standards	Set and achieve personal challenging short- and long-term goals that may exceed goals set by others; maximize effort to reach personal goals.	Set and achieve short-term, task-oriented goals that meet average-to-high standards; situationally minimize efforts and standards to reach assigned or negotiate standards.	Follow and try to achieve simple, task-oriented goals assigned by others; try to please and to conform; maximize efforts in supportive relationships with safe standards.
Learner Autonomy and Responsibility	They are self-motivated to assume learning responsibility and self-direct goals, learning, progress, and outcomes. They experience frustration if restricted or given little learning autonomy.	They are situationally self-motivated to assume learning responsibility in areas of interest. They willingly give up control and extend less effort in areas of less interest or in restrictive relationships.	They are cautiously motivated, prefer less responsibility and self-directed learning, like to be more compliant, and are ready to follow others.
Knowledge Building	Commit great effort to discover, elaborate, and build new knowledge and meaning.	Selectively commit measured effort to assimilate and use relevant knowledge and meaning.	Commit careful, measured effort to accept and reproduce knowledge to meet external requirements.
Problem Solving	They prefer case studies and complex, whole-to-part, problem-solving opportunities.	They prefer competitive part-to-whole problem solving.	They prefer scaffolded support for simple problem solving.
User Interface	Recommendation: Open learning interface for high stimulation and processing capacity.	Recommendation: Hands-on learning interface for medium stimulation and processing capacity.	Recommendation: Consistent and simple interface for minimal stimulation and processing capacity.
Adapted Presentation	They prefer occasional mentoring and interaction for achieving goals (MENTORING).	They prefer continual coaching and interaction for achieving goals (COACHING).	They prefer continual guidance and reinforcement for achieving short-term goals (GUIDING).

Table 2 (cont.)

Learning Issues	Transforming Learners	Performing Learners	Conforming Learners
Strategies to Achieve Objectives	Enable high-standard, strategic goal-setting and planning; support realistic personal goals; and ensure putting theory into practice.	Foster personal value (intrinsic benefits) and holistic thinking, offer hands-on, practical upport to encourage planning and effort into continual improvements.	Provide time and comprehensive, structured support for adapting training and transitioning skills for improved performance.
Feedback	They prefer inferential feedback.	They prefer concise feedback.	They prefer explicit feedback.
Motivational Feedback	Discovery	Coached discovery.	Guided achievement.
Learning Module Size	Short, concise, big picture, with links to more detail if necessary.	Medium, brief overview with focus on practical application.	Longer, detailed guidance, in steps.
Information Need	Holistic, specific information needed to solve a problem.	General interests, practice, short-term, task-completion focus.	Guidance to fill a requirement.
Content Structuring	They prefer freedom to construct their own content structure.	They prefer general instruction, have a limited ability to reorganize.	They prefer to let others decide the content structure.
Sequencing Methods	Hypertext, adaptive, multiple access. Avoid step-by-step instruction.	Semi-linear, logical branching, access by subtopic: Limit exploration.	Linear, page-turner representations, general access. Avoid learner control and exploration.
Inquiry	Ask probing, in-depth questions about content. Expect inferential, theoretical challenges.	Ask questions to complete assignments. Expect specific, practical directions.	Ask mechanistic questions about assignments. Expect explicit guidance.

Summary

The dream to deliver personalized learning using learning objects that fits the real-time, anywhere, anytime, just-enough needs of the learner is about to become a reality. Today, along with many important developments in instructional psychology—open standards, structured markup languages for interoperable data representation, and the shift of instructional flow control from the client to the server-side—an entirely new foundation is making truly personalized online learning possible. The most obvious benefit of these innovations is the creation of a learning ecology that shares resources from large reservoirs of content where learning objects are shared individually, widely, and more economically.

Technologically, researchers are making rapid progress toward realizing the personalized learning dream with object architecture and adaptive technology. However, two key elements still need to be addressed in the development and use of objects for personalized learning. The first is a whole-person understanding of how individuals want and intend to learn. Primarily cognitive learning solutions (i.e., those whose primary focus is on how learners process and build knowledge) are no longer enough. The second key element is the lack of consideration for instructional issues in the dynamic presentation of learning objects. When we design learning objects with only a universal type of learner in mind, or without guiding their higher-level instructional use, we unintentionally set learners up for frustration and possible failure.

Learning objects are expanding the supportive learning role that technology can rightfully play in enhancing learning and correcting learning problems that have continually perplexed training markets in the past.

Personalized learning is important because it supports flexible solutions that dynamically adapt content to fit instructional objectives. For sophisticated learners, it also enables them to select components to customize their learner-centric environment. For all learners, it enables them to gain more sophisticated online learning ability over time. How else can learners keep up with the rapid pace of change?

If we are serious about providing good online instruction for learners, we must plan multiple, cost-effective ways to provide instruction and environments so that all learners have opportunities for success. Learning orientations may be a first step in recognizing and accommodating individual learning differences from a whole-person perspective. They may also be an important step in recognizing the expanded, dominant role and impact of emotions and intentions on learning, especially since online learners need to become more independent, self-motivated, and self-directed learners. Additionally, we need to develop common instructional models which can guide the instructional presentation of learning objects for personalized instruction, assessment, and learning environments.

As learners move online, personalized learning is a more sophisticated solution for learning and performance improvement and meaningful online relationships. Hopefully, these suggestions will contribute to more successful learning via the Internet and a greater understanding about fundamental learning differences and online instructional issues.

Acknowledgements
Margaret Martinez can be contacted at: Maggiez99z@cs.com.

References

ADL. (2000). *Advanced distributed learning network.* Web site [online]. Available: http://www.adlnet.org/

ARIADNE. (2000). *Alliance of remote instructional authoring and distribution networks for Europe.* Web site [online]. Available: http://ariadne.unil.ch/

Bandura, A. (1997). *Self-efficacy: The exercise of control.* New York: W. H. Freeman.

Bandura, A. (1986). *Social foundations of thought and action: A social cognitive theory.* Englewood Cliffs, NJ: Prentice-Hall.

Bangert-Drowns, R., & Rudner, L. (1991). *Meta-analysis in educational research.* Paper presented to ERIC Clearinghouse on Tests, Measurement, and Evaluation, Washington, DC (ERIC Document Reproduction Service No. ED339748). Available: http://www.ed.gov/databases/ERIC_Digests/ed339748.html

Bereiter, C., & Scardamalia, M. (1989). Intentional learning as a goal of instruction. In L. B. Resnick (Ed.), *Knowing, learning, and instruction: Essays in honor of Robert Glaser* (pp. 361–392) Hillsdale, NJ: Lawrence Erlbaum Associates.

Bereiter, C., & Scardamalia, M. (1993). *Surpassing ourselves: Inquiry into the nature and implications of expertise.* Chicago: Open Court.

Berryman, S. E. (1993). Learning for the workplace. *Review of Research in Education, 19,* 343–401.

Besser, H. (1993). Education as marketplace. In R. Muffoletto & N. Nelson Knupfer (Eds.), *Computers in education: Social, political, and historical perspectives* (pp. 37–69). Cresskill, NJ: Hampton Press.

Cronbach, L. (1957). The two disciplines of scientific psychology. *American Psychologist,* 671–684.

Cronbach, L. (1975). Beyond the two disciplines of scientific psychology. *American Psychologist,* 116–127.

Cronbach, L., & Snow, R. (1977). *Aptitudes and instructional methods: A handbook for research on interactions.* New York: Irvington.

DC-Ed. (2000). *Dublin Core Metadata Initiative Education Working Group* [online]. Available: http://purl.org/dc/groups/education.htm

Federico, P. (1980). Adaptive instruction: Trends and issues. In R. Snow & M. Farr (Eds.), *Conative and affective process analysis* (Vol. 1, pp. 1–26). Hillsdale, NJ: Lawrence Erlbaum Associates.

Flavell, J. H. (1979). Metacognition. *American Psychologist, 34,* 906–911.

Gagné, R. (1967). *Learning and individual differences.* Columbus, OH: Merrill.

IMS. (2000). *Instructional management systems project.* Web site [online]. Available: http://imsproject.org/

Ledoux, J. (1996). *Emotional brain: The mysterious underpinnings of emotional life* New York: Simon & Schuster.

LTSC (Learning Technology Standards Committee). *Standard for information technology—education and training systems—learning objects and metadata* (IEEE P1484.12) [online]. Available: http://ltsc.ieee.org/wg12/index.html#S&P

Maddux, C. 1993. Past and future stages in education computing research. In H. C. Waxman & G. W. Bright (Eds.), *Approaches to research on teacher education and technology.* Charlottesville, VA: Association for the Advancement of Computing in Education, pp. 11–22.

Martinez, M. (1999a). Mass customization: A paradigm shift for the 21st century. *ASTD Technical Training Magazine, 10*(4), 24–26.

Martinez, M. (1999b). Using learning orientations to investigate how individuals learn successfully on the Web. *Technical Communication, 46*(4), 471–487.

Martinez, M. (in press). Building interactive Web learning environments to match and support individual learning differences. *Journal of Interactive Learning Research, 11*(2).

Popkewitz, T. S., & Shutkin, D. S. (1993). Social science, social movements and the production of educational technology in the U.S. In R. Muffoletto & N. Nelson Knupfer (Eds.), *Computers in education: Social, political, and historical perspectives* (pp. 11–36). Cresskill, NJ: Hampton Press.

Reeves, T. (1993). Pseudoscience in computer-based instruction. The case of learner control research. *Journal of Computer-Based Instruction, 20*(2), 39–46.

Russell, T. (1997). Technology wars: Winners and losers. *Educom Review, 32*(2), (1997), 44–46, Available: http://www.educause.edu/pub/er/review/reviewArticles/32244.html

Snow, R. (1987). Aptitude complexes. In R. Snow & M. Farr (Eds.), *Conative and affective process analysis* (Vol. 3, pp. 11–34). Hillsdale, NJ: Lawrence Erlbaum Associates.

Snow, R. (1989). Toward assessment of cognitive and conative structures in learning. *Educational Researcher, 18*(9), 8–14.

Snow, R., & Farr, M. (1987). Cognitive-conative-affective processes in aptitude, learning, and instruction: An introduction. In R. Snow & M. Farr (Eds.), *Conative and affective process analysis* (Vol. 3, pp. 1–10). Hillsdale, NJ: Lawrence Erlbaum Associates.

Valdez, G., McNabb, M., Foertsch, M., Anderson, M., Hawkes, M., & Raack, L. (2000). *Computer-based technology and learning: Evolving uses and expectations* [online]. The Central Regional Educational Laboratory. Available: http://www.ncrel.org/tplan/cbtl/toc.htm

Wiley, D. (1999). *Learning objects and the new CAI: So what do I do with a learning object?* [online]. Available: http://wiley.ed.usu.edu/docs/instruct-arch.pdf

Woodward, A. (1998). Infants selectively encode the goal object of an actor's reach. *Cognition 69,* 1–34.

Evaluation of Learning Objects and Instruction Using Learning Objects

David D. Williams

E valuation is integral to every aspect of designing instruction with learning objects. Evaluation helps in clarifying audiences and their values,
identifying needs, considering alternative ways to meet needs (including
selecting among various learning objects), conceptualizing a design, developing
prototypes, and actual instructional units with various combinations of learning objects, implementing and delivering the instruction, managing the learning experience, and improving the evaluation itself.

Evaluation must assemble all the standards associated with objects,
learners, instructional theories, and other stakeholder values, and estimate the
quality of the instruction in terms of those standards both to formatively (for
development purposes) improve the instruction and to assess its value summatively (for accountability purposes), as well as determining degrees of compliance with technical standards.

This chapter summarizes current relevant evaluation theories and practical guidelines for building evaluation principles into the entire process of
designing instruction with learning objects throughout the life of any given
unit of instruction. It also emphasizes the need to include evaluation as an integral part of any design process by addressing the following questions.

What Is Evaluation?

And what does it have to do with learning objects? What is the most
current thinking about evaluation, particularly participant-oriented and democratic evaluation? What are they and how do they fit with learning object and
instruction evaluation needs? How does the world of values fit and not fit with
the learning object world?

Who Cares?

Who will use the information gathered through an evaluation of particular learning objects and instruction using those objects?

What Do They Care About?

Definitions

What are users' definitions of learning objects? How do their definitions fit with the growing literature? How are they different? What are the implications of these qualities for an evaluation? How do users define or view instruction using those learning objects? In what context? Should evaluation only address learning objects in the context of the instruction in which they are employed?

Values

Several criteria for evaluating learning objects are emerging in the literature and more are likely to emerge. How should they play into any evaluation? Whose values do the technical standards represent? What are users' values that are relevant to the learning objects? How do those values fit with the various versions of standards for learning objects that are being promoted? How do they differ? What criteria do they have for deciding if the learning objects or the instruction using them are successful? Teachers automatically evaluate learning objects on the fly, what are their criteria? Can their criteria be built into the metadata?

Some criteria for learning objects being discussed in the literature include reusability, repurposability, granularity, instructional or learning value, existence and quality of metadata, ability to adjust to the needs of the context in which they are being used, fundamentality, the spirit of the learning object idea, the philosophy of the learning management system in which the learning object is being reused, agreement among collaborators on units of measurement, architecture, and approach, sequencing *(instructionally grounded)* and scope *(size of the learning object)* issues. How should these fit into an evaluation of learning objects?

In addition to the learning object criteria, instructional criteria, etc., what are the evaluation criteria valued by those who care? Will the Program Evaluation Standards (Sanders, 1994) work here? Shouldn't evaluation take place while the needs assessment, design, development, and refining of learning objects and instruction using them are taking place?

Likely Use

What are those who care likely to do with any evaluative information gathered about the objects or the instruction? Learning object use will vary by user, and users' criteria must be included in any evaluation effort. Their interests may or may not overlap with the technical standards discussed in the literature. What to do about that?

Other Issues

How do those who care about learning objects already evaluate them and instruction using such objects? Should they change? Why or why not? What would it take to change? How can the evaluation process be automated or at least made more scalable? Should it be? What are the implications of doing so? What are the relationships between various evaluation theories and instructional theories that could be used to make sense of learning objects? What difference does it make which evaluation theory is used by a given stakeholder for a given learning object?

How to Evaluate Learning Objects?

Once the questions regarding audience and their values and criteria are addressed, evaluation methodology is relatively straightforward. The rest of the chapter will examine additional steps to be followed in carrying out an evaluation based on particular audience needs and values.

An Illustration

An illustration of a potential learning object and its evaluation circumstances will be used to organize the discussion around these questions throughout the chapter. The illustration is based on the learning object presented as Figure 1.

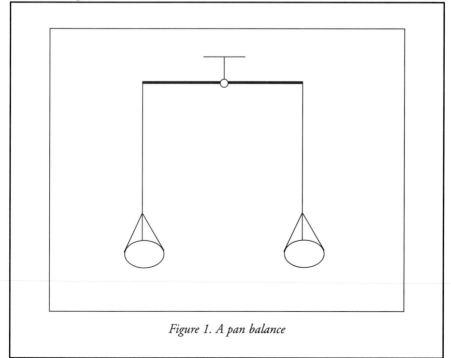

Figure 1. A pan balance

What Is Evaluation?

What is the most current thinking about evaluation? What does evaluation have to do with learning objects? What is participant-oriented evaluation?

What is the current thinking about evaluation? Various definitions of evaluation have emerged in the last few years (see Worthen, Sanders, & Fitzpatrick, 1997, for a good summary), but they all boil down to comparing what something is to what it ought to be, in order to facilitate a judgment about the value of that thing.

Gathering data about what something is constitutes a major challenge for science. It involves carefully defining the dimensions along which the object will be described, and then using methods that are dependable and accurate for gathering and interpreting data about the object. As difficult as these tasks may appear, the much greater challenge in evaluation is the necessarily prior task of defining the values or dimensions along which the object should be described or deciding *"what ought to be."*

Deciding *"what ought to be"* for a given object involves clarification of values, criteria, and standards from various points of view. What an object ought to be or do is clearly a matter of opinion that will vary with the perspectives of different potential or actual users of that object. One of the first major tasks of evaluation involves exploring alternative values and clarifying which will be used in a given evaluation of an object.

What does evaluation have to do with learning objects? As indicated elsewhere in this book, learning objects are being defined in many different ways by different users and others with interests in promoting their use. There is a need for a body of experts to clarify the criteria that should be used for judging the quality of a learning object. Essentially, people from several fields are setting the stage for evaluating learning objects and are actually evaluating them in the process. But are the principles associated with formal evaluation that have been developed over the years forming the basis for all this evaluation activity? This chapter will set forth some of those principles and will invite those who are involved or may become involved in setting standards and using those standards to use these evaluation principles in their efforts.

What is participant-oriented evaluation? Many approaches to addressing these evaluation challenges have been proposed and employed since the 1960s when evaluation was mandated by the United States Congress in conjunction with funds allocated for educational programs (for a summary of most approaches, see Worthen, Sanders, & Fitzpatrick, 1997). The approach taken will determine to a great extent the selection of values or criteria, the kinds of information that can be gathered, and what recipients of evaluation results will do with the evaluative information.

Over the last several years, goal-based, goal-free, decision-making, theory-based, and many other evaluation approaches have been adapted into participant-oriented approaches, which encourage all evaluation efforts to attend to the interests and values of the participants. Some of these participant-oriented approaches are responsive evaluation (Stake, 1984), democratic evaluation (House & Howe, 1999; Ryan & DeStefano, 2000), fourth generation evaluation (Guba & Lincoln, 1989), empowerment evaluation (Fetterman, 1996), utilization-focused evaluation (Patton, 1997), participatory evaluation (Cousins & Whitmore, 1998) and collaborative evaluation (Cousins, Donohue, & Bloom, 1996).

Although these approaches to evaluation vary in many ways, they all emphasize the fact that evaluations are done for particular participants whose values vary and must be addressed in fair and systematic ways if justice is to be met and the participants are to have sufficient interest in using the evaluation results. Indeed, over time, evaluation has become increasingly attentive to the needs and interests of wider and more diverse groups of people associated with the things being evaluated.

Some fundamental elements of one participant-oriented approach to evaluation are summarized below. This approach takes a broad perspective on the nature of most kinds of evaluands *(things being evaluated)*, ranging from organizations to instructional products (including learning objects) and from their conception to their completion, as first proposed by Stufflebeam (1971) in his CIPP *(context, input, process, product)* approach as shown in Figure 2.

The CIPP approach assumes that anything that might be evaluated could be usefully evaluated at various stages in its development. As indicated in the figures below, the proposed evaluation framework organizes the interests, questions, values, and participation of potential evaluation users and stakeholders around four types of evaluation which parallel four stages of development:

- *Context* evaluations that investigate the socio-political, organizational, and other contextual variables associated with the need for learning objects, courses, and support efforts;

- *Input* evaluations that compare alternative inputs or means for meeting the needs identified in context evaluations, including but not limited to learning objects;

- *Process* evaluations that formatively assess the planning, design, development, and implementation of learning objects and associated efforts to use them, including attempts to adapt instruction based on individual differences as expressed in learner profiles, and so forth.; and

- *Product* evaluations that allow summative judgments to be made regarding the quality, utility, and value of learning objects and infrastructures that support them.

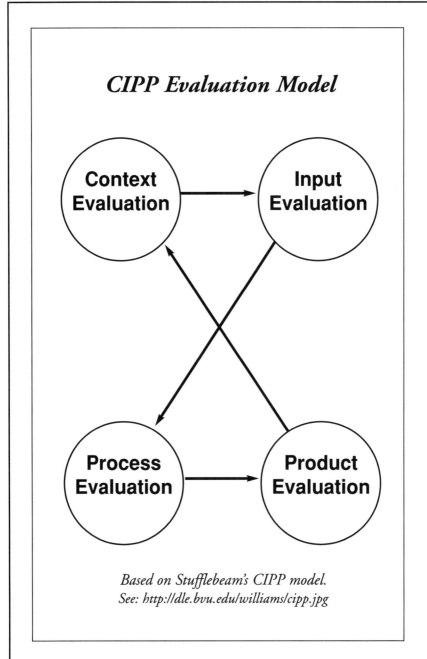

CIPP Evaluation Model

Based on Stufflebeam's CIPP model.
See: http://dle.bvu.edu/williams/cipp.jpg

Figure 2. Stufflebeam's CIPP (Context, Input, Process, Product) Model

Ideally, evaluations of all four types will occur simultaneously and repeatedly throughout the life of an organization (at the macro-level) that has multiple projects, programs, initiatives, and courses, and throughout the life of a learning object (at the micro-level).

The participant-oriented approach presented in this chapter combines Stufflebeam's approach with Patton's user-focused approach (Patton, 1997), illustrated in Figure 3 into a comprehensive model, presented in Figure 4.

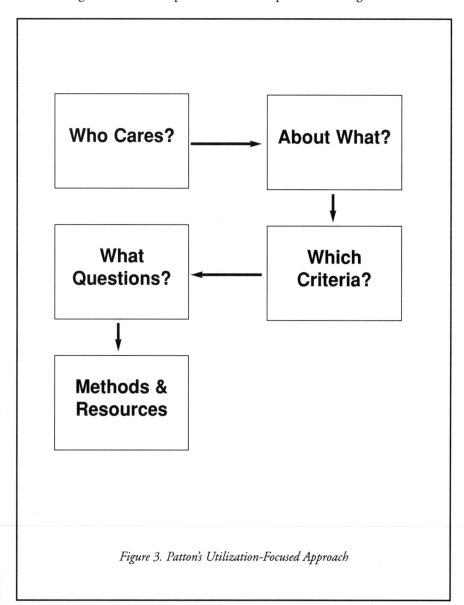

Figure 3. Patton's Utilization-Focused Approach

As represented in Figure 3, Patton argues that the key to evaluation utility is to identify people who are disposed to learning from evaluations. He outlines several procedures for identifying these users and then working with them to clarify what they want to know and what they are likely to do with information gathered by an evaluation. He gives many examples to persuade evaluators to not only organize their studies around users' questions and criteria but to also involve the "clients," stakeholders, or participants in gathering and interpreting the evaluation data as much as possible.

As shown in Figure 4, combining Stufflebeam's and Patton's approaches suggests that different users with different questions, criteria, and information needs may be more or less crucial at different stages in the life of an evaluand. To be most helpful, evaluations should be organized to meet the greatest needs of the most people at each of these stages.

For example, let's imagine that the image of a pan balance in Figure 1 is an evaluand of potential interest as a learning object. The proposed evaluation approach would suggest that potential users of the image as a learning object should be identified and their questions and concerns about learning contexts in which they are involved should be explored in a "context" evaluation to see if there is a need for the pan balance image as a learning object and what the nature of that need might be. Likewise, if it is determined that there is a need for the image as a learning object, a subsequent "input" evaluation of alternative ways to meet that need should be conducted. During this stage, potential users should be involved in clarifying their criteria for the image of the pan balance and comparing different pan balances or other kinds of learning objects that might most powerfully meet the need. Subsequently, assuming that one particular pan balance image is selected for inclusion in the users' instruction as a learning object, those users should be involved in a "process" evaluation to ascertain how well the pan balance is being implemented as a learning object. Finally, when it is clear that the pan balance image is being used as intended as a learning object, a "product" evaluation should be conducted in which the users clarify what they want the learning object (pan balance image) to be accomplishing and evidence is collected to ascertain how well it is doing so.

A Joint Committee on Standards for Educational Evaluation (Sanders, 1994) has developed, tested, and published standards for judging evaluations based on the concept of "metaevaluation" as expounded by Scriven (1991) and Stufflebeam (1975). As shown in Figure 4, the approach to evaluation proposed in this chapter includes evaluation of the evaluation as well as evaluation of the learning objects or original evaluands. This inclusion of metaevaluation helps ensure that the evaluation adds value to the instructional process by identifying ways to improve the evaluation as well as the instructional process itself.

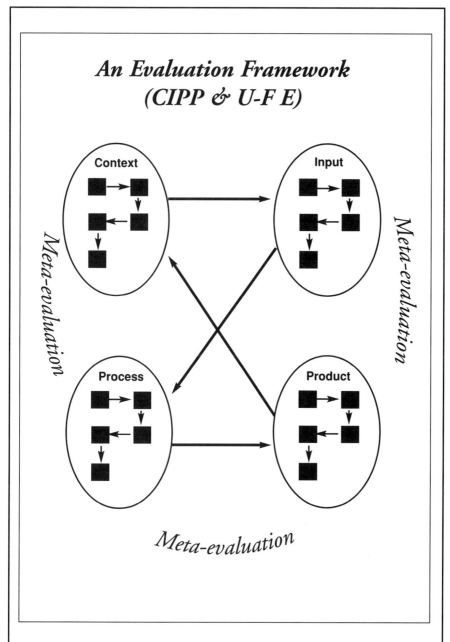

Figure 4. CIPP and Utilization-Focused Evaluation, combined

The proposed evaluation framework combines Stufflebeam's and Patton's approaches into a model which uses a basic evaluation logic (Scriven, 1980) of comparing what is to what ought to be, much as one would compare the weight of an item to a standard weight in a pan balance as represented in Figure 5.

As indicated there, on the lower left side of the pan balance, the users' criteria, definition of the evaluand, ideal performance levels, information needs, questions, and metaevaluation standards are juxtaposed with the lower right side of the pan balance which contains data collection methods and resulting descriptions of the evaluand. The key evaluation activity takes place at the fulcrum, where the users make their evaluations by comparing their criteria to the descriptions of the evaluand with the assistance of evaluators.

A further elaboration shown in Figure 6 outlines a process for carrying out evaluations of many kinds of evaluands for many different kinds of audiences using this evaluation framework.

According to the approach being proposed here, as part of each evaluation the following activities should be conducted by qualified participants

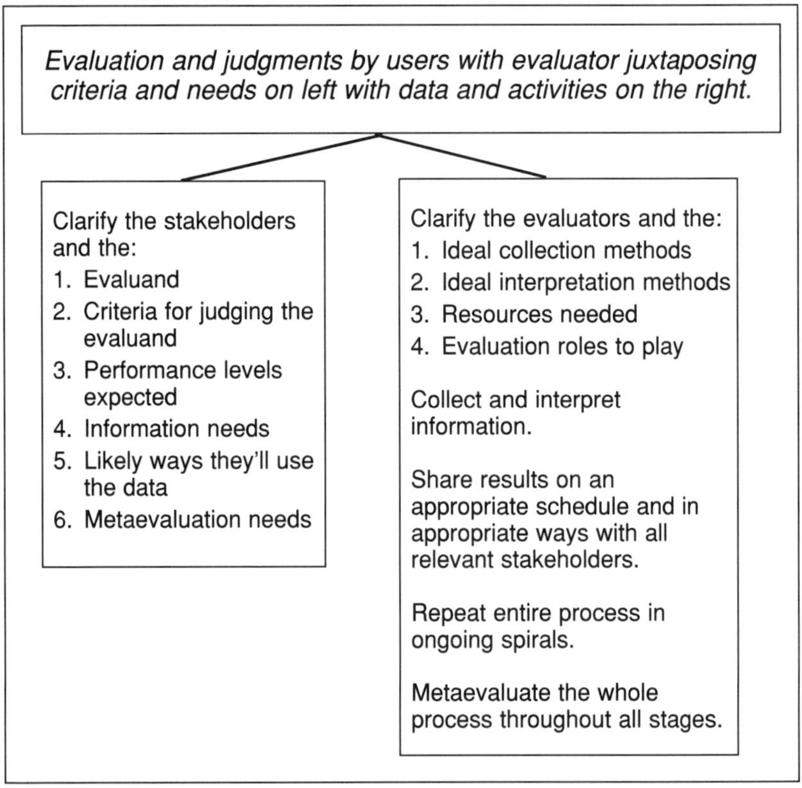

Evaluation and judgments by users with evaluator juxtaposing criteria and needs on left with data and activities on the right.

Clarify the stakeholders and the:
1. Evaluand
2. Criteria for judging the evaluand
3. Performance levels expected
4. Information needs
5. Likely ways they'll use the data
6. Metaevaluation needs

Clarify the evaluators and the:
1. Ideal collection methods
2. Ideal interpretation methods
3. Resources needed
4. Evaluation roles to play

Collect and interpret information.

Share results on an appropriate schedule and in appropriate ways with all relevant stakeholders.

Repeat entire process in ongoing spirals.

Metaevaluate the whole process throughout all stages.

Figure 5. Basic evaluation logic in a pan balance

Process Evaluation

focuses on evaluating the processes being used to address needs clarified in the context evaluation and the use of various inputs to carry out a program or project. Examples of processes include organizational structure, instructional strategies, cooperation among organizations, use of technologies, involvement of faculty, curriculum development, course development, organizational change, etc.

Product Evaluation

focuses on evaluating the results of products yielded by the three other evaluation activities— such as instructional objects, instruction using objects, entire courses, etc.

Context Evaluation

focuses on evaluating needs, priorities, shared vision of participants, expectations of people and organizations, and how their efforts fit into broader time and location contexts.

Input Evaluation

focuses on evaluating alternative inputs that could be considered for addressing concerns such as vision, purposes, alternative curricula, instructional strategies, participants, technologies, etc.

Ideally, evaluation of all four types will occur simultaneously and repeatedly throughout the life of an organization that has multiple projects, programs, initiatives, courses, and so on coming and going. As part of each evaluation, the following activities should be conducted by qualified participants (sometimes internal to the organization and sometimes by external consultants or experts, depending on whether it is formative, meta-evaluative, etc.).

- *Clarify the evaluation users (who cares?). For example, administrators, faculty, students, instructional developers/designers, etc.*

- *Invite users to clarify what the evaluand (thing being evaluated) is (what do they care about?). For example, various contextual variables, alternative inputs, elements of the process, or alternative products or dimensions of those products, such as particular learning objects.*

- *Work with users to clarify criteria or indicators of success to judge the evaluand against (what is success?). For example, the process should cost less than the status quo, the course should teach more people faster at a higher level of performance, the learning objects should be easily accessible, etc.*

- *Work with users to clarify the questions they want to answer and what they would do with alternative results (what to ask?)*

- *Use 1-4 to determine the inquiry methods, needed resources, timeline, costs, etc.*

- *Meta-evaluate the plan, the process, and the actual evaluation formatively and summatively on a continual basis to improve it while improving the evaluands.*

Figure 6. An evaluation framework

(sometimes internal to the organization and sometimes by external consultants, ideally by some of the people who will use the evaluation results to make decisions about learning objects or other evaluands):

1. Clarify who the evaluation users are *(who cares?)*, such as administrators, faculty, students, instructional designers, etc.

2. Invite users to clarify what the evaluand is *(what is the thing they care about to be evaluated and at what stage[s] in its life?)*. For example, learning objects of many kinds as well as various contextual variables, alternative inputs, elements of the process, or alternative products or dimensions of those products could be considered.

3. Work with users to clarify criteria or indicators of success against which to judge the evaluand *(what is success?)*. For example, which definition of learning object do they agree to use? What metadata and other standards will they hold to?

4. Work with users to clarify questions they have (in addition to or to elaborate on the main questions about how well the evaluand is meeting their criteria) and what they will do with results *(what to ask?)*.

5. Use steps 1–4 to determine the inquiry methods, needed resources, timeline, costs, etc., to carry out a particular evaluation project, assuming that many different projects by different participants over time will be part of an ongoing evaluation system that is an integral part of the instructional design process and the work of faculty, students, and administrators with interests in the instruction.

6. Metaevaluate the evaluation plan, process, and activities formatively and summatively on a continual basis to improve them while improving the evaluands.

Summary. So, what does all this information about evaluation have to do with learning objects? How does the world of values fit or not fit with the learning object world? Answers to these questions should become clearer throughout this chapter. But it should be clear now that learning objects are evaluands of particular interest to particular users of those learning objects and evaluative information about them. The field of evaluation recommends that a first step in evaluating learning objects is to clarify who wants to evaluate them and use them. Next, how the users define the learning objects and the criteria they have for judging the learning objects need to be clarified so it is clear what they expect the learning objects to do. Finally, data about how learning objects measure up to those criteria need to be collected and used to make evaluation judgments in accordance with established metaevaluation standards. In conclusion, the worlds of learning objects and evaluation are very compatible if it is reasonable to assume that users of learning objects want to judge their quality and have ideas about what quality means.

Given the contexts for the evaluand and evaluation processes outlined above, most evaluation projects (including evaluations of learning objects) can be organized and reported easily around the following topics which will be used to organize the rest of this chapter:

- Who cares? Or, who are the audiences or users who have or should have interests in the learning objects?

- What do they care about? Exactly what do users have an interest in (which learning objects or aspects of them), what criteria will they use in judging the learning objects, and what questions will the evaluation be organized around?

- What methods will be used to gather and analyze data to answer the evaluation questions, to report results, to make recommendations to the users based on the results, and account for resources used to conduct the study?

- How will evaluation be built into the instructional process and how will metaevaluation be used to continually ascertain the quality of the evaluation as part of that process?

Who Cares?

Who are the audiences or users who have or should have interests in learning objects? Although many different groups of people may have interests in learning objects, the two most obvious user groups are instructors and students. A third group we will consider in this chapter are instructional support persons (including instructional designers, librarians, technical support personnel, etc.), because people in these groups are more involved in the learning object community than most instructors and students at this time.

Instructors. Instructors or teachers are primary users of learning objects because they often design their own instruction and draw upon objects of all kinds to do so. Instructors may design instruction formally in lesson plans, syllabi, and Web sites. They also design instruction "on the fly" during lectures and group activities with the entire class and during individual or small group consultations.

Instructors vary in their needs as users of learning objects as they vary in experience, the age level they teach, the subject matter, the instructional needs they are trying to address, their instructional technique, and so on. For example, a third grade teacher is a different kind of instructor with very different needs associated with learning objects than a private corporation trainer who helps adult learners from the business community upgrade their skills and knowledge of changing laws affecting business practices. But instructors from both groups may actually use some of the same learning objects in their instruction.

Helping instructors evaluate learning objects requires adjustment to each of these variations. In addition, all instructors need different kinds of evaluative information to help them make decisions at different stages in the instructional process, which may vary dramatically from student to student with whom they work.

Students. Students or learners are some of the most important users of learning objects. And of course, they vary in their needs and values even more than instructors do because there are more of them. Because of their numbers and the tradition that instructors develop learning experiences for students in most formal learning settings (such as schools) rather than invite the students to develop their own instructional environment, the role of students in evaluating and choosing among learning objects may be easily overlooked. But eventually students have to evaluate any given learning opportunity and choose to learn from it or not. Therefore, this chapter attends to the learners as key users of evaluations of learning objects.

Instructional support persons. Instructional supporters include instructional designers, teacher educators, textbook and other instructional materials developers, instructional Webmasters, librarians, technical support personnel, and many others who create, maintain, and index objects. Interestingly, it is to this group that most of the current learning objects community members belong. These are the folks who are setting the standards and clarifying the roles for learning objects that instructors and students are supposed to use.

What Do They Care About?

What do these users care about? Exactly what do they have an interest in, what criteria will they use in judging the evaluands, and what questions will the evaluation be organized around? These questions are at the heart of the evaluation task. As indicated at the beginning of this chapter, there are many such questions associated with this issue to be explored. Several of these are presented below in three categories: definitions, values, and other issues.

Definitions. What are users' definitions of learning objects they are interested in? How do their definitions fit with the growing literature? How are they different? What are the implications of these qualities for an evaluation?

A brief review of the emerging literature on learning objects (see other chapters in this book for current reviews) reveals very little consensus on what constitutes a learning object in general. Rather, whatever a particular user finds useful as a learning object *IS* a learning object for them. General definitions in the literature range from *"any entity . . . which can be used . . . or referenced during technology supported learning"* (LTSC, 1999) to *"any digital resource that can be reused to support learning"* (Wiley, 2000). But unless there is a user with one of these definitions in mind, these variations don't really have practical implications for the use of and evaluation of learning objects by actual users.

The lack of consensus on a definition of learning object reinforces the importance of involving potential users in defining what they mean by "learning object" in their particular context, and focusing evaluative attention on those specified items. Participant-oriented approaches to evaluation emphasize this definition activity early in the evaluation process.

How do users define or view instruction that employs learning objects? In what contexts? Should evaluation only address learning objects in the context of the instruction in which they are employed?

Learning objects may be defined in isolation but they can only be employed as such in instructional situations or contexts. For example, the pan balance image by itself has no instructional value until it is used by an instructor and/or a learner in a particular way, place, and time. The way, place, and time define the instructional context which constitutes instruction using learning objects. What the context and associated instruction are varies with the perspectives of different users. And these variations shape the definition of the associated learning object.

So, although working groups and learned bodies may define the concept of "learning object" in many different ways, what constitutes an actual learning object as part of instruction in a given context must be defined by the users of that learning object for it to have useful meaning for those users. Likewise, those same users need to be involved in the evaluation of the learning objects in the context of the instruction in which they learn from those objects.

For example, in this chapter, I chose to use the pan balance image presented as Figure 1 as a learning object in the context of the instruction I gave on the basic evaluation logic underlying the participant-oriented evaluation approach as illustrated in Figure 5. In this case, I took on the role of "instructor" to invite you as a reader to be a "student" of evaluation and to collaborate with me in examining some characteristics of evaluation through the pan balance learning object. Some readers may find this learning object useful while others may not. Instructional designers might have much to say about how to employ this potential learning object better than I've done if they too were willing to accept the pan balance as a learning object for this instructional context. Hence, the pan balance *IS* a learning object for particular users in a particular context if they agree to let it be so. To the extent that users reach consensus about defining a particular object in a particular context as a learning object, it becomes such for them.

The question of granularity or scope (what is the best size of object to create and catalog) is a pressing question for many instructional designers and implementers. Learning objects can range in size from individual images (such as the pan balance used in this chapter) to an entire curriculum. This fact raises the question, *"On what size of learning object does it make sense to spend evaluation resources?"* As indicated above, how the users define the context for an object defines the object. Likewise, participant-oriented evaluation relies on users to decide how big the object must be for various kinds of evaluation attention. Users may want to use metadata indicators for conducting context and input evaluations of potential learning objects while relying on larger more formal process and product evaluations of an entire curriculum in which those learning objects are organized. On the other hand, a producer of an object to be sold may want to conduct process and product evaluations on a single object in various contexts to generate credible evidence of the value of the object for potential buyers. Users have to decide what kind of evaluation is needed for any given learning object.

A related question is *"How do evaluators perform in-context evaluations of resources whose main purpose is to be reused in as many different contexts as possible?"* Evaluating the object in one context does not necessarily answer the question of how it performs in another context. This is a particular concern for smaller objects such as the pan balance image, which should be usable in many more contexts than larger objects, such as a curriculum. Once again, the answer lies in ascertaining the interests of the users of the evaluation (and the object). If a single object's main purpose is to be reusable in many different contexts, its usefulness should be documented by many users with different needs and perspectives in many contexts over time and that product evaluation information should be attached to the object as metadata. No single evaluation study of an object could provide that kind of information. In contrast, evaluations of a curriculum employing many learning objects could be less frequent by responding to fewer users' perspectives because the curriculum would not be applied in nearly so many contexts. Therefore, curriculum evaluations could be more formal and larger than single object evaluations.

In all these questions about definition of learning object and appropriate context, the users' values provide the key guidelines for defining the appropriate evaluation approach, scope, and timing.

Values. Several criteria for evaluating learning objects are emerging in the literature and more are likely to emerge. How should they play into any evaluation? Whose values do the technical standards represent? What are users' values that are relevant to the learning objects? How do those values fit with the various versions of standards for learning objects that are being promoted? How do they differ? What criteria do various users have for deciding if the learning objects or the instruction using them are successful? What are those who care likely to do with any evaluative information gathered about the objects or the instruction? Teachers automatically evaluate learning objects on the fly; what are their criteria? Can their criteria be built into the metadata?

Some criteria for learning objects being discussed in the literature include reusability, repurposability, granularity, instructional or learning value, existence and quality of metadata, ability to adjust to the needs of the context in which they are being used, fundamentality, the philosophy of learning into which the learning object is being inserted, agreement among collaborators on units of measurement, architecture, approach, sequencing *(instructionally grounded)* and scope *(size of the learning object)* issues. How should these criteria fit into an evaluation of learning objects?

In addition to the learning object criteria, instructional criteria, etc., what are the evaluation criteria valued by those who care? Will the Program Evaluation Standards work here? Shouldn't evaluation take place while the needs assessment, design, etc. are taking place?

As this list of questions suggests, values and criteria comprise huge areas of interest and concern for anyone interested in evaluation of learning objects. But the same principles discussed in the previous section on definition of learning objects and instructional contexts hold here as well. Criteria and values are held by people, users of the learning objects and their evaluations. There has to be a selection among all the possible criteria based on the values of people and the participant-oriented approach to evaluation argues that the values of the users should guide this selection of criteria.

Obviously, there may be potential conflicts among likely users. For example, the instructor may want to emphasize the instructional quality of an object while a student may be more interested in scope, and instructional supporters may be anxious about meeting emerging technical standards. Quite likely, none of these users would be aware of and therefore interested in criteria for evaluating their own learning object evaluation activities. Hence, it becomes critical to find ways for users with different interests to not only have information they need to evaluate learning objects against criteria that reflect their own values, but to also learn of and acknowledge the importance of criteria associated with values held by other users with whom they are collaborating. An evaluation process needs to be used that will encourage users to explicate their values, clarify their criteria, allow others to do the same, and make their evaluative decisions in concert with the decisions of fellow users. Guidelines for evaluating learning objects will be proposed later in this chapter. These suggestions are based on a participant-oriented approach to evaluation which seeks to encourage users in these directions.

Other issues. How do those who care about learning objects evaluate them and instruction using such objects? Should they change? Why or why not? What would it take to change? How can the evaluation process be automated or at least made scalable? Should it be? What are the implications of doing so? What are the relationships between various evaluation theories and various instructional theories that could be used to make sense of learning objects? What difference does it make which evaluation theory is used by a given stakeholder for a given learning object?

In addition to the practical issues of clarifying users of learning objects, their criteria and definitions, many basic research questions such as those listed above challenge the learning object world. Although the principle task of evaluation is to help particular users make formative and summative decisions about the evaluands of their interest, there is a growing interest in evaluation as a means of generating understanding and explanation (Chelimsky, 1997). Therefore, some of the basic research questions listed above and others could be profitably addressed as part of any evaluative efforts users might make to improve and judge the quality of learning objects and instruction based on such objects. Users should be invited to inform others of their insights into these and other issues as they engage in the process of identifying needs for learning objects, selecting among potential objects, implementing instruction using objects, and judging the impact of instruction using learning objects.

How to Evaluate Learning Objects?

So, how to do all this? Given the importance of involving potential users of evaluation information in clarifying their definitions, criteria, and questions, what methods should be used to gather and analyze data to answer those questions, to report results, to make recommendations to the users based on the results, and to account for resources used to conduct the study? As might be imagined, each evaluation setting calls for slightly different methods to most powerfully address the unique questions and to satisfy the information needs of users. However, rather than just say "it depends," this section of the chapter will be used to explore two alternative approaches to illustrate the diversity of possibilities.

One typical approach to evaluation is the one-shot stand-alone study conducted by an external evaluator under contract with the evaluation users. A second option is to build evaluation into the internal system involving the users as internal evaluators as part of their roles as participants in the system. Both approaches will be discussed and illustrated because a combination allows for offsetting strengths and weaknesses of each.

External evaluation. Often external consultants are invited to conduct evaluations for organizations or individuals. This approach is usually taken to provide a form of objectivity based on the belief that resulting data will be more credible to possible evaluation users. In terms of Stufflebeam's CIPP model, external evaluation is particularly attractive for "product" evaluations or evaluations designed to check accountability.

For a learning object evaluation, an external evaluation would be helpful if a vendor, a creator of a learning object or instruction containing learning objects, or some other instructional support person wanted to certify to potential users that their product would help learners learn and instructors instruct more powerfully or quickly or at a lower cost than some competitor. An external evaluation would also be helpful if a user or potential user wanted to hold others accountable for how they were using learning objects. For example, if students wanted to evaluate how well their instructor was helping them learn with particular learning objects, or if an instructor wanted to evaluate how well an instructional product containing learning objects was helping them teach, a summative product evaluation would be in order.

Although each of the evaluations mentioned as examples above could proceed in slightly different ways, they would likely follow a general pattern which will be described and illustrated below if they were to use the participant-oriented approach advocated in this chapter.

Step 1. Someone would initiate a request for proposals (RFP) to invite potential evaluation specialists to propose an external evaluation. In the RFP, the evaluators would be introduced to the key questions and issues from the initiator's point of view. They might also be told what resources were available for the study (time, personnel, funds, etc.). They would be invited to make a proposal with or without opportunities to ask questions or to explore the situation in person.

For example, let's assume there is a team of instructional designers who have created a set of learning objects packaged into instructional materials for teaching evaluation skills to educators. They want people to access these objects and use them, so they decide to commission an evaluation study to provide evidence that use of these objects will help both new and experienced evaluators do their job better. One of the team pulls together an RFP and the others review it before posting the request on their Web page and other sites where evaluators might learn of this opportunity.

Step 2. Several professional evaluators would respond to the RFP with proposals based on their philosophies of evaluation, their experience, their resources, and interests. They may or may not take a participant-oriented approach, even if the RFP emphasized the need for such an approach. They would propose activities to address the evaluation questions and would explain the need for resources such as time, participant involvement, and funds. They would describe the qualifications of the evaluation team members. They would likely leave some options open to negotiation once the project was funded, hoping to have a better understanding of the needs and interests from the inside perspectives of the users.

For example, a professor of evaluation might read the RFP put out by the instructional design team and decide to organize her students in a beginning evaluation class to collaborate with her in conducting an evaluation.

Because she is teaching the students about participant-oriented evaluation and goal-based evaluation, she might guide the class to prepare a proposal that has elements of both or she might propose two alternative strategies to compare the results that would come from each. She would be working to meet the needs of the instructional design team but also to meet the needs of her evaluation team.

Step 3. The group who sent out the RFP would choose among the resulting evaluation proposals and select one evaluation team with which they would establish a contract for services based on the evaluation proposal. The contract would specify responsibilities of both the evaluation team and the client group as well as milestones and reports to be produced according to a timeline.

For example, the professor and her students might note in the proposal (and thereby, in the contract) that they were responsible for conducting initial interviews by a certain date with students, instructors, and the instructional design team members to clarify their definitions of the learning objects and their criteria for judging them. At the same time, the proposal would stipulate that the interviewees would be responsible to cooperate with the evaluation team in meeting appointments and would be asked to review interview protocols and other instruments in a timely way so the evaluation team could use these reactions to modify their plans.

Step 4. Evaluation team members would conduct initial interviews with those who invited the proposals, with organization leaders and members, and with other representative users of the products being evaluated and anyone else who might be likely to use the results of their evaluation. These interviews would clarify who potential users might be, what their definitions of the evaluand are, what values and criteria they might use to judge the evaluand against, what questions they want answered, and what they might do with different kinds of results. The initial interview step is also an opportunity for the evaluation team members to establish a working relationship with the evaluation users, clarify at the individual level what the evaluation is about and how it should help each user, and refine the plans that were made in response to the RFP before the evaluators were able to actually talk with a wide range of users in person.

For example, the evaluators would want to meet with several instructional design team members who were not involved with writing the RFP, as well as the writers, to see how their perspectives might shape the evaluation too. They would also want to meet with representative students and instructors who might be using the learning objects in the instructional packages being produced by the design team to explore how they define the learning objects, which aspects of the objects should be attended to, what criteria they would use to evaluate the objects and the instruction based on the objects, and what they might do with different evaluation results that could emerge. During these interviews the evaluation team members would work to help all users understand that the evaluation is meant to serve them as well as the instructional designers or those who made the RFP.

Step 5. The evaluation team would revise their evaluation plan based on the interviews and would present the plan to the users or their representatives. Although the initial proposal should have been a good response to the RFP, it is likely that by interviewing a wide range of users in Step 4, the evaluation team will discover additional issues or the need to emphasize some issues over others to meet the needs and to answer the questions of the greatest number of users possible. The evaluators would then modify their evaluation proposal to take these new emphases into account—to focus data gathering activities on the highest priority values of the potential users as a whole.

Usually, the team will discover some conflicting criteria or value perspectives among different groups. To truly serve the participants, the evaluators should build in techniques for sharing alternative perspectives among them rather than focus evaluative attention only on the interests of subgroups. Techniques include the Delphi technique (Scriven, 1991) and the hermeneutic dialectic (Guba & Lincoln, 1989). Both of these are means for sharing with the whole group or their representatives the views of subgroups with the invitation to consider values that are different than theirs, and to search for consensus on the most critical issues and criteria to use in the evaluation.

For example, suppose the professor-led evaluation team conducts the interviews described in Step 4, and learns that the instructors for the evaluation courses and the instructional designers have very parallel definitions for learning objects and similar ideas about which aspects of learning objects and instruction should be evaluated, but suppose the instructors differ somewhat on the criteria that should be used in evaluating both objects and instruction. On the other hand, imagine they find that student representatives have quite divergent ideas about what learning objects actually are, so their criteria diverge even more from values shared by other users. The team could use the Delphi technique to summarize results obtained from interviews into a questionnaire, which they could administer to representatives of all user groups with the request that they prioritize and add to the list of issues or questions and criteria presented.

This cycle could be repeated several times, until some consensus emerges (assuming that the respondents could see what the majority of their associates indicate as priorities and that they would modify their views to come to consensus). This process won't always work, but it is a means of helping users see what their associates are thinking in contrast to their own views and it provides evaluators with guidance in narrowing the focus of inquiries to the highest priority items shared by the greatest number of participants.

Step 6. Once the interests of the users are focused, the evaluation team would synthesize them into the key evaluation questions to be addressed during their study (with the assumption that many more questions than can be answered in one study would be identified for future attention). They would then refine the data collection and analysis plans from the original proposal to guide the study in light of the resources available. Finally, they would conduct the study according to these plans and would report the results to interested participants or their representatives.

For example, perhaps the professor's team decides that one key question for all potential users of the evaluation is *"How effective is the pan balance learning object in conveying the key ideas behind evaluation in the early stages of instruction on conducting evaluation studies?"* The evaluators would explore various ways to gather data to address that question. Then they would gather the data, analyze it, and share it with the users or their representatives.

One way they might address this question would be to convert the criteria identified during Steps 4 and 5 into an instrument for rating effectiveness of the pan balance object. They could then ask students who receive instruction using the pan balance object to rate the object using that instrument. They could also test the students on the concepts the pan balance object was designed to teach, both before and after instruction, to see if it made a difference. They might decide to randomly assign and use a control group of students who either received no instruction or received instruction using a different learning object as a basis for comparing changes from before instruction to after instruction if using such an experimental design was deemed appropriate and necessary for helping users reach justifiable conclusions.

An appropriate analysis procedure for the design used would be developed as well. In this case (with a pre-post control group design), it would be most appropriate to use a repeated measures analysis of variance procedure. The results of the analysis would be combined with descriptions of how the study originated, was designed, and was conducted into a report to be shared with students, instructors, and instructional designers to assist them in making evaluative judgments about the value of the pan balance learning object in the basic evaluation instruction context.

Step 7. Finally, the entire process used to conduct the evaluation should be metaevaluated to ensure that it is planned and conducted according to standards established by consumers and proponents of evaluation. As noted earlier, a joint committee of representatives of nearly twenty organizations identified and tested the use of thirty standards for the formative and summative evaluation of evaluation projects (Sanders, 1994). In this case of an external product evaluation, the metaevaluation could be conducted by either an internal team (perhaps while the study is in the planning and implementation phases), or an external third or independent party (after the study has been completed).

For example, the professor's evaluation team would invite an oversight committee of representatives of users, such as instructors, students, and instructional designers to metaevaluate the team's evaluation plans at the proposal stage and then to monitor them throughout the project to ascertain how well the evaluation meets the standards in practice. Finally, the users would be invited to employ a third party which is independent of the professor's evaluation team to read the evaluation report, conduct their own interviews and observations to metaevaluate the entire project and its products after the study ends.

Internal evaluation. The process described in the previous section for conducting external evaluations of learning objects is comprehensive for a product evaluation, when it is clear that instruction using several learning objects is needed, that the particular combination of learning objects is ideal, and that the instruction is operational and learning objects are being used as designed. However, involving external evaluators in product evaluation to ensure credibility for accountability purposes is expensive and not as efficient as an internal process could be for evaluating contexts, inputs, and processes as Stufflebeam (1971) argued. Therefore, it is recommended that an internal evaluation process be used to evaluate contexts and needs, competing inputs or ways of meeting those needs, and processes of carrying out the selected inputs.

Also, evaluation for accountability purposes makes the most sense when large units of instruction using many learning objects are the evaluands of interest. But smaller scale evaluations of the need for a learning object (a context evaluation), of alternative learning objects to meet a given need (an input evaluation), and of how well a unit of instruction implements one or more learning objects are better served by internal formative evaluation projects.

Likewise, internal formative evaluations are more readily systematized into the instructional design process than are external summative evaluations, because the former can be conducted by instructional designers and instructors as part of the instructional process, while the latter require external evaluation teams to enhance credibility for accountability purposes. Several steps to follow in building internal evaluation of learning objects and instruction using them into the instructional design process are presented below. Note that the letting of an RFP, the creation of a proposal, the negotiation of a contract, the conducting of initial interviews, and the revision of an evaluation plan which constituted steps 1–5 in the external evaluation process are all built into Step 1 in the internal evaluation process, making it much more efficient once established as part of the instructional design and delivery system which employs learning objects.

Step 1. Create an instructional design process around the participant-oriented approach to evaluation that is advocated in this chapter. That is, build

Stufflebeam's CIPP model (1971) and Patton's utilization-focused approach (1997) into the process of creating and providing instruction (see Figure 4). The CIPP model fits well with the common ADDIE approach to instructional design but improves upon it by building systematic evaluation into each step. ADDIE stands for: *Assess needs, Design, Develop, Implement, and Evaluate instruction.*

A modified ADDIE approach built around CIPP and Patton's approach would look something like this (with examples illustrating how to apply this approach to the development of an evaluation course):

- Involve everyone who cares or ought to care (or their representatives) and their values and definitions of the evaluand at each phase of the instructional design and delivery process and the evaluation of both. For example, an instructional development group would want to include representative teachers and students along with instructional support persons on a team that would help with design, implementation, and evaluation activities at all stages of the evaluation course design and implementation process.

- *Assess needs* for instruction (or a learning object) by following all the required elements of a *context evaluation* in which the context for potential instruction is evaluated using all the principles and standards associated with evaluation. For example, the team members would share their own perspectives about needs and would collaborate to develop interviews and other instruments for assessing how widely their views about were shared among potential users. This might include online surveys sent to potential users (e.g., evaluation course instructors and students) and other Web-related information collection tools.

- *Design* instruction (or learning objects to be used in instruction or select learning objects to be used in instruction) based on the needs identified in a context evaluation and then follow all the required elements of an *input evaluation* in which alternative means for meeting the needs are systematically compared and evaluated using all the principles and standards associated with evaluation. For example, two alternative pan balances could be presented to members of the team who represent instructors and students and their feedback could be used to refine those alternatives or replace them completely with other learning objects. These would be fast turn around evaluation studies in which minor changes could be made quickly to identify the most likely candidates, which could then be presented online to a sample of potential users with a variety of perspectives for their judgments.

- *Develop and deliver or implement* instruction (and learning objects included in the instruction) following all the required elements of a *process evaluation* in which the fidelity of implementation of the evaluand is assessed throughout the process of design and/or implementation using all the principles and standards associated with evaluation. For example, once a pan balance was identified during the input evaluation as meeting the users' criteria better than any other learning objects for the introductory instructional unit, the pan balance would be built into the instruction and actual instructors and students would be invited to use that instruction. Members of the team would monitor their use of the pan balance in conjunction with other learning objects to see how they actually use it. They could use machine-generated data for some of this monitoring but would probably have to sample some users to interview or to observe as well. They would then compare actual use to intended use criteria to judge how well the instruction and the learning objects were implemented.

• *Evaluate results* of instruction (and associated learning objects) by following all the required elements of a *product evaluation* in which outcomes associated with the instruction and associated learning objects are assessed using all the principles and standards associated with evaluation. The external evaluations of products or results were discussed in the earlier section on external evaluation but the instructional process should also include internal evaluation of the value of outcomes associated with instruction and learning objects. For example, just as in the external evaluation, the design team would assess what students learned while using the pan balance and would compare those achievements to the instructional objectives while taking into account the degree to which the instructional objects were actually implemented. This might involve an experimental or quasi-experimental design if feasible but could be less formal for the internal purposes than the external evaluation would be.

Step 2. Carry out evaluation on a constant basis by implementing the instructional design and evaluation process systematically and continually. In particular, engage participants who play different roles in regular dialogue about their values, their concerns, their questions and their information needs. Students and faculty should be as well represented as instructional support persons. Build a teamwork atmosphere in which individuals with different views feel free to express themselves and seek to understand the perspectives of others. Create an atmosphere that encourages diversity of views but also consensus on priorities for the entire instructional process. The process should include reporting results to the users and their representatives on a regular basis, but the reports could be oral or short progress reports instead of massive formal reports, which are more typical of external evaluations.

Step 3. Metaevaluate internally as well as externally. Finally, for the internal evaluation to function properly, the design team needs regular feedback on how well they are building evaluation systematically into their design process. They should designate at least one team member who will spend regular time throughout the design cycle critiquing the process being followed and the results being obtained from the design, implementation, and evaluation activities. They should use the same Standards (Sanders, 1994) that the external metaevaluators use and should be protected from any recrimination that others on the team might feel justified in using. Regular reports to the team members about how well they are meeting the evaluation standards will not only improve the evaluation of the learning objects but will improve the learning objects and the instruction associated with them as well.

Conclusion

This chapter has provided a quick overview of some key issues to consider in evaluating learning objects. It has been argued here that participant-oriented evaluation is ideal for learning object evaluation because what an object is and what criteria should be used to evaluate it vary from participant to participant. Participant-oriented evaluation allows various users to have their values honored in the evaluation of learning objects and other evaluands in which they have an interest.

It has also been a major conclusion of this chapter that internal systematic evaluation built into the instructional design and delivery process should be combined with external evaluation of whole units of instruction that employ learning objects. Steps for conducting both kinds of evaluation were proposed.

As the study and development of learning objects evolves, evaluation can and should play a critical role in helping users refine their criteria for such objects and their ability to use disciplined inquiry to improve instruction using learning objects. Evaluation can also be a tool for empirically exploring how learners and instructors use learning objects in a variety of subject areas and across age groups. Finally, the systematic use of evaluation as part of the instructional design process should help the evaluation field refine emerging philosophies and theories of evaluation.

References

Chelimsky, E. (1997). In E. Chelimsky & W. R. Shadish (Eds.), *Evaluation for the 21st century: A handbook.* Thousand Oaks, CA: Sage.

Cousins, J. B., Donohue, J. J., & Bloom, G. A. (1996). Collaborative evaluation in North America: Evaluators' self-reported opinions, practices, and consequences. *Evaluation Practice 17*(3), 207–226.

Cousins, J. B., & Whitmore, E. (1998). Framing participatory evaluation. In E. Whitmore (Ed.), *Participatory evaluation approaches.* San Francisco: Jossey-Bass.

Fetterman, D. M. (1996). *Empowerment evaluation: Knowledge and tools for self-assessment and accountability.* Thousand Oaks, CA: Sage.

Guba, E. G., & Lincoln, Y. S. (1989). *Fourth generation evaluation*. Thousand Oaks, CA: Sage.

House, E. R., & Howe, K. R. (1999). *Values in education and social research*. Thousand Oaks, CA: Sage.

LTSC (Learning Technology Standards Committee). (2000). *Learning technology standards committee*. Web site [on-line]. Available: http://ltsc.ieee.org/

Patton, M. Q. (1997). *Utilization-focused evaluation* (3rd ed.). Thousand Oaks, CA: Sage.

Ryan, K. E., & DeStefano, L. (Eds.). (2000). Evaluation as a democratic process: Promoting inclusion, dialogue, and deliberation. *New Directions for Program Evaluation,* no. 30. San Francisco: Jossey-Bass.

Sanders, J. R. (Chair). (1994). *The program evaluation standards* (2nd ed.). Thousand Oaks, CA: Sage.

Scriven, M. (1980). *The logic of evaluation*. Inverness, CA: Edgepress.

Scriven, M. (1991). *Evaluation thesaurus* (fourth ed.). Thousand Oaks, CA: Sage.

Stake, R. E. (1984). Program evaluation, particularly responsive evaluation. In G. F. Madaus, M. Scriven, & D. L. Stufflebeam (Eds.), *Evaluation models*. Boston: Kluwer-Nijhoff.

Stufflebeam, D. L. (1971). The relevance of the CIPP evaluation model for educational accountability. *Journal of Research and Development in Education. 5*(1), 19–25.

Stufflebeam, D L. (1975). *Metaevaluation*. Occasional Paper Series, no. 3. Kalamazoo, Mich.: Evaluation Center, Western Michigan University.

Wiley, D. A. (2000). *Learning object design and sequencing theory*. Unpublished doctoral dissertation, Brigham Young University, Provo, UT. Available: http://davidwiley.com/papers/dissertation/dissertation.pdf

Worthen, B. R., Sanders, J. R., & Fitzpatrick, J. L. (1997). *Program evaluation: alternative approaches and practical guidelines*. White Plains, NY: Longmans.

4.0 Learning Objects: Implementation War Stories

Battle Stories from the Field: Wisconsin OnLine Resource Center Learning Objects Project

FIPSE/LAAP Learning Objects Project Core Team:
Kay Chitwood, Carol May, David Bunnow, & Terri Langan

Introduction

Formal approval of the $1.6 million grant came through in August of 1999.
That meant we had the money. That was good news . . . But now what?

The *Fund for the Improvement of Post-Secondary Education* (FIPSE) provided the money through its brand new *Learning Anywhere Anytime
Partnership* (LAAP) for our three-year proposal to develop an online
resource center of "learning objects." We intended this center to house learning
objects for nine courses called the General Education "core" in the Wisconsin
Technical College System. The project would require all 16 districts to collaborate, providing staff, faculty, and technical expertise to get the project up and
running.

The proposal to develop "learning objects" was based on new thinking
in the field of curriculum development and course design—thinking that asks
educators to focus on learning and the learner by creating self-contained,
reusable, high-quality learning chunks that can be combined and recombined
in courses, learning activities and experiences, and assessments that meet a
learner's immediate needs. This kind of shift in thinking represents a move
away from the traditional course-building approach to teaching and learning—
the approach that assumes design around a whole course or a whole unit of
instruction with carefully integrated, often complex activities working in concert with one another to accomplish a learning objective or goal. Instead, the
learning object approach is more of a building blocks concept. In a simple analogy, one originated by Wayne Hodgins, Director of Worldwide Learning
Strategies, think of how you build structures and things with Legos™. When
you have a pile of Legos™ in front of you, you have the smallest unit of the

building available. Legos™ come in various shapes, sizes, forms and colors and they can be used together to form an infinite number and variety of structures. Even the "odd" pieces fit together with all of the other pieces so the builder can be as creative as he or she wants to be. That's the concept behind the learning objects approach to designing courses—put a pile of learning objects in front of a course builder, learning objects that can fit with other learning objects across courses and learning objectives in an wide array of possibilities, and watch courses emerge in creative ways. The approach has been called "just in time/just for you" learning and can be facilitated by professional teachers or used by learners who are curious to know more about particulars of their field.

The project opened the way for the Wisconsin Technical College System to pursue the development of educational experiences for its learners in this new way. It meant that we had resources we'd need to both explore the concept and to provide support and inservicing to move our courses and our learning and teaching activities in this direction. It meant that we could look at the way we write and revise curriculum, as well as the ways we teach, learn, and assess content. It gave us the vision that whatever we could produce could be state of the art, both for traditional time- and space-bound courses as well as for technology-based and virtual courses.

We had the money—the project, once a dream, would become a reality! *But now what?*

Initially, almost all of the 16 district presidents had signed letters of support, which meant in concept that these technical college districts supported the proposed idea and the proposal itself. But in reality, what did a letter of support mean?

To us, it meant all 16 districts would be well represented on a project steering committee; faculty from all 16 districts would do the development of the learning objects for all nine courses; and there would be technical support from the Faculty Innovation Centers of all the colleges. Did letters of support mean the above to district presidents and others in each of the colleges? And, in some cases, did the presidents remember to share this information with their key people in their colleges?

Needless to say, some of the more difficult challenges in the early months of the project stemmed from the coordination issues that come with hundreds of staff from 16 very different districts across the state, legal hurdles to overcome, dealing with technology which is changing each day, and communication issues. Although we expected and planned for some of the issues we've encountered, part of the fun of any project is confronting and overcoming the unexpected, which included everything from writing the project in the first place to getting the learning objects onto the Web. So far, approximately a third of the way through three-year project, we've had our share of fun—here are our top 10 challenges within the first several months of the project.

Challenge #1:
From Idea to Written Project Proposal

The idea emerged from issues such as these that have been with the WTCS system for a number of years:

- the costs of developing and updating courses and programs;
- the inconsistencies and perceived duplication among courses and programs with the same titles, and in some cases, the same numbering;
- difficulty in getting courses into the online arena, both from a development standpoint and from the perspective of how to manage and deliver such courses;
- variability of technology from campus to campus, and as a result, variability of access for both students and faculty; and
- competition among districts for FTEs and funding.

As staff and faculty shared concerns and issues, read more and more on the topic, and listened to guest speakers such as Elliott Masie, the idea of providing flexible learning options for students and faculty began to take shape. Along with that idea came the realization that collaboration among districts might just be able to produce more creative learning and teaching resources using less time and money to do so. The idea for the project was beginning to develop.

In order to initiate a state-wide project, we needed to define the parameters of the activity and figure out how to fund it. One way of limiting the project was to look at one specific subject area. We looked at General Education because each of our sixteen schools has a General Education Division—it was a natural. Also, a state task-force effort completed in 1991 resulted in the establishment of common course competencies for the nine core General Education courses offered throughout our state system. Those competencies could provide a reasonably common language, or focal point, for a collaborative project.

The 1999/2000 FIPSE/LAAP RFP seemed a match made in heaven—the criteria for the grants include collaboration, innovation, and the use of technology. Several staff from Fox Valley Technical College worked with staff from the State Technical College system to explore and develop the idea for an online resource center for General Education instructors developing, updating, and adapting the nine core courses. The first step was to organize a conference call in which all 16 General Studies deans were invited to participate. The goal of the initial call was to share the basic idea, get additional ideas, and discuss the possibility of applying for the FIPSE grant.

As was expected, not everyone invited to the first conference call was able to attend, and as a result, a lower than hoped-for number of people actually contributed to the discussion. The good news, though, was those who did participate liked the concept and encouraged us to move forward with the submission of the proposal. Because our timeline to get the FIPSE proposal in was short, we needed to act fast. We needed to get feedback on the idea, suggestions for additional ideas or considerations, and most of all, commitments from each of the other schools in our system. There we were, on the verge of what we thought was a great idea, but we couldn't move forward as quickly as we wanted because people were either unable to or uninterested in becoming involved in our preliminary discussion. The communication process was already proving to be a challenge. Since we weren't able to involve everyone who needed to be involved up front, we found ourselves sending copies of proposals, reminders of meetings, and e-mail messages to follow up and assure thorough information dissemination among all 16 districts.

Given the interest and support we did get, the group did move forward, with Fox Valley Technical College taking the lead in designing the project and writing the proposal. One of the final steps of preparing the proposal for submission was getting letters of support from each of the other fifteen schools. Some of the letters came immediately following the request for them while others straggled in. In a couple of cases, another follow-up process had to be used.

Finally, all the letters of support were in hand and the proposal was in the mail. We were hoping for all 16 colleges, but as it turned out, we received 15 letters of support and one verbal commitment.

Challenge #2:
To Commit or Not To Commit

Even within the same overall state system, bringing 16 diverse and unique districts together in agreement on the details of a proposal such as this one is a monumental task. In theory, the districts agreed that the idea was a good one. In practice, well, that's another part of the story.

The project required a steering committee with representation from all 16 districts, live (real people) technical support in all 16 districts, and faculty representatives for all nine courses from all 16 districts.

Steering Committee membership was open to decision makers on each campus, with the expectation that deans would step forward immediately, and early on, most did. Where follow-up was needed, we found that once people reviewed the idea and the general intent of the project, they were happy to serve themselves or to appoint a representative to the committee. One thing stressed was that attendance at all steering committee meetings would be mandatory and that a major responsibility of members would be to advocate for faculty and to be sure they were assisting faculty in removing barriers to their participation wherever possible. While the membership has been stable for the most part, there are still a couple of members who are not always able to represent their districts at meetings. At the first Steering Committee meeting, it was decided to rotate the meetings among the 16 colleges. Therefore, when we meet every other month, a different steering committee member hosts the meeting. The meetings are open to anyone and the host steering committee member invites interested staff to attend from his or her college. This has helped to "get the word out" with technical college staff.

Ideally, each district's Faculty Innovation Center would serve as hub of activity as faculty representatives brought their ideas to the forefront and began developing them into Web-deliverable learning objects. Technical experts in each district were expected to help faculty learn more about what would be possible (or not) and how they might adapt ideas to work in a Web-based learning environment. Even though each district has a center and technical expertise staffing it, many districts are small enough that this expectation was met with some concern; some districts have only one person staffing the center and serving the needs of the entire district; how would this added responsibility affect current duties? Could they do it? Several months have passed and that question is still unanswered.

When invitations went to districts inviting faculty participation, the assumption was made that faculty would be invited to volunteer and would have explained to them the terms under which they would participate in the project. Some districts were quite good about that; others simply tapped a faculty on the shoulder and said, "Go," with little or no choice or explanation. We have noted, though, that in one or two districts there has been strong support for this project at the administration level, but the faculty have not demonstrated that same interest. And then, in a couple of other districts, there has been the opposite with strong faculty interest and little support from their supervisors. The most active and involved colleges are the ones with both groups—administration and faculty—strongly supporting this project, with amazing results.

As we near the end of the first year of the grant, commitment from all districts has, as a result, been somewhat uneven, both in terms of time and personnel. All districts share equally in the costs, but not all are sending representative faculty for all courses, and not all have designated technical support for the project.

Challenge #3:
Project Focus on General Education Competencies

The Wisconsin Technical College System ascribes to a performance-based curriculum design philosophy called The Wisconsin Instructional Design System. That system requires that any course developed for the WTCS be written using competencies and performance standards as foundational elements for the course. Since the competencies for each of the nine General Education courses central to the project had been developed and agreed to during culminating state-called meetings in the early 1990s, the FIPSE/LAAP proposal indicated that learning objects would be developed using these agreed-upon competencies. The reasoning was that they could serve as a common language and foundation for the development of learning objects. Faculty from any district could use learning objects created for the competencies that were already in place and in use.

The nine core courses involved are these:

Communication Skills

- Oral/Interpersonal Communication
- Speech
- Technical Reporting
- Written Communication

Social Science

- Contemporary American Society
- Economics
- Introduction to Psychology
- Introduction to Sociology
- Psychology of Human Relations

As the project began, the operating assumption was that the competencies for each of these courses were still being taught as agreed at the state-called workshops that developed them. However, at the initial Steering Committee meeting in October, information came out that strongly indicated that not only do some districts not teach those competencies, but some have rewritten them to meet local purposes. Several discussions occurred on whether to revamp the competencies that had been developed before we moved ahead, during the course of this project, or at another time. Thanks to the input of the General Education State Consultant, the current approach is to use the competencies identified by the project grant proposal as the ones that would be used by this project. Competencies would be used "as is" for this three-year cycle of learning object development.

Some reluctance to agree to this policy ensued and some people opted to leave the project as a result; but those who have agreed and who have stayed are moving forward, operating under the belief that a well-developed learning object will be able to be applied to the competencies for these courses regardless of how they've been altered since the early 1990s.

Challenge #4:
Recruiting and Keeping Faculty Developers

From the onset, everyone knew that for this project to be successful, it would need to be faculty-driven. We could have all the latest technology in the world, but the project would be only as good as the learning objects developed, and without faculty buy-in and commitment, we would have no learning objects at all. Getting faculty involvement, buy-in, and commitment presented challenges from a variety of perspectives.

First of all, just getting information to the faculty was a challenge. One method used was to hold a kick-off meeting to which all interested faculty were invited. That day-long meeting was used to explain the concept of "learning objects," to explain the project itself, and to begin the team formation and team building processes intended to support the developer teams as they tackled the task of actually developing learning objects.

The meeting itself raised issues: How should the meeting be timed to accommodate 16 districts' different calendars? In which of the districts should the meeting be held? How would instructors be able to take a full day away from classes to attend an informational session before they even decided whether to commit to a three-year project—which would, perhaps, require more of their time away from classes or teaching duties than they might be comfortable with? How would their time and travel for this meeting be handled?

The core team believed it necessary to meet before districts sent staff and faculty home for the holidays if there was to be hope for development of learning objects during the first year of the project. With between 400 and 500 learning objects that would have to be developed in three years' time, skipping that work during the first year was not an option; the project had committed us all to having a third of all objects developed by the end of the first year of the grant as well. We had to get moving, so despite the unpredictable Wisconsin winter weather, we scheduled the kick-off meeting for faculty in Madison in December. The project would reimburse travel and pay for hotel rooms and meals; districts would (or wouldn't) reimburse time based on project match dollars.

If each district sent one instructor per course, we knew we'd have a potential of between 120 and 150 instructors at the meeting; some districts don't offer all the courses, so a full complement of instructors wasn't expected. As it was, nearly 100 attended, some driving several hundred miles to get there. One instructor, from the farthest location, even flew in for the meeting.

To encourage faculty participation on a voluntary basis, the core team designed registrations that asked faculty to think about their contribution to the project and to give some information about their background. The registration form designed by the Core Team can be found on the Wisconsin OnLine Resource Center site (http://www.wisc-online.com). Registrations trickled in at first, but as the day grew closer and we read them through, we were confident of participants' enthusiasm and willingness to be involved.

One thing we hoped to measure in the project was how faculty skills in using technology to deliver courses might change as a result of this project. After much discussion, the Core Team decided to use the kick-off meeting to survey staff, adapting surveys already built for other purposes at Fox Valley Technical College. We enlisted the help of our measurement specialists on staff at the College and put together a benchmark survey that was given to all who attended the kickoff meeting. Participants will be surveyed again periodically during the project with the intent of discovering the effects of the project participation on their perceptions of their technology skills in the classroom. A copy of the survey is available on the Wisconsin OnLine Resource Center site (http://www.wisc-online.com).

The meeting itself, however, uncovered the fact that many faculty had come only to get more information, many had been told to come without knowing why, and a smaller number than we'd hoped actually arrived ready to learn and go to work. That meeting also gave us our first hint at the districts that would probably provide the majority of support, both in personnel and time. Some districts had sent six to eight faculty while three districts sent none at all. As developers clustered into course teams, the group sizes also quickly demonstrated inconsistencies in numbers of faculty who had come representing various courses. In some cases, one faculty member was expected to handle the load of all the Communication Skills courses or all the Social Science courses, or both. In other cases, no district was represented on the course team.

Team leadership was another challenge. Each course cluster of participants was asked during the day to identify one person who would lead the team efforts. Some groups identified a leader immediately; other groups shuffled members and leads several times; in one case, a dean volunteered rather than a faculty person. One district seemed to have the bulk of people volunteering for team lead positions, so before the day ended it was necessary to regroup and assure that team lead positions were spread across the state and that every team had representation from a variety of districts since none would have a team with representatives from every district. Final resolution occurred with every team having at least one leader and some teams having co-leads.

To assist the process of team building and team formation, the Core Team needed to design the basic roles and responsibilities for the team leaders and the team members. This type of information was designed to help everyone know right from the outset what was expected and to provide minimal guidance in how to get the job done. Other information needed included process guidelines, so the Core Team developed handouts for the kickoff meeting that we hoped would help both team leaders and team members through the development process.

Within a few weeks of the kick-off meeting, team membership pretty well stabilized (as shown by the following listing), so that teams could complete the first round of learning object development by May 1, 2000.

- Oral/Interpersonal Communication   9
- Speech   3
- Technical Reporting (2 leads)   7
- Written Communication   10
- Contemporary American Society   5
- Economics (2 leads)   5
- Introduction to Psychology   10
- Introduction to Sociology (2 leads)   6
- Psychology of Human Relations   7

Recruiting additional members, especially for smaller teams (remember, there are 16 districts, so potential team membership is 16), was, and continues to be, a challenge. Initially, districts left the recruiting to the Core Team, who offered to make personal presentations about the project to any district wanting such a thing. Initially, three districts accepted the offer, with two requiring travel and one held via instructional television connections. As time passed, other districts requested on-site presentations, so the Core Team has grown used to packing up the laptop and taking the show on the road on sometimes short notice.

Steering Committee members were also asked to recruit faculty and help eliminate barriers on their own campuses to invite more faculty participation. General Education deans have also been encouraged to invite faculty involvement. Despite best efforts, only a few new faces have joined the learning object development activities, and some have left the project.

Another part of this challenge is compensation of faculty for work and time on the project. One of the reasons faculty have been reluctant to get involved with the Wisc-OnLine Resource Center project is that they are already involved in so many activities and have heavy teaching loads, both in terms of numbers of preps and numbers of students each semester. Staff in the WTCS are like educators everywhere—they are asked to do more and more with less and less, and many are less and less willing to make commitments which might detract from their primary teaching responsibilities.

Additionally, each district has its own unique set of expectations for General Education faculty (e.g., how much its faculty should be involved and how those faculty should be compensated for work on the project). One option is provided by the project, which requires a 50% match from the districts; as a result, each district was "assessed" 1/16 of that match, and those dollars could be used to compensate faculty. Preferred methods in use include timecards and time assigned on schedule.

Several forms for logging time and travel needed to be developed for the project. Fortunately, many of these forms were already in place in template form at Fox Valley Technical College, so adaptations of them were fairly easy to do. The biggest challenge continues to be getting them filled out and submitted in a timely manner from all faculty developers and Steering Committee members from all districts.

Challenge #5:
Web-Masters—So Easy to Find and Hire!

We knew it was critical to have a Web-master as part of this project. All of us on the Core Team felt this individual was going to have to have not only the technical skills, but was also going to have to be a great communicator. After all, this person was going to have to work with teachers and be able to ask the right kinds of questions. Our first challenge came when we realized we had budgeted within our project a salary that was far below the market value for Web-masters.

Who would we attract for half the going rate? The answer came when we posted the position. Through our statewide search we ended up with a total of four applicants. One of the individuals we interviewed talked in flowchart language which was very difficult for our interview team to follow. One of our applicants was hoping to be able to do the job at a distance. That may have made sense since this was a Web-based project, but it was our intention to have the Web-master on our campus. The third applicant withdrew his name just prior to the interview. The fourth candidate seemed to be a good match for position, but was not a U.S. citizen. This did not appear to be a barrier as we offered to pay for the visa extension to continue working in this country. As it turned out, the salary issue did become a reality, as the individual was able to accept a different position for a higher wage.

Luckily for us, we were able to "create" a Web-master by reorganizing the functions of two technical staff within the college's Faculty Innovation Center. In some ways, our team approach to the Web-master search provides a greater breadth of knowledge—one staff member is highly skilled in Web development, and the other has a programmer's background. Each can support and mentor the other. Both individuals now work 50% of their time providing technical expertise with learning objects. Several trips have been made to Barnes and Noble to purchase technical manuals to support these individuals as they need to learn more and more about various software applications to support this project.

Challenge #6:
Developing Learning Objects—Oh, It's Easy . . . Isn't It?

The biggest part of this challenge was the definition of learning objects themselves. In researching the concept, the Core Team found almost as many definitions of "learning object" as there are Web sites that deal with the term. What would the definition be for *this* project?

The Core Team would "define" learning objects, and the Steering Committee would request further explanation. The Core Team would come back with another definition and the Steering Committee would, you guessed it, want more information. The Core Team looked to the examples presented for the faculty developers, yet the Steering Committee (and some faculty) wanted more, clearer information and examples. Defining a learning object has not been easy.

Definitions include the following taken from *VISIQ On Line Learning* (Online: http://www.visiq.com/learning_objects.shtml):

Learning objects are a new way of thinking about learning content. Traditionally, content comes in a several-hour chunk called a course. Learning objects are much smaller units of learning, ranging from two to fifteen minutes.

We decided that, for our purposes, learning objects

- are self-contained—each learning object can be taken independently;
- are reusable—a single learning object may be used in multiple contexts for multiple purposes;
- can be aggregated—learning objects can be grouped into larger collections of content, including traditional course structures; and
- are tagged with metadata—every learning object has descriptive information allowing it to be easily found by a search.

Learning objects let you have learning that is

- just enough—if you need only part of a course, you can use just the learning objects you need;
- just in time—because learning objects are searchable, you can instantly find and take the content you need; and
- just for you—learning objects allow for easy customization of courses for a whole organization or even for each individual.

This definition was not clear to Steering Committee members and has not been totally clear to developers or Core Team members!

Core Team members had designed a step-by-step process for developing learning objects and shared the process and the paperwork that went with it with faculty developers at their kick-off meeting. The same information went to Steering Committee members. The step-by-step process was in itself a learning experience since none of the Core Team had ever done this before. The Core Team designed learning object development forms that helped faculty think through the key information that would need to come into the programmers.

Examples of some of those forms are available on the Wisconsin OnLine Resource Center site (http://www.wisc-online.com).

As learning objects began coming into the technical team in early May of 2000, reviewers realized that what was coming in was often an entire learning activity complete with delivery instructions rather than a chunk of learning information that might or might not be interactive for students. Some developers were working under the impression that learning objects were developed solely for faculty, so these materials had to be redone completely. Other developers created highly innovative activities but did so by creating them thematically rather than looking at each as an independent, self-contained chunk of learning; many in this collection needed to be re-adapted for use as learning objects that could stand alone. Still other developers sent in ideas with no supporting information, such as what a student might need to do to activate the learning object or how they might interact with it once inside, so they needed to add detail to their submissions.

In the majority of cases, developers who initially believed they had a clear idea of what a learning object is actually submitted ideas and information that was far enough off the mark that they needed major revision before they went to the programmers.

One thing the Core Team tried to do was develop a sample learning object to show people what an actual learning object might look like. That process took far longer than it probably should have, but when two sample learning objects were actually developed for explanation purposes, many seemed to see immediately what a learning object actually is.

Challenge #7:
Who Needs to Worry About Intellectual Property Rights and Copyright Laws Anyway?

One of the visions of this project is that the learning objects developed by faculty will be "out there" to improve and to enhance the teaching and learning of students. It is also a fact that these objects will be accessible to all Wisconsin Technical College faculties at no cost. One of the questions that is asked, though, is *who owns the objects?"*

The Steering Committee has varying opinions on the topics of copyright and intellectual property. Some members feel that perhaps the objects should be public domain, while others feel the project could generate revenue and continue to support further development of learning objects. From the beginning of the project, our Core Team has always believed the learning objects needed to be copyrighted in order to protect them from someone profiting from them without our knowledge or permission. Who actually owns the copyright to the learning objects, though, has been a more difficult question to answer than we ever anticipated. Every one of the 16 technical colleges involved in this project has intellectual property language in its bargaining contract that differs from every other college's. Because of the complexity of this issue, attorneys have advised us to us to make certain that all faculty involved in the development of learning objects have a clear understanding up front about who owns the copyright to the learning objects these create and how they will be disseminated. How to do that is still an issue at this writing.

Challenge #8:
How Much Is Enough?

A basic premise of the project was that it be built on existing competencies so that learning object developers would be working with a common set of content fundamentals for each course in General Education. However, one of the first challenges from the people attending the first Steering Committee meeting in October was the question of why learning objects were not being developed for math and science areas, only for communications and social science areas.

Justification presented reminded members that common competencies did not exist for math and science and that, as a result, these areas were not considered for inclusion in this project. After much discussion, however, and much pressure from all districts, the Core Team agreed that math and science areas could be added during year two of the project. Early indications seem to point to much enthusiasm on the part of science instructors to become involved with the project; time will tell.

Enough funds remained from first-year project activities to open the door for math and science involvement. Therefore, at the state-called General Education deans' meeting at the end of May 2000, nine months into the project, the Core Team officially invited the deans of all 16 district to recruit faculty from the math and science disciplines to become involved in the project beginning in fall of 2000. A presentation explaining the project and its processes helped deans understand their role in recruiting and in compensating faculty for this project.

At the same time, the Basic Education deans are interested in providing this same opportunity for basic education faculty. Funding sources outside the FIPSE/LAAP project are likely to be available to support this additional effort within the state.

What is notable about these "spin-off" projects is the enthusiasm that the original project generated about the concept of developing learning experiences for students through the learning object approach. Whether they fully understand the concept or not, educators at all levels seem to understand that the whole goal of the project is to increase learning effectiveness and learner-centered approaches to learning and teaching. People are excited about how to help learners and teachers get more and more from their educational experiences, and they see this approach as a key way to do that.

Challenge #9:
Keeping the Evaluators Up to Speed

FIPSE/LAAP projects require external evaluators, people with expertise in the area who are not actually part of the project itself (or members of participating institutions). In our case, we were fortunate to enlist the talents and time of three people: Kathie Sigler, Ed.D., Vice-President of the Medical School at Miami Dade Community College; Wayne Hodgins, Director, Worldwide Learning Strategies; and Robert Sorenson, Ph.D., former director of the WTCS and a University of Wisconsin professor. Dr. Sorenson is also an evaluator for the North Central Association of Colleges.

Dr. Sorenson will evaluate the project as a whole, primarily in terms of process; while Dr. Sigler and Mr. Hodgins will evaluate the learning objects themselves. To help these people understand the process and the project, all were invited to the first Steering Committee meeting in October, and they attended a preliminary breakfast discussion with the Core Team before that meeting. All have a standing invitation to attend Steering Committee meetings, and Drs. Sigler and Sorenson attended the May meeting.

The Core Team has found it necessary to provide clarifying information and to draft a preliminary set of "quality standards" for the learning objects to help the evaluators know what to look for as they review the project and the learning objects. A copy of the preliminary draft can be found on the Wisconsin OnLine Resource Center site (http://www.wisc-online.com). What has been most helpful to know is that the evaluators are really looking for ways to help the project reach the greatest potential success possible, not for ways to "score" its success or failure. All have been extremely helpful.

Challenge #10:
Concurrent Statewide Virtual Campus Project Confusion

In August 1999, we received the official notification we had been granted the FIPSE/LAAP Grant Award. Less than one month later we learned our technical college system, with all 16 colleges, was going to cooperatively and collectively develop a Virtual Campus that would allow for a statewide online course and program delivery system. Because both of these initiatives were kicked off in same month (October), confusion about whether these were the same or different existed from the onset. The learning objects model used in the FIPSE/LAAP project intentionally avoids the development of whole courses and curricula; instead, its focus is on the development of reusable, portable, Web-enabled learning chunks—small bits and pieces of learning activities and assessments that can be used alone or combined and re-combined to customize courses and parts of courses. The Virtual Campus project intends to focus on the design, development, and delivery of whole courses via the Internet. The confusion arose largely because educators tend to think in terms of whole courses and whole activities in context rather than in terms of "granular" or smallest-piece-of-learning, so wherever discussion of either project took place (and still takes place), explanation of differences in focus and definition of learning objects occurs repeatedly. Part of the solution will surely come from the posting of actual learning objects in the Wisconsin OnLine Resource Center and the posting of courses to the Virtual Campus. Since that part of the solution is still somewhat in the future, a bigger part of the solution requires clear and frequent communication and explanation of similarities and differences.

One beneficial event that occurred was that one of the co-directors for the FIPSE/LAAP project was named to the Virtual Campus Curriculum Project Team. And, thanks to good and ongoing communication within that team, guess what—the learning object model became an adopted model for the Virtual Campus—the concept of providing for customization of courses through collaboration and development of learning objects that could be used and re-combined in a variety of ways.

Early on, this, too, continued to add to the confusion. In the many presentations that are done by the Core Team, there is always a question from someone in the audience on how this project is related to the Wisconsin Virtual Campus initiative.

Now we just say, *"We're the model!"*

Appendix:
Learning Object Development Process
(See pages 218–222)

> ### *Learning Objects*
> *"interactive, interoperable resources that may be in any on-line delivery format including text, graphics, photographic, animation, or video."*
> (FIPSE/LAAP Project, p. 14)

Learning Object Development Process

Team Responsibility: Create a minimum of <u>16</u> complete (tested and evaluated) learning objects related to your course assignment **this year.**

Suggested Checkpoints:

- Preliminary brainstorming and development of drafts; discussion, refinement, revisions
- Ready for testing—at least a month prior to "go live" expectation
- Evaluation—at least two weeks prior to "go live" expectation
- Final approval and addition to Wisc_OnLine Resource Center site—middle to end of May, 2000

➤ *Interim progress*—monthly progress report to Core Team— first one due week of January 17, 2000

Project Final Outcome:

450–500 learning objects, supporting nine General Education core courses (end of Year 3).

That means . . .

"For each course competency, a collection of Web-based options to master the competency would be developed to include a minimum of seven options as follows:

- Two learning style options
- Two assessment options
- Three content links to occupational focus content relevant to each of the three instructional divisions of technical education programming (business/health-service/industrial)" (FIPSE/LAAP Proposal, p. 11).

That translates to . . .

15 to 17 Learning Objects per course per year developed, tested, and "Web-able" for use by faculty across the state.

Learning Object Development Process

Phase 1: Learning Object Content Development
    (a.k.a: steps for each learning object)

Responsible: Course Developers
1. Select a competency.
2. Identify learning activities currently used in your classes that might be able to become learning objects.
3. Identify other learning activities (other instructors, other sources, e.g., the Internet) that might be appropriate.
4. To determine their suitability (learning styles, occupational focus, assessment), check the activities against the:
    a. Definition of learning objects
    b. Two-page blue handout: *Developing—Step 1* and *Developing—Step 2*
5. Select, number, and c enter the learning object into the <u>tracking matrix</u>.
6. Team lead: complete the <u>project development worksheet</u>.
7. Team lead: complete the <u>Skimmit</u>.
8. Team lead: forward the <u>project development worksheet</u> and the <u>Skimmit</u> to Dave Bunnow at FVTC.

End of Phase 1!

Phase 2: Technical Production
Responsible: Technical Team (Dave B., Web-master, District Technical Support)
1. Review the <u>Skimmit</u> and the <u>project development worksheet</u>.
2. Recommend format and communicate any issues that arise with course team leader.
3. Identify and forward the learning object project to the technical producer (the person who will actually make the object "Web-able").
4. The technical producer builds the object and posts it on the WiscOnLine server test site.

End of Phase 2!

Phase 3: Learning Object Testing
Responsible: Technical Team, Core Team Resources (C. May/Social Studies; T. Langan/Communication Skills)
1. Faculty review and test learning object; send a report of problems/bugs to Dave Bunnow.
2. Technical producer and Web-master modify object as needed.

End of Phase 3!

Phase 4: Go live!
Responsible: Web-master
1. Based on <u>Skimmit</u>, Web-master posts final learning object to Wisc_OnLine Resource Center.
2. Web-master updates and modifies learning objects as needed (e.g., adds it to other subject matter areas as appropriate).

Learning Objects – Quality Standards
First Draft (May 2000)

Θ	*Quality Standards: The learning object . . .*
	• Shows a clear purpose, i.e., is immediately relevant to the learner.
	• Reflects a specified learning style (visual, auditory, or kinesthetic).
	• Applies appropriate Principles of Good Practice (AAHE).*
	• Applies appropriate Learning College Principles (O'Banion).**
	• Helps learners understand the concept being presented.
	• Supports the competency at the appropriate level (Bloom).
	• Is able to be applied to courses in different subject areas.
	• Is able to be applied to different programs of study.
	• Is easy to use for the learner.
	• Is self-contained.

*"Seven Principles for Good Practice in Undergraduate Education" (AAHE 1987). *Available: http://www.aahe.org/technology/ehrmann.htm*

**See page 222 for O'Banion's Learning College Principles.

Learning Objects—Quality Standards
First Draft (May 2000)

1. Good Practice Encourages Contacts between Students and Faculty
Frequent student-faculty contact in and out of class is a most important factor in student motivation and involvement. Faculty concern helps students get through rough times and helps them to keep on working. Knowing a few faculty members well enhances students' intellectual commitment and encourages them to think about their own values and plans.

2. Good Practice Develops Reciprocity and Cooperation among Students
Learning is enhanced when it is more like a team effort than a solo race. Good learning, like good work, is collaborative and social, not competitive and isolated. Working with others often increases involvement in learning. Sharing one's ideas and responding to others' improves thinking and deepens understanding.

3. Good Practice Uses Active Learning Techniques
Learning is not a spectator sport. Students do not learn much just sitting in classes listening to teachers, memorizing prepackaged assignments, and spitting out answers. They must talk about what they are learning, write reflectively about it, relate it to past experiences, and apply it to their daily lives. They must make what they learn part of themselves.

4. Good Practice Gives Prompt Feedback
Knowing what you know and don't know focuses your learning. In getting started, students need help in assessing their existing knowledge and competence. Then, in classes, students need frequent opportunities to perform and receive feedback on their performance. At various points during college, and at its end, students need chances to reflect on what they have learned, what they still need to know, and how they might assess themselves.

5. Good Practice Emphasizes Time on Task
Time plus energy equals learning. Learning to use one's time well is critical for students and professionals alike. Allocating realistic amounts of time means effective learning for students and effective teaching for faculty.

6. Good Practice Communicates High Expectations
Expect more and you will get it. High expectations are important for everyone—for the poorly prepared, for those unwilling to exert themselves, and for the bright and well-motivated. Expecting students to perform well becomes a self-fulfilling prophecy.

7. Good Practice Respects Diverse Talents and Ways of Learning
Many roads lead to learning. Different students bring different talents and styles to college. Brilliant students in a seminar might be all thumbs in a lab or studio; students rich in hands-on experience may not do so well with theory. Students need opportunities to show their talents and learn in ways that work for them. Then they can be pushed to learn in new ways that do not come so easily.

Six Learning College Principles
(O'Banion, 1996)

1. The learning college creates substantive change in individual learners.

2. The learning college engages learners as full partners in the learning process, assuming primary responsibility for their own choices.

3. The learning college creates and offers as many options for learning as possible.

4. The learning college assists learners to form and participate in collaborative learning activities.

5. The learning college defines the roles of learning facilitators by the needs of the learners.

6. The learning college (and its learning facilitators) succeed only when improved and expanded learning can be documented for its learners.

A University-Wide System for Creating, Capturing, and Delivering Learning Objects

Joseph B. South & David W. Monson
(Brigham Young University, Center for Instructional Design)

Introduction

For organizations to take full advantage of the potential benefits of learning objects, learning objects must become an integrated part of the instructional technology infrastructure. At Brigham Young University in Provo, Utah, a coordinated effort (including our division of continuing education and our library) is underway across the university to create a unified system for developing, capturing, and delivering learning objects to both on and off-campus venues. This chapter will describe the theoretical framework we use to conceptualize and work with learning objects, the core issues that led to this effort, the principles that guide our approach, the solution that we are working toward, the particular role of learning objects in that solution, as well as the benefits that we anticipate as a result. The goal of the chapter is to provide a sense of the far-reaching impacts of our decision to use digital learning objects at the core of our instructional technology systems, including some of the obstacles that must be overcome and the tradeoffs that are required.

Theoretical Framework

Definition of Learning Objects

We define "learning objects" as digital media that is designed and/or used for instructional purposes. These objects range from maps and charts to video demonstrations and interactive simulations. Because of this wide range of sophistication, we use the more conservative term "media objects" when describing these objects at our university. However, the types of objects we are creating and using fall within the definition of "learning objects" given by David Wiley in the introductory chapter of this book. We presently produce all of the types identified in Wiley's (2002) taxonomy except the fifth type identified, the "instruction-al-generative," but we hope to begin producing this type in the near future.

Learning Objects and the "-ilities"

Various lists of "ilities" are often invoked within the working groups of the Advanced Distributed Learning Network (ADLNet), IMS,[1] and IEEE LTSC[2] P1484.12, organizations working on learning object specifications and standards. These lists generally include durability, interoperability, accessibility, reusability, discoverability, extensibility, affordability, and manageability. The central benefit of learning objects upon which most institutions focus, includ-ing our own, is their potential for reuse. Generally, the most expensive elements of instruction to produce are the media intensive assets. If these assets could be reused, the argument goes, production costs could be greatly reduced. This, in theory, provides the primary financial rationale that justifies investment in the infrastructure required to realize a learning object centered system. It is our experience that the degree to which learning objects actually achieve high reusability is largely a function of the degree of granularity of the objects. That is, the more granular the object, the more reusable it becomes (see Wiley et al., 1999, for a theoretical discussion of this relationship).

Choosing the Right Level of Granularity

Determining the degree of granularity of what should constitute a learning object is a foundational decision for any project. There is not neces-sarily a correct level of granularity. Certainly, it is essential to consider courses, lessons, and modules as learning objects. But these levels do not cross what we call the "context threshold" (see Figure 1). In other words, until you get past this level of granularity, the majority of your costly media assets are trapped in the surrounding context—too intertwined in the material that precedes and follows to be efficiently extracted and reused by instructional developers.

Obviously, a total lack of context would reduce the learning object to unassociated media (e.g., a background image, a sound file, a movable fore-ground element, etc.). While still of potential use to a media developer, it begins to lose its immediate usefulness to an instructional developer. At some point, the object crosses what we call the "learning threshold"—it no longer retains enough internal structure to be recognizably oriented to a learning pur-pose and loses its embedded instructional utility.

The optimal level of granularity must be determined for each project based on its individual goals. From the perspective of instructional developers, our experience is that it is most useful to move from the course level of granular-ity down to the concept level when designing, but not so far down as the indi-vidual media asset level. For our instructional needs, objects have the greatest

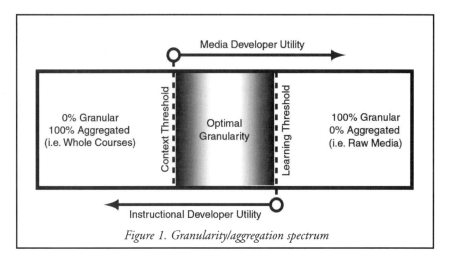

Figure 1. Granularity/aggregation spectrum

potential for reuse when they center on a single, core concept. At this level, they can easily slip into another context while still retaining significant instructional utility. For example, an interactive simulation that allows a learner to manipulate a pressure gauge, the shape of a container of liquid in which it is submerged, and the depth of that liquid is what we would consider a concept level media object (see Figure 2). It is granular enough to be useful in a variety of contexts, but aggregated enough to provide a robust exploration of multiple facets of a single concept.

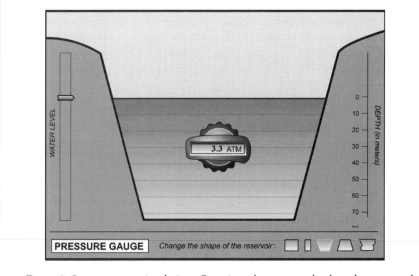

Figure 2. Pressure gauge simulation. Container shape, water level, and gauge can be manipulated to observe the resulting affect on pressure gauge reading.

The Metadata Tradeoff

Unfortunately, this greater level of granularity comes with at least two significant tradeoffs. The first is that you must provide a proportionately greater amount of metadata to retain high discoverability, that is, make it easy for instructional developers, instructors, and learners to find the objects in a vast database that match their needs. The second trade off is that you must store and manage significantly higher numbers of objects. For example, a recently developed physical science online course, while consisting of only 34 lessons and approximately 350 Web pages, contains over 1,300 media objects, ranging from simulations like the example given above to charts and diagrams that could arguably be considered more informational than instructional, but still of use to instructional developers. In the past year, we have produced more than 5,000 media objects that need to be associated with metadata to be reused in instructional contexts.

When tracking so many objects, the cost of creating high quality metadata for each object as well as the cost of storing and managing them becomes a significant issue. We will discuss our approach to this challenge later in this chapter.

As significant and complex as these issues are, the use of learning objects allows us to address systemic barriers to the long-term growth and viability of our institution. A discussion of these barriers follows.

The Challenge

Brigham Young University is a large regional university, owned and operated by the Church of Jesus Christ of Latter-day Saints (LDS Church), which serves an on-campus population of over 30,000 students as well as over 40,000 off-campus independent-study students. Like many other institutions of higher education, BYU sees the potential for learning objects to address core cost, infrastructure, and quality issues related to instructional media. This potential has led BYU to invest early and significantly in a campus-wide system that is based on a learning objects approach to courseware design and delivery. This initiative has required close cooperation and coordination between the university's Center for Instructional Design, the Office of Information Technology, the Lee Library, the Division of Continuing Education, and Independent Study. Cooperation on this scale was made possible by our shared understanding of university-wide challenges that need immediate attention. A summary of these challenges follows.

More Qualified Students than Seats

Each year, BYU turns away a number of students who meet our academic criteria, but for whom we have no space. Because most of these are also members of the LDS Church, we feel a particular obligation to accommodate their desire for higher education at our church-owned university. Unfortunately, the cost of physical expansion of the university in terms of both capital investment and maintenance is high. With the present campus comprising 339 buildings on 200 acres of land, the university's board of trustees has imposed a moratorium on physical expansion. Because of this limit, we need to find creative ways to provide a high quality university education to more students without physically expanding.

Growing Independent Study Program

At the same time, we are seeing sharp enrollment increases in both our paper-and-pencil and Internet-based Independent Study course offerings. Total enrollment is nearing 50,000 with about 10,000 online enrollments. This represents an expanding constituency of learners who desire high-quality, remotely accessible BYU courses. Presently, BYUs on-campus enrollment can accommodate only three percent of LDS men and women between the ages of 18 and 25. In 25 years, as the total number of LDS people in this age range is projected to swell to over 4.5 million, that percentage will drop to less than one percent.

This growth is further complicated by the fact that more than 70% of these men and women will live outside of North America, far from Provo, Utah. If BYU wants to be available to any significant percentage of qualified students among the members of the LDS Church, distance education appears to be the most viable option. If we are to meet this demand, our off-campus distance education offerings will need to undergo significant expansion.

Multiple Learning Environments

As a partial solution to the expanding student base, BYU has begun to explore using online courses to accommodate more students both on- and off-campus. Consequently, we find ourselves facing at least three distinct instructional settings where effective use of technology to aid learning is desired (see Figure 3). These are: (1) on-campus courses where media is used in classroom presentation; (2) hybrid courses where media may be used both during classroom sessions and in online sessions; and (3) independent study online courses where media supports the instruction of students who will never meet in a classroom. As technology continues to evolve, we anticipate more and more learning environment configurations, each with its own set of capabilities and constraints.

Rising Development Costs

As the demand for digital media to support these three venues grows, our development costs grow with it. Digital media designers and programmers are in high demand and, therefore, difficult and expensive to hire on university wages.

Multiple Learning Environments Using Instructional Media		
Traditional Classroom	**Hybrid Semester Online**	**Independent Study Online**
Traditional on-campus classroom in which an instructor desires to draw upon learning resources that require the use of technology, usually as part of the instructor's presentation of class material.	*An on-campus online course that meets once a week or less, that must be completed within a single semester, and that conducts the majority of course work online*	*An off-campus course conducted entirely online that must be completed within one year of the start date.*

Figure 3. Multiple learning environments.
We must insure that our approach to instructional media
meets the needs of all of these environments.

Additionally, research that we have conducted on students' reactions to digital media shows face validity is a very real issue; students expect high production values in instructional media design, and media that is perceived by students as "home-made" or "clunky" can significantly limit its instructional impact. This means that even simple objects can require several hours of expensive design and development by instructional and media professionals. We have also found that as media has converged to multimedia, production costs have risen in parallel with the increasing complexity.

Inefficient Delivery Methods

Yet even as these demands grow, a majority of the instructors on campus rely on analog, non-networked technologies for their instructional media.

An internal study of BYU faculty reveals that instructors tend to use the technologies they are most familiar with, and, for most of them, that means older, "off-line" technologies that require specialized and incompatible media formats and, therefore, specialized and incompatible media players. BYU employs an army of students that do nothing more than shuttle these players to and from classrooms all over campus. BYU maintains dozens of slide projectors, VCRs (including VHS, one-inch, and Beta formats), laser disc players, film projectors, CD players, tape players, record players, DVD players, and computer projectors for the sole purpose of bringing them to a classroom at an instructor's request. The system is cumbersome—requiring instructors to reserve the equipment well in advance—and requires many human resources. Further, the analog nature of most of the media often precludes learners from accessing the media outside of class due to the logistical complexity of making copies of it and having the appropriate player available.

Inconsistent and Incompatible Formats

In addition to the incompatible physical formats mentioned above, we have instructors buying and/or producing instructional media in digital formats that are incompatible with each other. Some of the media work only with a single browser or under a single operating system; some requires a proprietary plug-in or codec or obscure streaming protocol; some demand continuous Internet access while others do not, but these must instead be installed on each computer in each computer in a lab individually (BYU maintains over 600 computers in open labs).

Redundant Effort

Even if two departments happen to be using the same technology, and even the same content, resource sharing is not guaranteed. In fact, it is quite rare. We have found that one department, for example, an art history department, may have invested thousands of dollars in a slide library that has a 60% overlap with another department's slide library, such as that of the history department or the design department, in which more thousands of dollars have been invested. While considerable expense could be avoided if the two were to invest in a single library, each is apprehensive about the other causing loss or damage, or the simple unavailability of individual slides at times when the other department might need them. This redundancy is compounded when the two departments fund separate media development projects that overlap in content.

Expensive, Low-Impact Innovation

Even when instructional media development projects do not overlap, the projects can be problematic. Typically, their origin consists of a single faculty member from a single department coming up with a fabulous idea for using instructional media to improve a particular course. If that project is funded and developed, it is our experience that the resulting media is generally used exclusively by that faculty member. The media is often too specialized to the purposes of the originating faculty member to be used by another faculty member, even if the two are teaching in the same subject area, unless they are teaching the same course. Further, the media is rarely customizable or easily adapted for other contexts. If it is not useful as a whole in its original form, it is not useful. As a result, large sums of money are spent on relatively low impact innovation. This can cause jealousies within a department as well as a general reluctance by university administration to fund innovation, since each project appears to them to be a "pet project" of an individual faculty member.

Complex Media Management

The previous four problems can create a nightmare scenario for the management of a university's media assets. If media is incompatible, inaccessible, and esoteric, and if each asset requires a different delivery method, it is very difficult for a user or manager to know: (1) what assets exist; (2) where they reside; (3) what their physical condition is; (4) if they are useful for a particular context; (5) if the correct media player is available to display the desired media at the desired location; and (6) if the person who wants to use it will know how to work that player.

The cumulative effects of these problems can create an anti-media bias and an institution that views most instructional media as an expensive, clunky, irrelevant, impractical, inflexible, unfulfilled promise. Under the above circumstances, this view is probably correct.

The Approach

The range of possible solutions to the above problems is vast, extending far beyond our approach to instructional technology. While our approach to instructional technology alone cannot resolve all of the problems, it can have a significant impact on all of them. In determining what our approach would be, BYU established some core principles to guide our decisions.

Meet Present Needs While Anticipating Future Adaptation

Too often, institutions of higher education adopt an approach to instructional technology that benefits only the most technologically advanced. They may choose an approach that, in order to be successful, requires instructors and learners to come rapidly up to speed on complex technical tools. New and faster computers and sophisticated software is made available to faculty members who have the time and inclination to jump in, but their less techni-cally adept—or simply overworked—colleagues are left wringing their hands in the shadows of the new faculty techno-stars. Anyone still teaching in a normal classroom with normal students is in danger of becoming disenfranchised and being characterized as "old school" and out-of-date.

Because of this danger, we felt strongly that any instructional technol-ogy solution we chose needed to reach into and improve the present, face-to-face teaching environment, without requiring extensive training for instructors and learners. To accomplish this, we established a policy that we would focus our energies on meeting present needs, while anticipating that, as the faculty become more comfortable with technology, they will want to adapt their teach-ing to take more and more advantage of a digital environment. Our goal was to create media that could be easily pulled into a classroom, where an instructor might be using the traditional lecture format, while also making it available for use in an online lesson where the instructor may have left the physical class-room behind. In order to get the buy-in necessary for widespread utilization of digital instructional media, we felt it was important that faculty see immediate benefit, as well as long-term appeal, and that they feel they could participate in using new technology without a lot of technical ability.

Leverage Innovation for Broad Audiences

A related goal was to make sure that if significant funds were to be allo-cated to instructional media development projects, the resulting media would be useful to many instructors and learners at the university. For example, it became part of our funding criteria that large projects have an instructional impact that would transcend departmental boundaries.

Streamline Design, Development, and Delivery

Because demand for instructional media is increasing rapidly all over the university, it was imperative that we ensure that the process of designing, developing, and delivering media become more efficient. A common source of inefficiency in this process at many institutions is the tendency for both university faculty and instruc-tional designers to take an artisan approach to the development of instructional media. In this approach, the creator of the media works alone or perhaps with one other person. The instructional media is designed and developed with little outside feedback or technical expertise. The faculty member or designer is generally learning the technology as they create the media, and he or she focuses efforts on meeting only his or her needs. We felt we needed to streamline this process by bringing more tech-nical expertise to bear and by implementing a more disciplined development process. We also wanted to be sure that these efficiencies weren't lost in an unwieldy delivery system that introduced inefficiencies of its own.

Improve Quality

Finally, it was continually our focus to improve the quality of the instruction both in the classroom and online. A key feature of this was to involve an instructional designer in every university-funded project. This would increase the chances that instruction, rather than a particular favored technology, was in the driver's seat. We also recognized that while many faculty members are excellent teachers and researchers, their background in areas such as interface design or Internet-based instruction is usually limited. Some models of development do little more than put relatively high-end development tools in the hands of the faculty member or their teaching assistants, leaving them the entire task of design and development. Rather than forcing faculty into a role to which they were not suited or trained, it was our goal to bring to them the support of instructional designers, graphic designers, illustrators, 3-D animators, media designers, and programmers to create a product that was exemplary in content, instructional approach, visual design, and technical soundness.

Involve Students

Finally, as a university, we felt a strong commitment to integrating students into the process of developing instructional media. As a result, we organized the Center for Instructional Design in such a way that each area was overseen by professionals, but staffed by students. Our full-time instructional designers, artists, animators, audio/video producers, and programmers number less than 50 while the number of students working in those areas totals more than 150. This approach helps to keep wages down while providing invaluable practical experience for students seeking work in media-related fields.

The Solution

The title of this section may be a bit optimistic. The solution described next represents our best present thinking in this area. Because the solution will evolve over time, we have focused the discussion below on those aspects that we anticipate will remain stable over the course of several years.

All-Digital Delivery

In order to have any hope of efficiently using media resources, it became necessary to find a *lingua franca* of media format. As long as media and equipment were being shuffled from here to there by humans, stored and hoarded in climate-controlled basements, or just piled on a faculty member's office floor, we were never going to be able to leverage our resources in a meaningful way. The common language we chose was ones and zeros—we committed to an all-digital delivery system.

This meant that each classroom on campus would need to have, preferably, built-in equipment for accessing digital media. The change represents a tremendous investment in media infrastructure and a complete re-tooling of our media management entities.

In response to this initiative, BYUs Office of Information Technology is in the process of wiring every classroom on campus into the university's network, and installing each with a computer projector. Additionally, they have designed a "tele-podiums" (at a cost of less than $20,000 each) to be installed in each classroom. The tele-podium consists of the following:

- A VCR
- A computer with
  — Basic office software
  — A CD/DVD-ROM player
  — A Zip Drive
  — Speakers
  — Access to the Internet
  — Access to a network drive where instructors can upload materials from their offices for classroom use
  — A connection to our campus cable TV network
  — A set of connections to accommodate a laptop

The only analog media these tele-podiums accommodate is videotape, as present bandwidth constraints make the delivery of digital video untenable. We continue to provide media players on demand for other types of analog media, but encourage instructors to migrate to digital formats that can be delivered over the network. For example, the university is funding the digitization of large slide libraries owned by individual departments where copyright agreements allow us to digitize them. For individual faculty, the university has established a walk-in center where instructors and their teaching assistants can learn how to digitize their media and prepare it for viewing over the network.

While this does not fully resolve the issue of format obsolescence, since digital formats can also expire, it does greatly reduce the complexities associated with storing, caring for, and delivering physical media. It eliminates the need for hoarding and protecting personal or departmental stashes of media, while greatly reducing the number of media formats that need to be preserved and/or upgraded over time. It also opens the door for parallel development for classroom and online environments.

Standard Digital Formats

The format of digital media has been standardized across campus to help reduce technical support requirements and increase compatibility from one area to another. Media created by university-funded projects must meet these standards. We also promote these standards across the university, encouraging compliance by projects that are not funded by the university. Our current standards ensure that the media will be deliverable over the campus network, that it can be viewed by widely distributed versions of commercial Web browsers, and that, should it require plug-ins to view, it requires only those that are widely distributed and free to the user. This standardization, while limiting some cutting edge functionality, ensures that if there is a need to migrate to a new format, it will be much more likely that we will be able to do so at a relatively low cost, mass conversion. It also simplifies technical support demands and greatly increases the likelihood of reusing objects, since it eliminates the possibility of technical incompatibility—no small accomplishment—as long as the user's computer meets minimum specifications. The list of our standard media formats is published online at imc.byu.edu/questions/standards.html and is available to the public.

One Database

Going digital also allowed us to begin thinking in terms of a single source for instructional media. We are in the process of combining several smaller databases to create a single database of instructional media that serves objects for classroom presentations, for after-class viewing by learners, and for use in both semester-online and independent-study versions of our online courses. This database will allow for one-stop shopping for users seeking media to incorporate into their courses, and one-stop updating and correction of media in use in many venues.

Reusable Learning Objects

At the center of this infrastructure is a heavy reliance on reusable learning objects. In our experience, objects are most useful for instructional reuse when they center around a single, core concept. The exceptions to this are objects designed to assess learning. These, we have found, are most useful when they address several related concepts at once.

For example, we have several individual objects that encourage a learner to explore each aspect of Newton's First Law of Motion, including a slow-motion video of a car crash and an interactive simulation of a man "surfing" on ice in the back of a moving pick-up truck. However, to assess the learner's understanding, we created a context-dependent item set as a single object. In this object, the learner is asked a series of questions about a woman in a moving elevator, to cover several facets of the concept at once.

Each learning object is tagged with relevant metadata so that it can be found and reused. Once an object is discovered in the system, it is available for use in its present form through a URL link. All of the source files of the object are presently housed in a separate database. Those with access to this second database can, for any object, download, edit, and combine it with other objects or with additional media.

We are presently prototyping instructional templates that would dynamically generate media objects based on instructional criteria. A simple example would be a matching exercise. A user would select media items to be matched, labels for each item, media or text with which to match them, and feedback for correct and incorrect responses. The system would then generate for the user a fully functional, self-contained media object with drag-and-drop capability that tracks the student's answers and provides appropriate feedback. This is a simple beginning. Once successful with these relatively unsophisticated templates, we anticipate building templates for more advanced instructional tasks that include just-in-time instruction (or "wizards") for the creator in relevant instructional design principles and approaches.

Practical Metadata Identification

Creating metadata for highly granular learning objects is not trivial. Because of the complexity involved, we enlisted the help of our library staff. We found, that for whole courses, lessons, or modules, it is possible to use traditional methods such as using professional trained catalogers to create full MARC records with extensive Library of Congress subject headings. However, revisiting our earlier diagram, when we increased the granularity beyond the context threshold, we discovered these traditional library practices are not practical (see Figure 4).

In librarian terms, creating metadata for learning objects is the equivalent of cataloging not just a book but also all of its chapters, photographs, charts, diagrams, and so forth. Therefore, it becomes important to minimize the number of fields required for each object and, in general, streamline the entire process of gathering metadata. We have decided that MARC records should be reserved for collections of objects. These MARC records serve as pointers from the standard library catalog into specialized learning object repositories. Within the learning object repositories, we rely on IMS metadata standards to identify the individual objects.

Many developers tend to wait to create metadata until after a learning object has been created. However, it has been our experience that it is more time consuming and laborious to create metadata after an object is developed than to create the metadata in parallel with the object. Our approach utilizes the windows of opportunity where various fields can be most efficiently captured. For example,

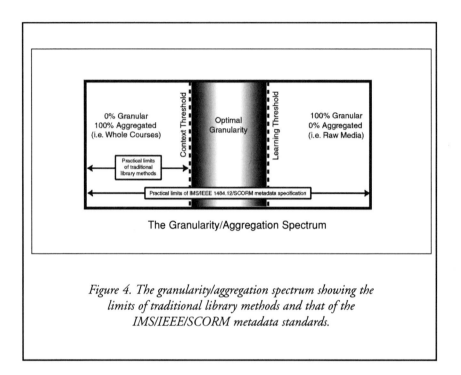

Figure 4. The granularity/aggregation spectrum showing the limits of traditional library methods and that of the IMS/IEEE/SCORM metadata standards.

the design specification for a new learning object provided by the subject matter expert and the instructional designer will in most cases include a title and description—with a little persuasion and a good performance support tool these fields and possibly others such as subject headings can be efficiently captured into a metadata record. This makes the final review of the data a relatively easily managed process.

Set Development Priorities

In order to insure that university resources designated for instructional media development have the greatest possible impact, we use a central planning committee to set development priorities.

The highest priority for university funds is high enrolling, bottleneck courses, usually general education (G.E.) courses. These courses receive the largest amount of allocated funds proportionately. This allows us to create and offer high quality, hybrid versions of these courses that are designed to require less time in the classroom. For instance, one G.E. science course now meets once a week rather than three times a week. This helps free up seat space, allowing more sections to be taught. An additional benefit is that, because these courses tend to be those of a basic, general nature, we find that learning objects created for these courses are often quite useful, not only in existing classroom versions of the courses, but in several other 100-level and 200-level courses. In other words, we find that the reusability of objects created for these courses is particularly high.

The second priority for university funds is medium-sized courses where the kinds of innovations proposed in these courses could have widespread impact. These projects are generally funded with smaller grants, and their content is generally less reusable, though it is still useful to other courses. The most beneficial aspect of these projects is the emphasis on exploring new approaches to instructional media development that may carry a slightly higher risk of failure than those we are using to develop the larger, general education courses, but that show long-term promise. As a result, these smaller projects produce high-quality objects while serving a research and development function as well.

The third priority for university funds is converting libraries of existing physical media into digital media where practical. Where materials are clear of copyright issues, we convert them for digital delivery to classrooms and for use in courses. Our School of Religion is presently digitizing thousands of slides of Jerusalem and other religious sites. These slides will be used in many religion courses, but are also in demand for courses in political science, geography, range science, history, and sociology. Ultimately, we anticipate that large online commercial libraries of these kinds of images will exist, and this somewhat tedious conversion process will no longer be necessary.

The fourth priority for university funds is the individual professor who is innovating by his or her self (or with some graduate students) to improve a course that may impact only a few students a year. In these cases, we provide the development tools, and, equally importantly, the technical standards so that the media they produce will be compatible with the media being produced for the larger, higher priority courses. This allows the faculty running these projects the freedom to create what they wish, but also helps insure that that their product will be in a format that allows it to be used by others at the university.

The combined effect of these initiatives is that: (1) many highly reusable objects are created; (2) bottleneck courses where impact is greatest and potential reusability of objects is high are addressed first; (3) medium-sized courses experiment with instructional methods that may become useful for high enrolling classes; (4) libraries of media become available to the entire campus community; and (5) individual innovators have freedom to explore while still contributing useful objects to a common digital library.

The Payoff

Lower Costs

As expected, the initial expenditure on this system has been higher than for previous technologies. However, we expect long-term financial benefits. These potentially include:

- *Lower development costs.* We expect that wide-spread use of instructional design learning object templates will speed development and allow non-experts to create fairly sophisticated media that can be used both in the classroom and online.

- *Lower delivery costs.* Once the digital delivery system and the digital library are fully in place, we anticipate that we will save money by eliminating the overhead of a large human delivery organization and maintaining a large amount of media delivery equipment. We also hope to lower our maintenance cost of the media itself, since it will no longer wear out with repeated use.

- *More reuse.* We expect a significant percentage of the learning objects that we are creating to be reused in many contexts. By having a large library available, we hope to reduce the cost of duplicate media considerably.

Higher Quality

We are already receiving very positive responses from instructors and learners using the objects designed by professionals in instruction and media design. We anticipate that the use of learning object development templates will amplify these gains over time.

More Participation

By publishing standards, making development tools available, and promoting an object approach to development, we expect to see much more participation on the part of the faculty. Many more faculty are interested in producing a few objects for their classes than are interested in a full-blown development project. By taking the object approach, we have essentially lowered the time commitment bar for faculty to participate in media development.

More Collaboration

We believe that as departments see the potential of the digital library, they will band together to leverage the use of resources common to all of them. We have already seen grassroots initiatives in this area, where faculty eagerly contribute their materials, knowing that they will have access to the materials of other departmental members, eliminating the need to maintain personal media libraries.

Possible Cost Recovery

Because of the high quality of several of our objects, we are attracting the attention of textbook publishers, e-learning companies, and individuals at other universities who are interested in licensing our content for their use. If this were done on a large enough scale, we believe that an open market for learning objects could provide significant revenues over time. Future partnerships may also allow us to use the large libraries of noninteractive media owned by major book publishers as source material for our objects, greatly speeding production while reducing acquisition and copyright costs.

Conclusion

Without learning objects at the center of the design, most of the problems we are trying to address would remain relatively unaffected, even if the other changes to the system described above were made. For example, migrating to a fully digital delivery system or setting development priorities, while significant steps, only address part of the need and do little to address cost effectiveness. Even though we are clearly still in the formative phase of our implementation, we are gratified to see that instructors are already reusing objects in their individual classrooms that were originally developed for online courses and vice versa. From a practical standpoint, this marks the beginning of the kind of reuse that, if prevalent, will signal the success of the system or, if absent, the failure. To reach this point, extraordinary coordination and cooperation by disparate university entities has been required. While difficult at times, we have discovered that as we overcome traditional barriers between academic entities and service organizations, we discover new efficiencies that invigorate the entire institution. As more academic publishers and institutions of learning commit to a similar model and make their objects publicly available for reuse, we anticipate these efficiencies will grow exponentially. By that time, we hope to have progressed to the point where using and reusing digital learning objects is as typical a part of on- and off-campus academic life as opening a textbook. And that simply opening a textbook can no longer be considered typical.

Acknowledgements

The ongoing work of the Digital Learning Environments Research and Development Group (dle.byu.edu) at Brigham Young University, of which we are both members, contributed greatly to the conceptual basis of our present system. *You can reach the authors at: Joseph B. South, Brigham Young University, Center for Instructional Design, 3800 HBLL, Provo, UT 84602 (801/378-9382, FAX: 801/378-8910, Joseph_south@byu.edu); David W. Monson, Brigham Young University, Center for Instructional Design, 3800 HBLL, Provo, UT 84602 (801/378-8338, FAX: 801/378-8910, David_Monson@byu.edu).*

Notes

1. Instructional Management Systems

2. Institute of Electrical and Electronic Engineers, Learning Technology Standards Committee.

References

Wiley, D. A. (2002). Connecting learning objects to instructional design theory: A definition, a metaphor, and a taxonomy. In D. A. Wiley (Ed.), *The instructional use of learning objects.* Bloomington, IN: Agency for Instructional Technology and Association for Educational Communications and Technology.

Wiley, D. A., South, J. B., Bassett, J., Nelson, L. M., Seawright, L. L., Peterson, T., & Monson, D. W. (1999). Three common properties of efficient online instructional support systems. *The ALN Magazine, 3*(2) [online]. Available: http://www.aln.org/alnweb/magazine/Vol3_issue2/wiley.htm

5.0 Learning Objects
and the Future

Collaboratively Filtering Learning Objects

Mimi M. Recker & Andrew Walker
(Utah State University) &
David A. Wiley (Utah State University)

Abstract

This chapter describes and discusses the application of collaborative filtering techniques to the design of metadata structures for learning objects, and its implications for instruction. This approach enables context-sensitive discovery and recommendation of learning objects. The discussion is based upon research in developing and evaluating a collaborative filtering system, which enables users to share ratings, opinions, and recommendations about resources on the Web. An additional benefit of this approach is that it also allows a user to locate other users who share similar interests for further communication and collaboration.

Introduction

Much recent research has focused on building Internet-based digital libraries, containing vast reserves of information resources. Within educational applications, a primary goal of these libraries is to provide users (including teachers and students) a way to search for and display digital learning resources, frequently called *learning objects*. As part of these efforts, researchers are developing cataloging and tagging systems. Much like labels on a can, these tags provide descriptive summaries intended to convey the semantics of the object. Together, these tags (or data elements) usually comprise what is called a metadata structure (LTSC, 2000). Metadata structures are searchable and thus provide means for discovering learning objects of interest, even when these are nontextual.

For example, an IEEE standards committee, called the Learning Technologies Standards Committee (LTSC), has developed a draft standard for "Learning Objects Metadata." For the purpose of this task, the committee defined a learning object as *"any entity, digital or non-digital, which can be used, re-used or referenced during technology-supported learning"* (LTSC, 2000). The LTSC standard is designed to provide a means of enhancing the discovery of learning objects. The LTSC learning object model currently defines over 50 data elements within its hierarchical metadata structure. Example data elements include title, language, rights management, and description (LTSC, 2000). Because of their status as official data descriptors of learning objects, we call these *authoritative* data elements (Recker & Wiley, 2000).

The LTSC standards are clearly focused on addressing knowledge management issues of learning object repositories. The standards are particularly focused on solving the technical aspects of object description, and cataloging within a networked environment. They are not, however, focused on capturing aspects surrounding the initial context of instructional use of objects. They do not support encoding a description of learning activities and context surrounding a learning object. The standards also do not provide explicit support for the re-use of learning objects within specific instructional contexts.

In this paper, we propose an alternate view of creating and sustaining a metadata structure for distributed digital learning objects. In particular, this paper describes and discusses the application of collaborative filtering techniques within a metadata structure for describing and cataloging learning resources. As we will describe, the approach supports metadata structures that incorporate what we call *non-authoritative* data elements. This form of metadata attempts to capture the context of use and surrounding activities of the learning object. The data elements can also describe the community of users from which the learning object is derived. Moreover, any user (and not just the authorized cataloger) can contribute a metadata record. As a result, a particular learning resource may have multiple *non-authoritative* metadata records, in addition to its *authoritative* record.

As we will explain, such an approach supports discovery and automatic filtering, and recommendation of relevant learning objects in a way that is sensitive to the needs of particular communities of users interested in teaching and learning. An additional benefit of this approach is that it allows a user to locate other users (students or instructors) who share similar interests for further communication and collaboration.

In the next section of this paper, we describe collaborative filtering and its implementation within a system called *Altered Vista*. We then describe an implemented example and present results of pilot user studies. We conclude with a discussion of planned system extensions, applicability to a framework for designing learning object metadata structures, and a discussion of implications for teaching and learning.

Altered Vista:
A Collaborative Filtering System

Within information science and human-computer interaction (HCI) research, a paradigm for categorizing, filtering, and automatically recommending information has emerged, called "collaborative information filtering" (Malone et al., 1987). This approach is based on collecting and propagating word-of-mouth opinions and recommendations from trusted sources. For example, if you wanted to try a new restaurant, how would you decide where to go? You would probably ask friends with similar tastes in cuisine to recommend their favorite spots. This solution to the "restaurant problem" forms the basic insight underlying research in collaborative information filtering. Systems built on a collaborative information filtering approach (also called recommender systems) have been demonstrated in a variety of domains, including filtering and recommending books, movies, research reports, and Usenet news articles (Maltz & Ehrlich, 1995; Resnick & Varian, 1997; Shardanand & Maes, 1995).

In recent work, we have been applying collaborative filtering techniques within a metadata structure for digital learning resources. In particular, we are developing and evaluating an Internet-accessible system, called Altered Vista, which allows users to share ratings and opinions about resources on the Internet. Using the Altered Vista system, users input reviews about the quality and usefulness of Internet-based resources. Their reviews become part of the review database. Users can then access and search the recommendations of other users. The system can also support the automated recommendation of learning resources. In this way, a user is able to use and benefit from the opinions of others in order to locate relevant, quality information, while avoiding less useful sites.

Altered Vista design goals were as follows:

- Because of the inadequacy of current content-indexing search engines (Lawrence & Giles, 1999), the system employs collaborative filtering techniques to support communities of users in discovering (and recommending) Web resources of value, while avoiding wasteful sites.

- By using the system to rate Web resources, users improve their information design skills. In particular, our target users, students, engage with Internet-based resources more mindfully and reflectively.

- By reviewing and searching for Web resources within a community of users (especially a learning community), the system supports and promotes collaborative and community-building activities in settings that utilize Internet resources. This is particularly true in distance education settings lacking face-to-face activities. Rather than focusing exclusively on Web resources, the system promotes interaction among people, with the resource providing common ground for reflection, discussion, and debate.

System Description

A fundamental design issue in a collaborative filtering system is defining the kinds of data elements used to describe resources of interest. These data elements are intended to convey the semantics and value of the resource. Following Resnick and Varian (1997), the following dimensions need to be considered in the design of a metadata structure for collaborative filtering. These are: (1) the ontology (data elements) of the metadata structure; (2) the collection of metadata records; (3) the aggregation of metadata records; (4) the usage of metadata records; and (5) whether user contributions (reviews) are anonymous.

Metadata Structure

Devising a metadata structure that can be used to describe a wide variety of resources used in a wide variety of ways by many users is a challenging problem. Moreover, the structure must be both usable and useful to potentially diverse communities of users. In many ways, the efforts to specify such metadata structures are reminiscent of the knowledge engineering efforts that were popular in the 1980s. These efforts were focused on building expert systems based on symbolic artificial intelligence (AI) research. Despite their promise, expert systems, by and large, have not become widespread. Two key reasons are (1) the knowledge elicitation bottleneck, and (2) the frame problem.

In the first case, the design of expert systems relies on a description of what experts in the domain know and how they use their knowledge. In practice, it has proven to be very difficult for experts to provide a description of their (often tacit) knowledge divorced from the actual context of use (Dreyfus, 1993). We suspect that providing a unique description of learning objects and resources that support their instructional use and re-use will raise similar sets of issues.

In the second case, symbolic AI and related applications are subject to what is known as the "frame problem" (Lormand, 1998). When providing symbolic descriptions of a changing world, the standard calculus requires axioms that describe changes that are dependent on prior events. For example, an axiom might state that flipping a light switch turns on a light. To support deductive reasoning about these events, axioms are also needed that describe "non-changes." For example, flipping the switch does not change its color, and so forth. Without these frame axioms, a reasoning system is unable to deduce which states persist through time. Unfortunately, using axioms to describe which occurrences relate to which non-changes quickly leads to combinatorial explosion.

As with knowledge engineering, we suspect that attempts to provide an authoritative description of a learning object divorced from context of use will again raise the frame problem. As suggested by research in situated cognition and activity theory, it can be very difficult to devise descriptions of representations arising out of activity (Brown, Collins, & Duguid, 1989; Suchman, 1987). Indeed, the activity (for example, instructional design or a learning activity) that led to the representation (the learning object) plays a central role in the creation of that representation. Often, these representations contain indexicals (e.g., "this," "today"), much like language. Indexicals derive their meaning from context. They are powerful in that they provide an efficient and compact representational form. As a result, the representations are dependent on their context of use.

When creating descriptions of learning objects, the immediacy and context of an indexical term must be replaced by a data element value. However, because indexicals are virtually transparent, the resulting descriptions may be obscure and ambiguous. Therefore, the consumer of a metadata record will sometimes be required to induce the meaning and reference of data element values.

As a result, we argue that for a metadata structure to be effective, it must incorporate what we call "non-authoritative" records, comprise of "non-authoritative" data elements. These data elements attempt to capture the embedding context and surrounding activities of resource use in order to help convey meaning. They can also capture a description of the community of users that designed or used the resource (cf. Recker & Wiley, 2000).

In our work, we have adopted an approach where the metadata structure used is specific to the review area (or domain) under consideration. In other words, rather than defining a single, overarching structure for all learning objects, we define data elements for each review area. These elements then define that metadata structure.

We have been experimenting with a variety of data elements for particular review areas. For example, Table 1 shows our current data element definition set in one example review area, online education. Any user can contribute a metadata record using our pre-defined set of data elements for this particular review area. As a result, an individual learning resource may have multiple metadata records. Moreover, the resource may be reviewed within multiple review areas.

Collection of Metadata Records

Altered Vista currently relies on explicit, active collection of resource reviews from users. To enter their data element values, users interact with a series of interface elements, including radio button Likert scales, text entry boxes, and multiple selection lists.

Aggregation of Metadata Records

Once a review is complete, the user submits the form and the metadata record is stored in the network-accessible, review database.

Table 1. Data Elements in Example Review Area, "Online Education"

Name	Description	Format
Web site title	*The title of the site*	Text box
Internet address	*The URL of the site*	Text box
Keywords	*Keywords to classify resource*	Multiple selection list
Added by	*User name*	Automatically generated
ADA Accessibility	*Meets Disabilities Act design criteria*	5-point Likert scale
Usability	*How usuable is the resource?*	5-point Likert scale
Authoritativeness	*Authority base of document author*	5-point Likert scale
Educational relevance	*Educational relevance of the resource*	5-point Likert scale
Description	*Simple description of resource*	Text box
Quality	*The subjective quality of the resource*	5-point Likert scale
Overall rating	*Overall opinion*	5-point Likert scale

Usage of Metadata Records

Metadata are used to support searching within a specific review area. In the current implementation, a user can see all reviews, search by keywords, or search reviews by a specific reviewer. Future versions will add additional searching capabilities (for example, searching by rating value).

In addition, user reviews can be analyzed statistically in order to identify clusters of users who have similar opinions. This is calculated by finding pairs of users whose data element values correlate strongly (Hill, Stead, Rosenstein, & Furnas, 1995). These clusters form the basis for automatically recommending to a user unseen resources rated highly by people within similar clusters. In addition, via these clusters, users can locate other users that share similar interests for further communication and collaboration. While much learning object work has been set in a direct instruction paradigm, this kind of community building through learning object rating and use provides a model for learning object use in constructivist learning environments.

Anonymity of Contributions

To maximize the value of user reviews, we believe it is important to recognize that contributors to the metadata database are members of a community. Information about who contributed is as important as the contribution itself. Hence, users must log in prior to using the system, and their reviews are not stored anonymously. Instead, we believe that the identity of contributing authors provides important contextual information within a metadata record. Thus, the author of reviews is both a searchable item and available for inspection within search results.

Altered Vista: System Description

There are three distinct usage modes for Altered Vista: Guest, User, and Administrator. While each mode supports specific functions, many functions are available in all modes. Figure 1 shows a simplified view of the system architecture. In our description of the system, we will use examples from one implemented review area, online education.

Login

To use the system, users must first log in using a pre-assigned ID and password. On the first login, users must complete a short demographics survey. A guest login is also available, in which reviews can be browsed but not added.

Session State

When users first start using the Altered Vista system, a unique identifier is generated. This unique identifier is then passed via the URL from page

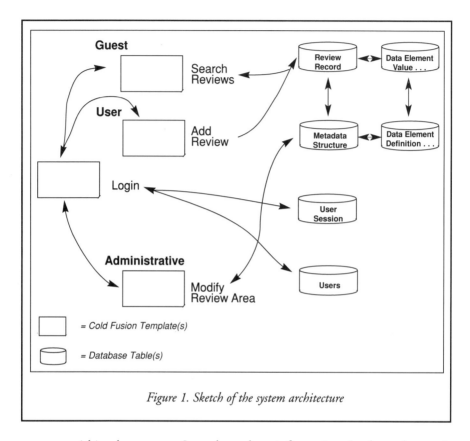

Figure 1. Sketch of the system architecture

to page within the system. State-dependent information (such as the user's access privileges or the current review area) is then stored along with this unique identifier in a database on the server. When the information is needed, it is retrieved using the unique identifier available on each page. This eliminates the need for storing cookies on the client machine.

Search Reviews

Using guest, user, or administrator access, users of the system can search through reviews that have been added by other (registered) users. Users first specify the topic or review area they want to search, then specify the keywords they are looking for. These keywords are selected from a list that is specific to the review area that they are searching.

After submitting their search request, users are given a list of matching results. This resulting list shows a summary list of matches. For each match, the system displays a rough aggregate of the community's opinion on a given resource by computing the median of responses for the "overall rating" category. From this large result list, the user can click for a more detailed look at a particular resource.

Figure 2. Example review record

Figure 2 shows an example composite review of a learning resource in an implemented review area, online education.

The detailed view first displays the median value for data elements that have numeric values. In the example online education review area, these are the median of Likert scale values (e.g., overall rating). In addition, each reviewer's name is listed along with the date/time that the review was submitted, the overall rating for the resource, and any textual data element values. For the online education review area, these are the site descriptions submitted by reviewers.

Each reviewer's name can also be clicked on. This action displays a list of all the reviews that the author has submitted in the current review area. This enables a user to view the reviews of a favored (or disliked) reviewer.

Add Review

Registered users and administrators can both add new reviews to the database. As with searching reviews, a reviewer must first identify the review area. Once the review area is identified, the screen is split into two areas. Depending on screen resolution, about three quarters of the screen space on the right side is given over to browser space for the user to look at the Web site under review. The remaining screen space displays a browser window in which the user is asked to identify the resource that they want to review. In the case of online education, Uniform Resource Locators (URLs) are used. Once the user submits a URL, Altered Vista checks the database to see if there is an exact match for it. If no exact match is found, then the system displays to the user the eight "nearest neighbors" to the URL. The user is then asked to either confirm that he/she is in fact reviewing a resource that is new to the system or select a neighbor that might be the same resource with a slight variation in the URL.

Once the URL is identified, in the left-side browser, a list of the data elements that comprise the metadata structure for that review area is displayed (see Figure 3). The user is asked to complete the review and submit it.

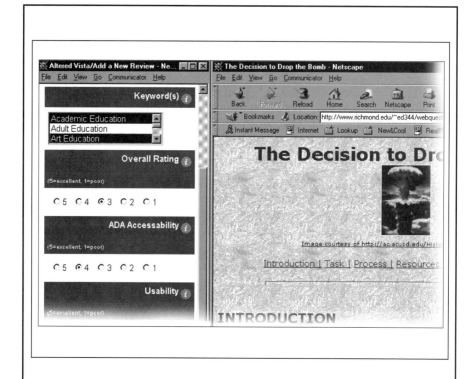

Figure 3. Screen shot of area for entering a review

Modify Review Area

Altered Vista is a template system. This means that administrators of the system can manipulate (update and insert) the review areas themselves. The fundamental metadata structure behind each review area is defined by its data element definitions. These currently consist of two types: Likert scale and memo. Each review area can contain any number of these definition types.

Each data element definition consists of a label and a description of how it should be used by reviewers. Likert scale definitions add a list of discrete values, a corresponding list of labels for those values, and may include an explanation of the scale (e.g., 5=excellent, 1=poor). Memo definitions have no additional parameters.

Each data element definition type has a corresponding table in the database for data values. These data values consist of a relationship to the data element definition that describes it, which in turn contains a reference to the review area in which the definition is used. These data values also contain a reference to the review area that they belong to, which in turn contains a reference to the user who added the review.

Administrators define the list of keywords for a particular review area.

System Specifications

The current version of Altered Vista is implemented on a Windows NT server. The metadata database is stored in Microsoft Access. Communication between server and database is accomplished using Cold Fusion server software.

Users must be connected to the Internet and may access the system using Internet Explorer 4.0 or Netscape 4.6 (or later) Web browsers. Javascript and Cascading Style Sheets must be enabled in the browser. The system is optimized for Windows, but will also run on other platforms.

Pilot Studies of Altered Vista

Method

The Altered Vista system was tested over a three-month period by 15 students enrolled in a course on "Creating Resources for Online Education," at Utah State University. The course was comprised of a mix of graduate and upper-level undergraduate students. In this trial, the collaborative filtering review area was "online education." Participants were asked to find and rate Web sites that contained online instruction. To maximize the chance of overlap, participants were asked to rate sites from a compiled list of online education sites (see http://edweb.sdsu.edu/webquest/matrix.html). Users also participated in an online discussion forum in which various aspects of Altered Vista usage were discussed. Table 2 shows usage results from the trial period.

Table 2. Results from Trial Usage Period

Total number of users	15
Total number of reviews	172
Total number of resources reviewed	97

At the end of this period, users anonymously completed a usability evaluation survey. The survey consisted of several 5-point Likert scale and short-answers questions. For example, students were asked to rate the usability of the system, its support for finding useful resources and people, and the extent that usage of the system promotes information design skills.

Results

Users appeared to hold a diversity of views about the sites that they reviewed. Figure 4 shows the frequency of Likert scale values for two data elements ("overall" and "usability," from 1 [poor] to 5 [excellent]). As can be seen, users appeared to be generally more critical in their overall rating of sites, while more positive in their view of the usability of sites.

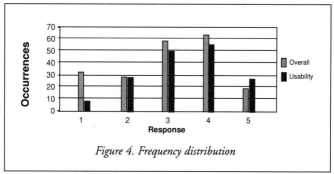

Figure 4. Frequency distribution

Overall, users appeared to find the system easy to use. In a Likert scale response to the statement *"I found the Altered Vista system easy to use"* (from 1 [strongly disagree] to 5 [strongly agree]), the median was 3.77. As one user commented: *"Generally speaking, I enjoyed using the altered vista, for it provides bunches of informative Web sites, based on which we can make comparisons according to certain criteria."*

Users also reported that use of the system has made them think more deeply about Web site design. In a Likert scale response to the statement *"Using Altered Vista has made me think more deeply about Web site design"* (from 1 [strongly disagree] to 5 [strongly agree]), the median was 4.00 on the 5-point scale. One user noted: *"Altered Vista seems to be a good way to review different Web pages and sharpen our design and usability skills by making comments about them."*

Users also thought that the system would be a useful tool for finding quality resources. In a Likert scale response to the statement *"Altered Vista, once fully deployed,* will be *a useful tool for finding quality Web sites"* (from 1 [strongly disagree] to 5 [strongly agree]), the median was 4.00. Students seemed less convinced that the system, once fully deployed, will be a useful tool for finding people with shared interests (median = 3.00 on the 5-point scale). The latter result may be due to the fact that automatic recommendation of similar people was not implemented during pilot testing. As a result, the respondents may have not understood the scope of the question.

Finally, user reviews can be analyzed in order to cluster users with similar interests (Konstan, Miller, Maltz, Herlocker, Gordon, & Riedl, 1997). These clusters then form the basis for recommending unseen resources. Specifically, we correlated pairs of users on the basis of the values they gave for their overall ratings of different resources. Pairs of users with high correlations in their overall ratings can be seen as having shared views. These high correla-

Table 3. Overlap in Reviews from Trial Usage Period	
Number of resources with 1 review	58
Number of resources with 2 reviews	19
Number of resources with 3 reviews	12
Number of resources with 4 reviews	3
Number of resources with 5 reviews	3
Number of resources with 6 reviews	1
Number of resources with 7 reviews	1
Number of user pairs with 1 review in common	34
Number of user pairs with 2 reviews in common	13
Number of user pairs with 3 reviews in common	13
Number of user pairs with 4 reviews in common	5
Number of user pairs with 5 reviews in common	4

tions form the basis for automating recommendations of resources. Thus, for each pair of users with high correlations in their overall ratings, the complement of one member of the pair's set of reviews can be recommended to the other member.

Here, we must be cautious in interpreting our results as, in our pilot studies, few resources obtained multiple reviews. Indeed, only 20% of the resources reviewed had three or more reviews. Similarly, few pairs of users had more than one review in common (see Table 3). Naturally, this affects the system's ability to recommend both resources and like-minded people.

Nonetheless, of the 22 pairs of users with more than three reviews in common, several strong correlations were found. In particular, five pairs of users correlated highly (r > .80), while three pairs had high negative correlations (r < −.80). Thus, resources rated by one member of the pair but unseen by the other provide the basis for automated recommendations. As our database of reviews expands, we will explore automation of this functionality.

Conclusion

We believe that collaborative filtering techniques, as demonstrated within Altered Vista, offer a viable approach for designing and sustaining a framework for metadata structures for learning objects. We showed how this approach enables users (and not just official catalogers) to contribute metadata records for learning objects within particular areas of interest. In this way, a particular learning object may have multiple metadata records. These may be referenced within multiple contexts. The customizable metadata structure also enables non-authoritative data elements to be included. These, we argue, better allow the context of use and re-use of particular learning objects to be described. This then supports the discovery of learning objects in a way that is sensitive to the needs of particular communities of users.

Moreover, the collaborative filtering approach also supports the automatic recommendation of relevant learning objects. It allows a user to locate other users that share similar interests for further communication and collaboration. These capabilities, we believe, are critical to the success of a learning object digital library.

The instructional and learning implications of such a system are significant. From the instructor perspective, such a system makes locating relevant, high quality learning objects much easier. In addition to standard digital library / metadata search capabilities, a system that also captures and allows the searching of instructional-context specific metadata should provide a significantly enhanced design experience for the instructor. Not only would instructors be able to inspect and select individual learning objects for utilization, they would also be able to review groupings of learning objects made by other instructors with similar instructional styles. This capability provides an important complement to existing online repositories of syllabi and lesson plans, and opportunities to cross-reference are obvious.

The implications for students are equally substantial. When a collaborative filtering system captures role information in the demographics for each user, students utilizing a grouping of objects could locate other students using the same or similar groups of learning objects. There exists an opportunity for informal group formation and inter-class pollination. This type of functionality could also compliment learning object-based environments in which students interact only with the learning environment, providing the opportunity for collaborative or cooperative learning to occur.

However, as noted in the research literature, to be successful, collaborative filtering systems must address the key problems of cold-start, sparse review set, and scalability: *"Reviewing Web sights (sic) is not something I would do without some kind of motivation"* (participant comment in an online discussion board).

As exemplified by the above comment, people are loath to explicitly contribute reviews without some kind of incentive; hence it is difficult to seed and grow a metadata database. As a result, the review database is sparse, impacting its reliability when searching for and recommending resources (Konstan, Miller, Maltz, Herlocker, Gordon, & Riedl, 1997).

Unfortunately, we propose no immediate solution to these problems. We simply note that the primary target context for our system is educational environments. The design goal thus is to promote a kind of learning community, as well as help users locate liked-minded colleagues. Thus, the actual quality of the automated recommendations may be less important than the process it supports.

Future Work

In future work, we wish to explore several additional issues. First, as previously noted, we wish to automate recommendation of people and resources. This requires a more substantial database, and we plan several sustained studies involving a larger pool of users. In addition, since review records incorporate numeric values for a number of data elements, we will need to conduct multivariate analyses of these values to fully support automated recommendation. Currently, we simply rely on the values provided by users in response to the "overall rating" category.

Second, we wish to experiment with a version of Altered Vista that supports a user-modifiable metadata structure. This means that users will be able to specify the data elements that they think are relevant. We hope this will enable users to devise a vocabulary that better captures the user or community's context of use. While providing greater flexibility, it will also introduce greater complexity within the system.

Finally, to help reduce the cognitive load of explicitly entering reviews, we wish to explore the use of implicit rating methods. These methods will be based on collecting metrics about prior usage of the resource. In particular, in previous research (Recker & Pitkow, 1996), we showed that object desirability is strongly correlated to recency and frequency of prior object usage. The collection of such usage metrics is generally easily implemented within a digital library. These metrics will thus provide data in an analytical model for deriving additional implicit reviews about the quality of learning objects.

Acknowledgements

We thank the students who participated in the pilot studies. We also thank Jen Walker and Richard Cutler for helpful advice. *You can reach the authors at: Mimi M. Recker and Andrew Walker (Department of Instructional Technology, Utah State University, 2830 Old Main Hill, Logan, UT 84332-2830); and David A. Wiley (Department of Instructional Psychology & Technology, Digital Learning Environments Research Group, Brigham Young University, 150Q MCKB, Provo, UT 84602-5089).*

References

Brown, J. S., Collins, A., & Duguid, P. (1989). Situated cognition and the culture of learning. *Educational Researcher, 18,* 32–42.

Dreyfus, H. (1993). *What computers still can't do: A critique of artificial reason.* Cambridge, MA: MIT Press. (Revised edition of *What computers can't do,* 1979, 1972.)

Hill, W., Stead, L., Rosenstein, M., & Furnas, G. (1995). Recommending and evaluating choices in a virtual community of use. In *ACM Conference on Human Factors in Computing Systems* (pp. 194–201). New York: ACM.

Konstan, J., Miller, B., Maltz, D., Herlocker, J., Gordon, L., & Riedl, J. (1997). GroupLens. *Communications of the ACM, 40*(3).

Lawrence, S., & Giles, L. (1999). Accessibility and distribution of information on the Web. *Nature, 400,* 107–109.

Lormand, E. (1998). Frame problem. In *MIT encyclopedia of cognitive science.* Cambridge, MA: MIT Press.

LTSC. (2000). IEEE P1484.12 *Learning Objects Metadata Working Group Homepage* [online]. Available: http://ltsc.ieee.org/wg12/index.html

Malone, T., Grant, K., Turbak, F., Brobst, S., & Cohen, M. (1987). Intelligent information sharing systems. *Communications of the ACM, 30*(5).

Maltz, D., & Ehrlich, K. (1995). Pointing the way: Active collaborative filtering. *ACM Conference on Human Factors in Computing Systems* (pp. 202–209). New York: ACM.

Recker, M., & Pitkow, J. (1996). Predicting document access in large, multimedia repositories. *ACM Transactions on Computer-Human Interaction, 3*(4), 352–375.

Recker, M., & Wiley, D. (2000). *A non-authoritative educational metadata ontology for filtering and recommending learning objects.* Manuscript submitted for publication.

Resnick, P., & Varian, H. (1997). Recommender systems (special issue). *Communications of the ACM, 40*(3).

Shardanand, U., & Maes, P. (1995). Social information filtering: Algorithms for automating word-of-mouth. *ACM Conference on Human Factors in Computing Systems* (pp. 210–215). New York: ACM.

Suchman, L. A. (1987). *Plans and situated actions: The problem of human-machine communication*. Cambridge, England: Cambridge University Press.

Knowledge Objects and Mental-Models

M. David Merrill
(Utah State University)

Cognitive psychology suggests that a mental-model consists of two major components: knowledge structures *(schema)* and processes for using this knowledge *(mental operations)*. A major concern of instructional design is the representation and organization of subject matter content to facilitate learning. The thesis of this paper is that the careful analysis of subject matter content *(knowledge)* can facilitate both the external representation of knowledge for purposes of instruction *(knowledge objects)* and the internal representation and use of knowledge by learners *(mental-models)*. If a student is taught a concise knowledge representation for different kinds of instructional outcomes (originally intended for use by a computer), can the student use this representation as a meta-mental-model to facilitate acquisition of specific mental-models?

Merrill (1987) elaborated the Gagné (1965, 1985) categories of learning assumptions as follows:

> There are different kinds of learned performance (instructional outcomes). Different instructional conditions are necessary to adequately promote a given type of learned performance. There are different types of cognitive structure associated with different types of learned performance. There are different types of cognitive processes necessary to use each type of cognitive structure to achieve a given type of learned performance.

Merrill (1987) suggested the following cardinal principles of instruction:

- *The Cognitive Structure Principle*—The purpose of instruction is to promote the development of that cognitive structure that is most consistent with the desired learned performance.

- *The Elaboration Principle*—The purpose of instruction is to promote incremental elaboration of the most appropriate cognitive structure to enable the learner to achieve increased generality and complexity in the desired learned performance.

- *The Learner Guidance Principle*—The purpose of instruction is to promote that active cognitive processing that best enables the learner to use the most appropriate cognitive structure in a way consistent with the desired learned performance.
- *The Practice Principle*—The purpose of instruction is to provide the dynamic, ongoing opportunity for monitored practice that requires the learner to demonstrate the desired learned performance, or a close approximation of it, while the instructor monitors the activity and intervenes with feedback both as to result and process.

This paper will elaborate the Cognitive Structure and Elaboration Principles.

Knowledge Structure

Instructional designers have long recognized the importance of analyzing subject matter for the purpose of facilitating learning via appropriate knowledge selection, organization, and sequence. An early, widely used set of categories was proposed by Bloom and his associates (Bloom et al., 1956, Krathwohl et al., 1964). Gagné (1965, 1985) proposed a taxonomy of learning objectives that found wide acceptance in the instructional design community. For each of his categories Gagné proposed unique conditions for learning based on information processing theory. The author elaborated and extended Gagné's categories in his work on Component Display Theory (Merrill, 1994).

While instructional designers tend to focus on delivery systems (especially technology) and to a lesser extent on instructional strategies and tactics, it is our hypothesis that the greatest impact on learning results from the representation and organization of the knowledge to be learned. Knowledge structure refers to the interrelationships among knowledge components. Gagné (1985) proposed a prerequisite relationship among knowledge components. For Gagné, the components of knowledge are facts *(discriminations)*, concepts, rules, and higher order rules.

Reigeluth, Merrill, and Bunderson (1978) proposed that a prerequisite relationship among knowledge components represents only one type of knowledge structure. Adequate instruction would require other types of knowledge structures to be identified and made explicit to the learner. For them knowledge components are facts, concepts, steps *(procedures)*, and principles. They proposed the following types of knowledge structures:

List. Lists often show no relationship among their components or there may be a simple ordering relationship such as size, chronology, etc., based on some attribute of the components of the list. A given set of knowledge components can be listed in a number of different ways.

Learning-Prerequisite.[1] This knowledge structure arranges components in a hierarchy indicating that a component lower in the hierarchy must be known before a component higher in the hierarchy can be learned.

Parts-Taxonomy. This knowledge structure arranges components in a hierarchy so that the coordinate components represent the parts of the superordinate component.

Kinds-Taxonomy.[2] This knowledge structure arranges components in a hierarchy such that the coordinate components represent kinds of the superordinate component.

Procedural -Prerequisite. This knowledge structure arranges the components (steps) of some activity to be performed in the order in which they must be executed. Procedural relations are often represented via a flow chart.

Procedural-Decision. In this structure alternative procedures are identified and the learner must consider a number of factors *(conditions)* in order to make a decision about which alternative is appropriate in a given situation.

Causal. In this structure the cause-and-effect relations among components are indicated.

These knowledge structures were further elaborated in a conversation between Gagné and Merrill (Twitchell, 1990–91). The structures were identified as lists, taxonomies *(kinds, parts, properties, functions)*, algorithms *(path, decision)*, and causal nets *(event chains, causal chains)*.

Knowledge Objects

Merrill and his colleagues in the ID_2 Research Group proposed a knowledge representation scheme consisting of knowledge components arranged into knowledge objects (Jones, Li, & Merrill, 1990; Merrill & ID_2 Research Group, 1993, 1996; Merrill, 1998; Merrill, in press-a). In the remainder of this paper we will refer to this work as Component Design Theory (CDT_2).[3]

CDT_2 suggests that almost all cognitive subject matter content *(knowledge)* can be represented as four types of knowledge objects. *Entities*[4] are things *(objects)*. *Actions* are procedures that can be performed by a learner on, to, or with entities or their parts. *Processes* are events that occur often as a result of some action. Properties are qualitative or quantitative descriptors for entities, actions, or processes.

CDT_2 defines knowledge via the components of a knowledge object. A knowledge object and its components are a precise way to describe the content to be taught. The components of a knowledge object are a set of defined containers for information.

- The knowledge components of an *entity* name, describe, or illustrate the entity.

- The knowledge components of a *part* name, describe, or illustrate a part of an entity.

- The knowledge components of a *property* name, describe, identify a value, and identify a portrayal corresponding to this value for the property.
- The knowledge components of an *action* name and describe the action and identify the process(es) triggered by the action.
- The knowledge components of a *process* name and describe the process and identify the conditions (values of properties) and consequences (property values changed) of the execution of the process and any other process(es) triggered by the process.
- The knowledge components of a *kind* name, describe, and define via a list of property values a class of entities, activities, or processes.

This knowledge object framework (see Table 1) is the same for a wide variety of different topics within a subject matter domain, or for knowledge in different subject matter domains.

Table 1. Major Components of Knowledge Objects		
Entity: Name Description Portrayal	**Part:** Name Description Portrayal	**Property:** Name Description Value Value portrayal

Action:
 	
Name
Description
Process trigger
	Action:
	
	Name
	Description
	Condition
	  (value of property)
	Consequence
	  (property value changed)
	Process trigger
		Property:
		
		Name
		Description
		Definition
		  (list of property values)

Some name or symbol identifies every entity *(thing)*, action, process, or property. A given knowledge component may have several different names.

The description component is a default category in which the author can put information about an entity, a part of an entity, the property of an entity, an action associated with some entity or set of entities, a process associated with some entity or set of entities, or a class *(kind)* of entities, actions, or processes. For a given knowledge component there may be several different classes of information available, hence the description category may be subdivided into several sub components.

A *portrayal* is how a learner senses the component. A given portrayal may be symbolic, verbal, graphic, video, animation, audio, or even olfactory or kinetic.

A *property* has a set of legal values that it can assume. These values may be discrete or continuous. Each of these values may also change the portrayal of the entity, action, or process.

An *action* often serves as a trigger for a process, hence one component of an activity is a pointer to the process that it triggers.

A *process* has one or more conditions. If the conditions are true, the process executes, if one or more of the conditions are false then the process will not execute. A condition is defined as a value on some property in the knowledge object. If the property has the specified value, then the condition is true and the process executes. If the property has some value other than the specified value, then the condition is false and the process does not execute.

A process always results in some consequence. The consequence is defined as the change in the value of one or more properties. When the property is changed, then the portrayal of that property is also changed.

A process can trigger another process, thus resulting in some kind of chain reaction. Hence, one component of a process is a pointer to the next process or processes in the chain.

One of the unique capabilities of human beings is the ability to conceptualize or to place entities, actions, and processes into categories. This capability seems to be part of the neural equipment furnished to human beings. One component of a knowledge object is a list of different category names that may be used to describe the varieties of the primary entity of the knowledge object. In a knowledge object, a definition is identified as the name of the super-ordinate category (often the name of the principal entity of the knowledge object), a list of discriminating properties by which an instance in one category is distinguished from another instance in a different category, and the value of each discriminating property that defines a given class.

Knowledge Structures

Dijkstra and van Merriënboer (1997) proposed an integrative framework for representing knowledge. The cornerstone of their framework is a problem to solve. The framework attempts to identify different kinds of problems and their relationship. They have identified three types of problems: categorization problems, interpretation problems, and design problems. Categorization involves assigning instances to classes. Interpretation involves predicting the consequence of a process or finding faulted conditions in a process. Design involves performing a series of steps to accomplish some purpose, often creating some artifact.

Dijkstra and van Merriënboer identify three levels of performance associated with the three types of problems. Level 1 is characterized as learning by examples. It involves remembering a definition, a statement of a principle, or the steps in a procedure. It also involves identifying instances of a concept, identifying or describing a process, or identifying the correct or incorrect execution of a procedure. For level 1, examples of the solution and the procedure for reaching the solution are available as models for the learner.

Level 2 is characterized as learning by doing. It involves inventing concepts, predicting the consequence of a process or trouble shooting a process, or using a procedure to design a new artifact. For level 2, the procedure to reach the solution is given but the learner must find new solutions using the procedures given.

Level 3 is characterized as learning by exploration and experimentation. It involves inventing descriptive theories, hypothesizing and testing explanatory theories, and developing prescriptive theories for creating artifacts. For level 3, the task is to find both the process and the solution.

Each of these categories and levels correspond to relationships among the components of knowledge objects and among knowledge objects. These relationships are described by knowledge structures. This paper describes knowledge structures for problems of categorization and problems of interpretation. Problems of design are not included.

Concept Knowledge Structure

The knowledge components for a concept *(kind)* are name, description, and definition *(a list of property values)*. A knowledge structure for a concept identifies the relationships among these knowledge components. Table 2 illustrates a knowledge structure for a concept.

This concept knowledge structure attempts to show the following relationships. A concept *(kind)* is always some subclass of another class *(the superordinate class)*. There must always be at least two kinds or coordinate classes. Each coordinate class shares a set of properties with the superordinate class.

Table 2. Knowledge Structure for Concept				
		Property 1	Property 2	Property 3
	Coordinate Class A	$Value_1$	$Value_1$	$Value_1$
Name of superordinate class	Coordinate Class B	$Value_2$	$Value_2$	$Value_2$
	Coordinate Class C	$Value_3$	$Value_3$	$Value_3$

Properties that have different values for two more of the subordinate *(coordinate)* classes are called discriminating properties. Not all properties are discriminating properties, only those who have different values for different coordinate classes. Class membership in a given coordinate class is determined by the set of values that the discriminating properties assume for members of this class.

Table 3 provides an instantiation of this knowledge structure for the superordinate concept *tree* and the coordinate concepts *deciduous* and *conifer*, kinds of trees. A third kind of tree is identified, one that has broad, flat leaves, that retains the leaves in the autumn and whose leaves do not change color. The question indicates that it is possible to identify a category *(kind)* but not know the name for this category.

Table 3. Instantiation of Knowledge Structure for Concept				
		Shape of leaves	Retains leaves in Autumn	Leaves change color in Autumn
	Deciduous	Broad, flat	No	Yes
Tree	Conifer	Needle like	Yes	No
	?	Broad, flat	Yes	No

Conceptual Networks

Conceptual networks are more complex knowledge structures. Conceptual networks are still composed of the same basic knowledge components. Table 4 illustrates a more complex conceptual structure. Note that property 1 has the same value for each of the coordinate classes A, B, and C. This is the property that determines class membership in this set of coordinate class. Property 2 further discriminates among the subordinate classes for class A, B, and C. This property defines the coordinate classes Aa, Ab, Ac, etc.

Table 4. A Complex Conceptual Network Knowledge Structure

	Coordinate concepts	Coordinate concepts	Property 1	Property 2
		$Concept_{1Aa}$	V_1	V_1
	Coordinate concept$_{1A}$	$Concept_{1Ab}$	V_1	V_2
		$Concept_{1Ac}$	V_1	V_3
		$Concept_{1Ba}$	V_2	V_1
Superordinate concept 1	Coordinate concept$_{1B}$	$Concept_{1Bb}$	V_2	V_2
		$Concept_{1Bc}$	V_2	V_3
		$Concept_{1Ca}$	V_3	V_1
	Coordinate concept$_{1C}$	$Concept_{1Cb}$	V_3	V_2
		$Concept_{1Cc}$	V_3	V_3

Table 5 is an instantiation of a more complex concept network. Note that the first property distinguishes among the first level of coordinate concepts: birds, insects, and mammals. The second property distinguishes among the second level of coordinate concepts. Please note that for purposes of illustration, the properties and property values are significantly over-simplified.

			Table 5. Instantiation of a More Complex Concept Network		
		Coordinate concepts	Coordinate concepts	Locomotion	Source of food
			Finch	Fly	Plants
		Bird	Hawk	Fly	Animals
			Sparrow	Fly	Both
			Ant	Crawl	Plants
Animal		Insects	Spider	Crawl	Animals
			Bug	Crawl	Both
			Cow	Walk	Plants
		Mammal	Lion	Walk	Animals
			Dog	Walk	Both

Processes and Activities

A process is knowledge about how something works. It answers the question, *"What happens?"* Processes are often taught at an information-about level. The process is sometimes demonstrated, but the learner frequently has an incomplete or inaccurate mental-model of the process.

The components of a process include its name and description, a consequence that is defined as a change in a property value with the corresponding change in the portrayal of the entity *(what happens?)*, and a set of conditions that is defined as values on properties *(when?)*. A knowledge structure for a processes causal network is illustrated in Figure 1. This structure is called a PEAnet (for *Process, Entity, Activity Network*). This structure is a very generic knowledge structure that can be used to represent almost any process. Processes are defined in terms of properties. A condition for a process is some value on a property. A consequence for a process is a change in the value of a property. When the value of a property of an entity changes the portrayal, either its appearance or its behavior also changes in a corresponding way.

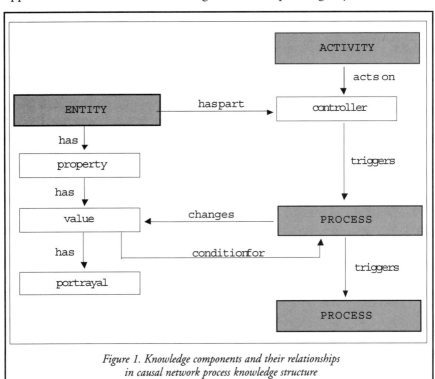

Figure 1. Knowledge components and their relationships
in causal network process knowledge structure

Figure 2 is an instantiation of this PEAnet knowledge structure for the simple process of lighting a lamp when a switch is flipped. The action is for the user to *flip the switch* by moving the toggle a part of the switch. This triggers the process *change toggle position* which changes the value of the property *toggle position* from up-to-down or down-to-up, which in turn, changes the appearance of the switch as shown in the portrayals pictured. The change in toggle position also triggers another process, *light lamp,* which in turn changes the value of the *lamp lighted* property from on-to-off or from off-to-on with a corresponding change in the appearance of the lamp as depicted by the portrayals shown.

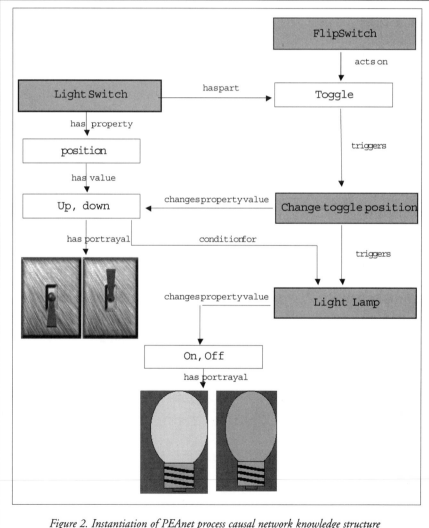

Figure 2. Instantiation of PEAnet process causal network knowledge structure

PEAnet knowledge structures can be used to represent processes involving human interaction as well as devices. PEAnet knowledge structure can also be represented in table form as illustrated in Figure 3. Figure 3 and Table 6 are representations of the following situation:

A research group has acquired a new contract. Mark is being informed about the role he will play in completing this work. Three entities are involved: the manager who is performing the actions which are statements to Mark as shown in Figure 3, the boss who is merely present or absent during the conversation, and Mark who is shown reacting to the news about the new contract.

Table 6 lists the actions, the process triggered by each action, the consequence of the action, and the conditions under which the consequence will occur. The actions in this PEAnet are statements of the manager to mark. The manager is not portrayed but does the actions. Note that the actions could occur in any order but in this case the usual order is as listed.

Table 6. PEAnet Actions, Processes, Consequences, and Conditions for a Simulation of an Office Conversation

Action		Process		Consequence	Condition
Statement "We have a new contract."	*triggers*	Make Mark Happy	*changes*	Mood = happy	
Statement "But you don't get to direct the project."	*triggers*	Make Mark Sad	*changes*	Mood = sad	
Statement "Jean will direct this project."	*triggers*	Make Mark Surprised	*changes*	Mood = surprised	
Statement "You get to work for Jean."	*triggers*	Make Mark Angry	*changes*	Mood = surprised	Boss present = yes
				Mood = angry	Boss present = no

Entities	Properties	Legal Values	Portrayal
Mark	Mood	Happy	
		Sad	
		Surprised	
		Angry	
Boss	Present	Yes	
		No	

Figure 3. Entities, associated properties, legal values, and value portrayals for a Process Causal Network PEAnet Knowledge Structure

What happens? When the first statement *(action)* is executed the process *Make Mark Happy* changes the property *mood* to the value *happy.* The happy portrayal of Mark corresponding with the value happy is shown. When the next statement *(action)* is executed, the process *Make Mark Sad* changes the property *mood* to the value *sad* and the corresponding portrayal showing a sad Mark is displayed. A similar chain of events occurs for the third statement. For the fourth statement the process *Make Mark Angry* changes the value of *mood* to the value *angry* only when the property *boss present* has a value of *no.* When the *boss present* property has a value of *yes,* then the value of *mood* remains or is changed to *surprised.*

This is a significantly oversimplified PEAnet to illustrate the role of properties, property values, conditions, and consequences. Actions can trigger more than one process. Processes can change more than one property. There can be many or few conditions. Conditions for a process may have been set much earlier in a complex process that consists of many events. Hopefully, the reader can extrapolate to the more complex case from the information given.

Mental-Models

Cognitive psychologists have proposed a variety of theories of how knowledge is represented in memory (See Mayer, 1992). Schema theory postulates that learners represent knowledge in memory as some form of cognitive structure. A knowledge structure is a form of a schema. A knowledge structure represents the information that is required if a learner is to be able to solve problems. If the required information *(knowledge components)* and the relationships among these knowledge components are incomplete, then the learner will not be able to efficiently and effectively solve problems requiring this knowledge.

Mental-models combine a schema or mental representation with a process for manipulating the information in the schema. Solving a problem requires the learner to not only have the appropriate knowledge representation *(schema or knowledge structure)* but he or she must also have algorithms or heuristics for manipulating these knowledge components in order to solve problems.

Categorization Problems

Classification. A common instructional strategy for teaching concepts *(kinds-of)* is to present a set of examples representing the different coordinate classes of the superordinate class. The learner is told the class membership for each example. The learner is then given a previously unencountered set of examples and asked to classify or sort each of them into the appropriate coordinate class.

Tables 2 and 3 illustrate a knowledge structure for a set of coordinate concepts. The knowledge components and relationships in this knowledge structure are necessary if the learner is to be able to correctly classify new examples. The algorithm necessary for concept classification requires the learner to do the following:

- Remember or have available the properties and values associated with each category *(the definition)*.

- For a given example, find the portrayal of each property in the portrayal of the example. Determine its value. Repeat for each of the properties required to determine class membership.

- Compare the property values of the example with the property values associated with each concept class. When a match is found, then give the name of the coordinate class associated with these property values.

Having a concept knowledge structure such as that illustrated in Table 3 also allows the learner to explore *"What if?"* problems about the concepts under consideration. Having a schematic representation of the properties and their values allows the learner to speculate about coordinate classes that may not have been specified by the instruction. For example, in Table 3 the third row enables the learner to ask, *"Are their trees that have broad leaves that don't change color and drop in the Autumn? Is so, what are they called?"* The learner can also explore other combinations of property values. The schema and this cognitive exploration process enable the learner to extend and elaborate concept understanding.

Generalization. Table 5 and Table 7 illustrate a more complex knowledge structure that enables a learner to make generalizations. A generalization is when classes from different set of coordinate concepts are seen as coordinate concepts for a new set of coordinate concepts. In Table 5, finches, ants, and cows each appear in a different coordinate set corresponding to birds, insects, and mammals. However, each of these classes share the same value, *plants,* on property 2, *Source of Food.* By sorting on the second property we can identify a new set of coordinate concepts as in Table 7. Note in this case that the first property discriminates on the second set of coordinate concepts while the second property discriminates on the first level of coordinate concepts.

What is the algorithm by which the learner solves problems of generalization? First, if the value on a property, or the values on two or more properties, are the same across different sets of coordinate concepts, then sorting on this property will yield a new set of coordinate classes. Having a complex knowledge structure of one set of concepts allows the learner to manipulate the knowledge components in this manner in an attempt to identify other coordinate concepts. The learner then searches to find the names associated with these new coordinate concepts (Dijkstra & van Merriënboer, level 2). If this is a new categorization then the learner may invent names and thus invent new concepts (Dijkstra & van Merriënboer, level 3).

Table 7. Instantiation of a Complex Conceptual Network Knowledge Structure

	Coordinate concepts	Coordinate concepts	Locomotion	Source of food
		Finch	Fly	Plants
	Herbivore	Ant	Crawl	Plants
		Cow	Walk	Plants
		Hawk	Fly	Animals
Animal	Carnivore	Spider	Crawl	Animals
		Lion	Walk	Animals
		Warbler	Fly	Both
	Omnivore	Bug	Crawl	Both
		Dog	Walk	Both

Interpretation Problems

Explanation. The knowledge components of property, value, portrayal, condition, and consequence provide a vocabulary by which the learner can provide a precise explanation of a given process. Having a learner determine the knowledge structure PEAnet of a given process provides a very precise way to assess the completeness and accuracy of the learner's mental-model for a given class of problems.

Prediction. What is involved in problem solving at the application level? Merely explaining a process, even with the precision of a PEAnet, is at the first level of Dijkstra and van Merriënboer's representation of problems. Making prediction moves the learner to the learn-by-doing level. For a given situation, making a prediction involves determining first the conditions that are relevant to the consequence. This involves finding the portrayal of the property(s) involved and determining its current value(s). The learner must know the principle involved, that is, if *<conditions>* then *<consequence>*, and determine which of several such relationships is applicable in the situation under consideration. The learner can then indicate the change in property(s) value that will occur and the corresponding change in the portrayal of the entity(s) under consideration.

 Troubleshooting. Another type of problem solving at the learn-by-doing level is troubleshooting. Troubleshooting is the inverse of prediction. In this situation the learner is shown some consequence (a change in property value and its concurrent change in portrayal). The learner must then determine what property was changed. The learner must recall the relevant principles: If *<condition(s)>* then *<consequence(s)>*. He or she must match the consequence that occurs to a statement of principle. This enables the learner to identify the conditions that may be faulted. He or she must then examine the situation to find the portrayal of the potentially faulted condition(s) and determine if the value of the associated property value matches the principle. If not, this is possibly the fault. The learner can then correct the fault, that is, change the value of the property that is the faulted condition and then test to see if the desired consequence occurs.

 In single event processes, this troubleshooting problem solving requires little more than memory. However, in very complex processes, involving many events, the above mental process may need to be repeated many times until the faulted conditions are identified and corrected.

 PEAnets provide a very specific way to define both prediction and troubleshooting. They also provide a vocabulary for use by the learner to be more precise in their problem solving activities.

Meta-Mental-Models

 A meta-model is a model for a model. The knowledge structures described in this paper for concepts and processes and their associated cognitive processes for different types of problem solving using these knowledge structures provide a potentially useful meta-mental-model for a learner. If the learner has acquired the knowledge components and knowledge structure for a conceptual network, then he or she has a meta-mental-model for acquiring a conceptual network in a specific area. This meta-mental-model allows the learner to seek information for slots in the model. It provides a way for the learner to know if they have all the necessary knowledge components to instantiate their mental-model. It enables the learner to extend their model of the concept under consideration by processing the concept schema for additional classes or by processing the schema to determine potential generalizations.

If the learner has acquired the knowledge components and knowledge structure for a PEAnet then he or she has a meta-mental-model for acquiring a process mental-model for some specific phenomena. The PEAnet structure enables the learner to determine if all the necessary knowledge components are present. By representing the phenomena in a PEAnet, the learner can run mental experiments to see what consequences should occur under given sets of conditions. The learner can conduct mental *"what if"* experiments to predict what happens when the conditions change. The learner can represent very complex phenomena in a very systematic way providing a much better understanding of the phenomena under consideration. Furthermore, the learner can describe devices or situations that don't work correctly using the PEAnet meta-mental-model. This allows the learner to help determine why a given process is not working by identifying the conditions that may be faulted.

Automated Instructional Design

Knowledge structures also make it possible to build smart instructional systems. A knowledge structure represents a precise way to represent a conceptual network or a causal network. The processes identified for manipulating the knowledge objects in a knowledge structure provide the basis for computer algorithms that can emulate some of the processing done by a learner.

In previous papers, we have described instructional simulations based on PEAnet knowledge structures. There is not space in this paper to elaborate these ideas here (see Merrill, 1999; Merrill, in press-b).

Summary

This paper describes knowledge components that are thought to be appropriate and sufficient to precisely describe certain types of cognitive subject matter content *(knowledge)*. It also describes knowledge structures that show the relationships among these knowledge components and among other knowledge objects. It suggests that a knowledge structure is a form of schema such as those that learners use to represent knowledge in memory. A mental-model is a schema plus cognitive processes for manipulating and modifying the knowledge stored in a schema. We suggested processes that enable learners to manipulate the knowledge components of conceptual network knowledge structures for purposes of classification, generalization, and concept elaboration. We further suggested processes that enable learners to manipulate the knowledge components of process knowledge structures *(PEAnets)* for purposes of explanation, prediction, and troubleshooting. The hypothesis of this paper is that knowledge components and knowledge structures, such as those described in this paper, could serve as meta-mental-models that would enable learners to more easily acquire conceptual and causal networks and their associated processes. The resulting specific mental-models would facilitate their ability to solve problems of conceptualization and interpretation.

Notes

1. Gagné (1985) referred to this structure as a learning hierarchy.

2. This structure is often called a concept hierarchy.

3. Component Display Theory (CDT) is the original work that extended Gagné's categories of outcomes (see Merrill, 1994). Component Design Theory (CDT$_2$) is our current extension of this work and has been called Instructional Transaction Theory (ITT) and instructional design based on knowledge objects. We apologize for the proliferation of terms for this work.

4. We adopted the word *entity* rather than the word *object* to avoid confusion with the use of the word *object* as used in *object-oriented computer programming*.

References

Bloom, B. S., Englehart, M. D., Furst, E. J., Hill, W. H., & Krathwohl, D. R. (Eds.) (1956). *A taxonomy of educational objectives: Handbook I. Cognitive domain.* New York: David McKay.

Dijkstra, S., & van Merriënboer, J. J. G. (1997). Plans, procedures, and theories to solve instructional design problems. In S. Dijkstra, N. M. Seel, F. Schott, & R. D. Tennyson, *Instructional design: International perspectives. Volume 2: Solving instructional design problems.* Mahwah, NJ: Lawrence Erlbaum Associates.

Gagné, R. M. (1965, 1985). *The conditions of learning.* New York: Holt Rinehart and Winston.

Jones, M. K., Li, Z., & Merrill, M. D. (1990). Domain knowledge representation for instructional analysis. *Educational Technology, 30*(10), 7–32.

Krathwohl, D. R., Bloom, B. S., & Masia, B. B. (Eds.). (1964). *Taxonomy of educational objectives: Handbook II, affective domain.* New York: David McKay.

Mayer, R. E. (1992). *Thinking, problem solving, cognition* (2nd ed.). New York: W. H. Freeman.

Merrill, M. D. (1987). The new component design theory: Instructional design for courseware authoring. *Instructional Science, 16,* 19–34.

Merrill, M. D. (1994). *Instructional design theory.* Englewood Cliffs: Educational Technology Publications.

Merrill, M. D. (1998). Knowledge objects. *CBT Solutions,* (March/April), 1, 6–11.

Merrill, M. D. (1999). Instructional transaction theory (ITT): Instructional design based on knowledge objects. In C. M. Reigeluth (Ed.), *Instructional design theories and models: Volume II, a new paradigm of instructional design.* Mahwah, NJ: Lawrence Erlbaum Associates.

Merrill, M. D. (in press-a). Components of instruction: Toward a theoretical tool for instructional design. *Instructional Science.*

Merrill, M. D. (in press-b). A knowledge object and mental-model approach to a physics lesson. *Educational Technology.*

Merrill, M. D. & ID$_2$ Research Group. (1993). Instructional transaction theory: Knowledge relationships among processes, entities, and activities. *Educational Technology, 33*(4), 5–16.

Merrill, M. D. and ID$_2$ Research Group. (1996). Instructional transaction theory: Instructional design based on knowledge objects. *Educational Technology, 36*(3), 30–37.

Reigeluth, C. M., Merrill, M. D., & Bunderson, C. V. (1978). The structure of subject matter content and its instructional design implications. *Instructional Science, 7*(2), 107–126.

Twitchell, D. (Ed). (1990-91). Robert M. Gagné and M. David Merrill in conversation. *Educational Technology.* A series of seven articles: No. 1 *30*(7), 34–39; No. 2 *30*(8), 36–41; No. 3 *30*(9), 36–41; No. 4 *30*(10), 37–45; No. 5 *30*(11) 35–39; No. 6 *30*(12) 35–46; No. 7 *31*(1)34–40.

The Future
of Learning Objects

H. Wayne Hodgins
(Director, Worldwide Learning Strategies, Autodesk Inc.)

Introduction:
The End of the Beginning?

Any ending can also be viewed as the beginning of something new, and such is the intent of this final chapter. As the summary of the current state of learning objects in the year 2000, this book will serve to mark the end of the introductory phase of learning objects, and as the precursor to their implementation and application to learning and working. As this first phase draws to a close, it has become clear that learning objects are not a passing fad, nor a new name for something old. Rather, learning objects represent a completely new conceptual model for the mass of content used in the context of learning. They are destined to forever change the shape and form of learning and, in so doing, it is anticipated that they will also usher in an unprecedented efficiency of learning content design, development, and delivery. However, the most significant promise of learning objects is to truly increase and improve human learning and performance.

The Long and the Wide View

Having been heavily involved in learning objects from their beginning and perhaps from the inception of the name and idea, and because I am extremely active in addressing the needs for standards in these areas and movements for change, I could not be more delighted by this collection of work from such an eclectic and talented range of authors and experts. It provides new perspectives and a constant source of inspiration for the use and application of learning objects, and provides an exciting catalyst to new thinking and new perspectives.

Let me start by adding some context to what follows in this final chapter. As the strategic futurist and Director of Worldwide Learning Strategies for Autodesk Inc., I have the privilege and opportunity to develop a wonderfully unique perspective on the world of learning, training, education, and performance support, a situation to which I ascribe the request to write the final chapter to this amazing book and collection of thought. My focus at Autodesk Inc. is on human performance improvement, and my time frame starts about two years from today and extends through the next 10 to 20 years. This charter affords me the pleasure of meeting, working, observing, and talking with people from all over the geographical world, as well as from the worlds of learning, training, education, and performance improvement—people who work in government, academia, and business. Therefore, it is with this long and wide view that I am honored to write this final chapter. In doing so I aspire to:

- Provide some *additional and new perspectives* from which to view the enormous set of challenges we face in creating a world filled with learning objects that work.

- Frame a *longer and wider view of the future* world of learning and learners.

- Develop an understanding of how learning objects *fit within this larger context* and within a *holistic view* of the future.

- Pose some provocative yet pragmatic *points to ponder* as you read and reflect upon the ideas captured within the preceding chapters.

- *Stimulate new thinking and ideas* to emerge, such that the process of knowledge creation continues long after you have read this book and keeps you coming back for more.

Power of a Shared Vision

We can only create what we can imagine. Hence, this collection of work from some of the best thought leaders in the area of learning objects seeks to stimulate your imagination on what is possible in the not-too-distant future for the betterment of learning and human performance through the effective instructional use of learning objects. As Michelangelo reportedly remarked, sculpting a statue is easy (for him at least)—it is a matter of looking at a block of marble and taking away everything that does not belong there! What he humbly leaves out is that this is true *IF* you have a very clear vision and can see what you imagine within the marble. More germane to our current times, and to this book, is that Michelangelo worked with a group of 16 to paint the ceiling of the Sistine Chapel. Thus, it was not the work of a single individual, however gifted, but the creation of a project team working on a shared vision. It will also become important later in this chapter to note that Michelangelo lived in an environment filled with peers the likes of da Vinci, and during the time of the Renaissance. You may want to consider, as you reflect upon the ideas and the opportunities captured here, that we are potentially entering a similar environment of creativity, innovation, and shared vision. Could this be a second Renaissance?

Great Groups

It is usually sage advice to "never try to write a book by committee." However, with the masterful guidance of this collection's editor, and with the exceptional expertise and experience of the group of thinkers he assembled, this exception has been a wise choice. Indeed, this as much as anything may be a great example of how much things have changed and how they need to be when it comes to capturing and transferring knowledge through learning objects.

> As they say, 'None of us is as smart as all of us.' That's good, because the problems we face are too complex to be solved by any one person or any one discipline. Our only chance is to bring people together from a variety of backgrounds and disciplines who can refract a problem through the prism of complementary minds allied in common purpose. I call such collections of talent Great Groups. The genius of Great Groups is that they get remarkable people—strong individual achievers—to work together to get results. But these groups serve a second and equally important function: they provide psychic support and personal fellowship. They help generate courage. Without a sounding board for outrageous ideas, without personal encouragement and perspective when we hit a roadblock, we'd all lose our way. (Bennis, 1997)

I hope you will believe, as I do, that the collection of authors who contributed to this book, and the community to which you now belong as a reader, comprise such a "Great Group." Together, we can create that magic phenomenon when bodacious, humungous, achievable goals collide with passionate, talented, and supportive people. As we venture forward, let each of us aspire to contribute to the creation and deep understanding of the shared vision that is emerging from our collective work. As we passionately pursue this vision, we will want to establish the delicate balance between sufficient clarity to ensure that our multiple efforts have a unity of purpose and direction, and sufficient sagacity to allow for the serendipitous discovery of new directions and ways to get there. With this as our foundation, we can develop and execute plans to transform our vision into reality, and our potential into performance.

> We can let the future happen or take the trouble to imagine it. We can imagine it dark or bright—and in the long run, that's how it will be. (Gelertner, 2000)

The Future Does Not Happen *to* Us; We Create It

The future is not just happening to us any more; we make decisions every day that determine what decisions we will be able to make tomorrow. As we stand at the inflection point of a new learning economy, we realize that it will be shaped as we choose to shape it; it will be as rewarding and humane as we make it; the decisions we reach will determine what the world will be like for all of us. The world of learning with learning objects described in these chapters does not rest easily within the public system of education and training that exists in this country today. Much of this system was put into place as a result of demand; many original demands have, over time, changed dramatically or disappeared.

I believe that the positive forces of human nature are far more powerful and they outweigh negative forces. For this reason, I believe passionately that much of our task is to learn to disregard outmoded caveats against allowing disorder, tangential thinking, and even down time in our lives, since the genuine creativity that we need to shape the future can emerge only among people whose way of being incorporates adaptability, flexible thinking, and confidence that, with encouragement, the positive forces of our nature will triumph.

Witnessing "Future Histories"?

Isaac Asimov once remarked that he did not write science fiction, he wrote "future histories." This collection of work in my opinion represents a great deal of thinking about our future histories. As a believer in synchronicity over coincidence, I believe it is no coincidence that during the same week I was writing this chapter for this exciting new collection of work, we were also going through one of the single largest collections of historical milestones ever:

- The Human Genome Project has succeeded in breaking "The Book of Life" (as they call the DNA decoding), down into very small identifiable "tags."

- Water has been confirmed to exist on Mars, requiring us to completely rethink what we know about physics, atmosphere, and other planets, a revolution that is the equivalent of going from the flat world view.

- Innovations like Napster and Gnutella are revolutionizing content distribution, challenging age-old bastions of control such as publishing, and portending revolutionary changes to the world as we know it, to a degree possibly equivalent to that of the Gutenberg press. (Don't think this is about music; this is about rethinking the conceptual model of the Web and connecting everything to everything, directly).

- The first Advanced Distributed Learning Network (ADL) "Plug fest" has provided the first true "proof of concept" that it really is possible to have interoperable, reusable learning content across multiple learning management systems.

Together, these events reflect not only a re-ordering of the way we think and do things; they spark our imagination to contemplate possibilities for expanding the boundaries of who we are. We do not know where all this will lead, but surely, those of us in the fields of learning, training, education and human performance improvement cannot help but look at these changes and know this is a historic and truly a great time to be alive.

Putting Learning Objects in Context

Defining Learning Objects

The struggle and seeming futility in trying to nail down a precise definition for learning objects is obvious as you read the various chapters in this book, and it is reminiscent of the similar chase to define "multimedia" not many years ago. I believe this is a very good thing, and that it bodes well for the lasting power of learning objects. Not that it is undesirable to have some common understanding of the term; several very good ones are offered in previous chapters. However, this ongoing struggle, along with the multitude of applications and the desire to use the term, suggest that there is something very substantial going on, to which attention must be paid. It is also interesting to observe the natural tensions and dynamics between opposing views on learning, such as those of behaviorists and constructivists, and the instructional design and performance support models.

> *Information causes change; if it doesn't, it isn't information.* (Claude Shannon)

> *"You are sitting in a chair"* is not information.

Information that Informs: What a Concept!

Information informs. Otherwise, it is just interference or noise competing for your all-too-scarce and precious time and attention. Information resides in many varieties of media: graphic, audio, anything that you perceive that has value. A painting is information, a concerto is information, a recorded conversation is information, experience is information.

Entering the Knowledge Economy

The ability to capture knowledge such that it can be analyzed, reused, and shared with others, thus developing a spiral of more new knowledge creation, is perhaps the most powerful promise information technology can provide. The impact on learning of just-right information flowing to the right place, person, and time, cannot be overstated.

Learning as Nourishment

In our new way of thinking about learning, we can compare our need to learn with our need to eat. When we recognize that learning, like hunger, is not a problem to be permanently "solved" but a condition to be continually addressed, we can extend our range of flexibility in meeting our needs depending on our current situation. Just as we decide what and how to eat relatively quickly in any given situation (Fast food? Linen napery and red-coated servitors? A run to the grocery store?), we need to be able to get the learning we need that suits our current situation. Today, we have many more choices than our ancestors, but these choices have not led us to abandon any one method of nourishment; rather, they have allowed us to experience many different kinds, from freeze-dried camping fare to old-fashioned home cooking. However, after the information revolution, as after the industrial revolution, our habitual ways of eating have changed to accommodate the lives we lead.

Just as we have created grocery stores to provide us with the raw materials (and sometimes more) for our meals, and these stores are carefully geared to meet the predictable demands of their customers, so in the future we will receive learning objects as our needs arise, based on the predictability of those needs as determined from past behavior. The dramatic efficiencies of automation, such as bar codes and scanners that have assumed the functions of price tags and cash registers, will be mirrored in the learning arena by metadata standards, collaborative filtering of information, and so forth, all of which require standardization just as grocery stores require standard labeling and coding of the products they sell.

To carry the analogy further, learning objects themselves can be likened to essential amino acids, without which we cannot assimilate the value of what is taken in. Learning paths and structures will be comparable to recipes for food: they will list but not include the ingredients themselves, they will be portable and transferable, and they will allow for customization, that is, individual touches and preferences. Such "learning content recipes" will be able to be captured, saved, reused, and moved across systems to meet the individual needs of learners in different locales, milieux, and cultures.

My Lego™ Epiphany

My journey into this world of learning objects started with an "epiphany moment" watching my children play with Lego™ blocks many years ago. As with most families, my son and daughter have very different needs, one for instructions, directions, and a pre-determined end state (a castle as I recall), and the other for complete freedom and creativity of constructing whatever he imagined (a robot in this case). As it struck me that both had their wonderfully different needs met equally well with these simple blocks of plastic, I began what has been almost ten years of refining a dream of a world where all "content" exists at just the right and lowest possible size, much like the individual blocks that make up Lego™ systems. These fundamental size or "molecular data" blocks are not so small as to be "sub-atomic," yet they are the smallest possible to be of use. In this dream, these "prime-sized" blocks of content have a fundamental "standard," the equivalent of the "pin size" of the Lego™ blocks, such that they can be assembled into literally any shape, size, and function. Some people may find the most value in taking a pre-assembled unit and putting it to direct use; others will want to assemble their own, possibly from scratch, but more likely from sub-assemblies. Some will want instructions and guidance on how to assemble the blocks, while others will want to determine their own results. However they may be used and applied, the empowerment of literally every individual by such a world full of learning objects is staggering. Please join me and the other authors of this book in the quest to transform this dream into a shared vision, and to transform the potential into reality.

Water, Water, Everywhere, Nor Any Drop to Drink!

Switching metaphors and expanding the dream, in my vision this granular content forms a vast ocean of the world's data, with a seemingly infinite number of source streams of all sizes flowing into it. Data is to people as water is to fish: an environment within which to live and support life. It is the oxygen and nutrients contained within the water, and most notably the ability of fish to extract these, which allow the fish to live. Without this fundamental capability they die, and we understand that yes, a fish can drown in water. Similarly, we find ourselves swimming in a rich and plentiful sea of data, so much so that we are in danger of drowning in data. The key to our ability to survive and thrive depends on our attaining abilities equivalent to those of fish, to extract the information out of the data and then convert this into knowledge.

The Baby Bear Analogy

For those who recall the story of *Goldilocks and the Three Bears,* this is the "Baby Bear" analogy—we get it "just right": not too big, not too small, not too hot, not too cold, etc. In the case of learning objects, we get them in "just the right"

- size/amount
- time
- way (learning style)
- context, relevance
- medium of delivery (paper, DVD, online, synchronous, on screen, etc.)
- location (desk, car, house, palm, field, etc.)

The Final Frontier:
Technology that "Learns"

As this vision of the future develops, it leads to one of the ultimate characteristics of the dream: tools and technology that truly have the ability to learn. It is all in the turn of a phrase, some say. Learning *about* technology is important. Technology *for* learning enables amazing results and advances. However, technology that *can* learn is going to provide the most revolutionary and significant change!

Imagine tools, technologies, environments, data sets, that get better the more you use them, that learn about you and adapt and improve as a result of your interactions and use. Imagine intelligent technological tutors and coaches. Think about being able to create new knowledge based on capturing observed patterns, recognizing behaviors, gleaning and understanding the context of events and actions. Imagine having your ideal mentor available every minute, supplying you with ideas, suggestions, true information, at just the right time, without having to ask for it.

Wow! or Whoa?

This future is potentially frightening and even sinister at first, to be sure, rife with inherent dangers and concerns at least equal to the power and benefits, but when has this not been the case?

Would we propose not to have discovered fire because it can burn down houses and forests and kill people and animals? Would we be willing not to have discovered and adopted electricity so widely because is can similarly cause damage and death, or because when it suddenly stops working we are rendered almost helpless? No, we instead choose to be mindful of such consequences, to impose appropriate discipline on ourselves, and to plan and research accordingly. Surely, we must equally push forward, explore, learn, develop, and advance the capabilities presenting themselves today. Just imagine the impact on human life if we had technology that could learn!

Discovery vs. Invention

It is important to distinguish the difference between invention and discovery. Invention, for the purpose of this discussion, can be understood as the creation of something completely new, be it an idea or a device. Discovery is when we first "see" something new to us. Typically, this also happens when we figure something out that has been there all along. The world has, to the best of our current knowledge, always been (almost) round, yet we only discovered this thousands of years after living on it. Gravity, electricity, theory of relativity, atomic structure . . . all discoveries. Considering past great discoverers such as

Copernicus, Einstein, and Newton, history would appear to show that a flurry of invention follows great discovery. It also tends to show that there were many signs and indicators that such discoveries were imminent. Concurrent or synchronistic arrival at similar conclusions by independent groups and individuals who are formulating similar theories, asking similar questions, is a harbinger of great things to come. As evidenced by the contents of this book, one could argue that we have many of these same characteristics going on right now in the worlds of learning, performance improvement, and learning objects.

Coincidence or Synchronicity?

As asked earlier in this chapter, can it be mere coincidence that we are also experiencing an unprecedented number of discoveries that promise to be as significant as the historic ones mentioned above? The discovery of water on Mars promises to be such a revolutionary discovery for the sciences of space and the study of the evolution of the cosmos. The deciphering of DNA promises to forever change our view and understanding of life. This entire happening in the span of one week strikes me as more than mere coincidence. In keeping with this pattern, it is worth pondering whether we now have signs that we may be on the verge of the next revolutionary discovery in the world of data, information, knowledge and learning. Let us imagine what one such discovery might be.

On the Verge of Discovering the "Periodic Table of Data"

I believe we are on the verge of grand discovery in the areas of learning, content, knowledge, and objects. Just as revolutionary as our discovery of the atomic and molecular models will be our discovery of the equivalent of the periodic table for all content or data. Mendeleyev's 1870s creation of the periodic table laid out the basic building blocks of all physical matter and revolutionized our view of that world. Similarly, an equivalent understanding of our data and informational world will give us a fundamental understanding and ability to manipulate, create, and build any substance possible. In the case of data, this model will be based on the ability to take everything down to fundamental units, understanding their basic structural makeup and components, the equivalents of their electrons, neutrons, protons that combine to form compounds. This understanding will be similarly simple and equally powerful. It will provide some of the basic "rules" that govern what can be combined and how, natural pairings and groupings, nesting structures, etc.

This "periodic table" will help us understand these natural groupings just as the table of the elements shows us the natural occurrence of minerals and chemicals. It will allow for a literally infinite number of new discoveries as we experiment with new combinations to create the informational equivalents of aluminum and nylon, the wonders of chemical reactions and the inventions stimulated by this new understanding.

Existing Evidence and Supporting Theories Are Growing

There are many "hints" and glimpses of this new discovery within many of the chapters and works in this book:

- In previous works, *David Wiley* has proposed the notion of such a hierarchy and entities such as "fundamental information objects" and "combined information objects.

- *David Merrill* writes about a very detailed hierarchy of "knowledge objects " and "knowledge structure."

- The chapter by *Brenda Bannan-Ritland (et al.)* on "constructivist learning environments" provides a very good summary of several such granular models and goes on to describe how to utilize a very fundamental and granular structure to attack the problem of personalization and highly flexible learning objects with such things as the Cognitive Flexibility Theory (CFT).

- *David Wiley* has created a first attempt at such a taxonomy and he describes a similar analogy and the existence of "learning crystals" that aggregate the smaller units of data together into a "natural" structure in the right conditions.

- *Mimi Recker (et al.)* then goes on to show the power that can come from having this basic structure and using "collaborative filtering" to provide context-sensitive discovery and recommendation of the appropriate learning objects to the right person at the right time.

Entering the Information Age and the Knowledge Economy . . . *Finally*

The ability to capture knowledge such that it can be analyzed, reused, and shared with others, thus developing a spiral of more new knowledge creation, is perhaps the most powerful promise information technology can provide. The impact on learning of just-right information flowing to the right place, person, and time cannot be overstated.

As these changes and discoveries noted above overlap in time, they have obvious synergies and relationships that begin to converge to create the inflection point or take-off of the information or knowledge age. As this occurs, we will also witness a level of revolution equivalent to the agrarian or industrial revolutions in the form of the information and knowledge revolutions and information automation. As with previous revolutionary creations, we will realize order of magnitude increases in productivity and performance, but in the information revolution these will include increased productivity of knowledge and service workers. This is not to be confused with merely generative processing of information, just as the factories of the industrial revolution were not merely the automation of previous process and practice. This will involve the invention of entirely new processes for knowledge capture, converting raw data into information, and the subsequent creation of new knowledge in an ever-spiraling crescendo.

Planning Backwards from the Future

How might we better understand and plan for the arrival of such a future? I suggest that the most practical strategy for claiming the potential riches offered by the information revolution, and avoiding its very real perils, is to *"plan backwards from the future,"* positing the future we want and figuring out how to get there. Inventing the future is not a new suggestion; however, the important difference is the second step in the planning process. Rather than going back to the present and figuring out the next step from there, planning backwards would require us to imagine what the step immediately before arriving at the future would be. Then we imagine what would be required of the stage just before that, and so on, until we get back to the present. Having laid out some elements of the future state of learning objects in the preceding text, we can follow this planning backwards model to look at what would be required immediately before arriving at the future state. For example, imaging this future world filled with literally millions of small granular fundamental data objects, selecting a "just right" set, and assembling these into a learning object, would require a rich set of information about each of these data objects. These attributes, or "metadata" as they are properly called, would be required in order to know which ones to select to match up with each person and situation. Similarly, we would quickly conclude that the interoperability, flexibility, and reusability of learning objects could only take place if there were a set of fundamental standards universally in place for this to work.

Standards

Widely adopted, open, and accredited standards are a fundamental requirement. History has clearly shown that revolutionary changes do not "take off" or hit their inflection point without widespread adoption of common standards. In the case of electricity, this was the standardization of voltage and plugs; for railroads, the standard gauge of the tracks; and for the Internet, the common standards of TCP/IP, HTTP, and HTML. Common standards for metadata, learning objects, and learning architecture are mandatory for the similar success of the knowledge economy and future. Fortunately, the work to create such standards for learning objects and related domains has been going on around the world for the past few years. This includes the creation of accredited standards from the IEEE Learning Technology Standards Committee (LTSC) for such areas as Learning Object Metadata, Computer Managed Instruction, Course Sequencing, Learner Profiles, and many more.

The Magic of Metadata

I can imagine a world in which there is a constantly refreshed supply of all the attributes (*a.k.a.* metadata), both subjective and objective, to adequately describe every piece of data, every object, every event, and every person in the world. It is especially the subjective attributes or metadata that create the ability to capture what is otherwise tacit knowledge, context, perspectives, and opinions. Thus, everyone is able to discover, find, and access true information, and the processes of learning and knowledge creation are significantly enhanced and accelerated.

Subjective and Objective Metadata

Metadata come in two flavors: objective and subjective. Objective metadata are factual data, most of which can be generated automatically—things such as physical attributes, date, author, operational requirements, costs, identification numbers, and ownership. Subjective metadata are the more varied and valuable attributes of a learning object determined by the person or group who creates the metadata. The labels on the cans are objective metadata; your opinion of the product (for example, whether it worked as well as a fresh ingredient in your favorite spaghetti sauce) is an instance of subjective metadata.

It is also worth noting that new technology can extract and recognize these attributes, and it is possible to find, combine, and use not only text-based information, but also a person's face, a sound, a smell, a shape, or "things like _____." Imagine the possibilities . . .

Unlimited and Limited Metadata

As we continue to plan backward by imagining what has to happen before all this is possible, we come to realize that another critical characteristic of metadata is the ability to have any number of metadata records for any single information or learning object. This is particularly obvious for subjective metadata as they capture such things as opinions, and there is *any number* of these available and desirable for any single object.

However, we also come to realize the need to understand the limits of metadata and not try to have them capture too much. For example, information about sequencing of learning objects and the creation of learning paths is extremely important for the effective use of learning objects. These attributes are not describing the content itself, but rather the use of the content, and are therefore not part of the metadata, but rather the application of the learning object to a specific use.

As personalization becomes the key element of learning, subjective metadata become increasingly important. The value of the learning object goes up as its associated metadata increase in richness and completeness; the value of the data objects also goes up as it approaches its smallest potentially useful size.

Capturing Experience

When technology is able to capture and learn from its own experience and from its user, it gains a critical new power: accurate prediction of what will be needed next, in terms of information it can provide or suggestions it can offer. This is possible through the analysis of the experiential knowledge that has been collected, and it creates new knowledge in the form of patterns and profiles. It has often been overlooked that just-in-time learning and performance support are *only* possible with this predictability. With it, learning is truly as adaptive as the technology itself.

Profiling Learners

As we all learn from helping others learn, the degree to which you can be effective is directly related to how much you know about the situation and circumstance of the person you are trying to help. Personalization of the learning experience requires knowing something about the learner. To avoid redundancy, the system must know what the learner already knows. To assemble relevant learning experiences, it must know about the learner's past experiences, learning preferences, career goals, and more. Personal profiling enables new approaches to productivity. A profiling system that automatically identifies people's areas of expertise based on the issues they research on the Internet, the ideas in their documents, the e-mail messages they create, and the topics they follow in their knowledge bases facilitates creation of virtual workgroups, encourages communication, and reduces duplication of effort.

The more a learning system knows about a learner, the greater the opportunity to provide on-target information. At the same time, one's learning record should be at least as secure as one's credit medical records.

Strategies for Success:
Relevant, Connected, Simplified

These three attributes appear to be the keys to determining success both currently and in the future.

> For most people, their computing environment is just a tool. A highly versatile and unimaginably flexible tool, but just a tool to help them do a job, or write a book, or entertain themselves, or sip at the Internet's straw. Computing,

for most, is no longer an end game. And the businesses that make it easy for people, while still maintaining the expected levels of quality, functionality, price, and support, will win out over those who do not.

Who will be most likely to write the next AOL-style success story? Answer: Those businesses that do all these things PLUS provide innovative solutions that go to the core of peoples' computing needs (both the needs their customers already know they have, and new needs they haven't yet realized they have—how many people knew they wanted Instant Messaging before it became AOL's most popular service?) Products and services that are innovative, easy to use, and focused on the end-users' current and future needs—sounds like quite a formula to me! (Harrow, 2000)

Make It Relevant, Make It Easy:

Jeff Harrow captures the essence of what will determine success of any product, service, or new idea. If it is not compelling to the masses based on its obvious and high practical value (relevant), and if it is not easy for them to use, then do not expect it to catch on. Learning objects will be no different. Their success beyond this point will be dependent upon the masses being able to see their fundamentally high value and the ability of the masses to put them to use quickly and easily. This should *not* be confused with the underlying complexity that is required to make all this work and make it work transparently and easily. Indeed, there is likely an inverse relationship between the external simplicity and ease of use of any technology or system, and the underlying complexity required to make it happen. Therefore, there is a critical need for raising awareness, education, dissemination, and the tools and technology with which to start implementing.

Connecting Everything to Everything

One of the fundamental characteristics of innovations that have truly changed the world is that of connecting things, especially data and people. Trains, planes, and automobiles; television, telecommunications, the Internet, and the World Wide Web. Learning objects have, at their root, an enormously high potential to take connectivity to a new level. On the data level, metadata (as previously discussed) will be the key to enabling the connectivity of learning objects by supplying the basis for making these connections between other learning objects and between people. On the technical and system architecture side, it will likely be new paradigms of the Web and its related technologies that will make these connections possible.

For example, while most of the hype to date (September 2000) has been about the new Napster Web site for downloading music files (most of which are illegal copies), the real news will prove to be the lesser known

"Gnutella" technology. Do not be misled because all the focus has been on the impact of these technologies on the music world. Their lasting impact will be *much* larger and more revolutionary as we come to understand how this fundamentally changes "everything" in terms of how we think about the Web, and the connectivity it enables. As per their Web site:

> Gnutella is a real-time search, peer-based file-sharing client that allows a user running a Gnutella client to search for and download files from other Gnutella users. Gnutella was originally conceived, authored and released by Justin Frankel and Tom Pepper of *Nullsoft* in March 2000. *(http://gnutella.wego.com)*

Similar to Gnutella is FreeNet (http://freenet.sourceforge.net), the brainchild of Ian Clarke, a London-based Web designer who created FreeNet as a final project for his degree in artificial intelligence and computer science. The goal of FreeNet is *"to allow people to distribute and retrieve information with complete anonymity, and to operate without any central control."* Sounds like the seeds of revolution to me! This type of file sharing technology enables the connectivity of everyone and everything on the Web.

Imagine what it means to have no concept of "servers," where *everything is "just" a node on the net.* A world where every person and every file can be connected directly, one-to-one. Think of the impact on learning, learners, and learning content. Think about every learning object connected to every other learning object, able to communicate, pass data, and manipulate the other. Think about a world where control of content is truly put into the hands of every individual, where everyone in need of a given piece of content can be connected directly with those who have it. What will it mean to have potentially billions of authors and publishers?

"Learnativity": The New Frontier?

Living in a World of Convergence

In a world of constant and increasing rates of change, one of the most prevailing trends and traits is that of convergence. Technologies converge to create new technologies and products; concepts converge to form completely new concepts; people converge into new local, global, and virtual communities; and professional skills converge to create new professions. However, these convergences pale in comparison to the implosion of learning, working, and capturing knowledge, and the management of their sum total. These previously disparate and relatively independent activities are converging to become one, and in so doing will create a completely new existence, a new way of being. Just as in nuclear fusion, their intersection will create a previously unimagined new state producing unimaginable amounts of creativity, innovation, productivity, and performance. This fusion will create an infinite supply of the new energy source of the new economy: knowledge. In this new knowledge-based economy the idea of "learning a living" will become more than a cute phrase, it will become our reality; it will become "learnativity."

Learnativity?

It is perhaps revealing that we do not have a word or a name for this new state we find ourselves living within. What do you call that which you and every other person are doing every day as you solve problems, work, plan, innovate, create, communicate, and learn? When they used to stand still long enough, when they were independent activities, we simply called them by their own names. However, when they happen all at once and all the time, fused together into one single state of just being, what do we call it? For the purpose of simplicity and consistency, let us call it *learnativity.*

Redefining Learning, Working, and Knowledge

Expertise used to demand constant improvement of one's ability to perform the tasks or skills of a profession or trade. However, as multiple professions converge and fuse, as tasks and skills are constantly replaced with new ones at an ever-increasing rate, expertise becomes a matter of steadily renewing one's knowledge base and extending it to new areas. Critical expertise has transformed into the continuous creation and acquisition of knowledge and skills. This lifelong cycle of learning is the new foundation of professional self-worth and that of all teams and organizations. One's primary responsibility, and perhaps the only sustainable competitive advantage, is to improve one's ability to learn and apply the right things faster.

Putting Learning (Back) into Context and Motion

A classic and historical problem with most approaches to education and training has been to see learning as an end in itself, an activity that is designed and studied independent of the learner and most importantly, independent of the overall system within which it works. Learnativity is *not* a mechanical, static, linear process, nor one that can be understood by examining any of its components outside of its systemic context. It is a very human, dynamic, and complex flow that resembles an organic structure more than a mechanical one.

Knowledge Creation in Action

Learnativity is knowledge in action, a continuous spiraling conversion of tacit knowledge (such as know-how and experience) into explicit knowledge that can be captured, shared with others, diffused within groups, and turned back into new tacit knowledge gained from learning by doing. Learnativity is a way of continuously creating new, actionable knowledge. The key is to see this as a single state, with the following four primary elements swirling within (Figure 1):

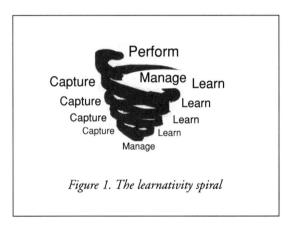

Figure 1. The learnativity spiral

Performing. Let us start where we want individuals, teams, and organizations to end: peak performance. Performing refers to the application of knowledge. We put knowledge to work, solving problems. Performing is the integration and application of knowledge in the activities, products, and services of the project team or organization. Explicit knowledge converts to tacit as successful performance achieves results and the workers move on.

Capturing. Capturing knowledge means converting it from a tacit state into an explicit, comprehensible form—such as a video, a simulation, a model, or words and illustrations in a document—so that others can understand it.

Managing. Management of information, learning, and performance is the conversion of explicit knowledge (formal and expressed) into complex and valuable combinations of ideas, insights, and experiences so they can be shared with others.

Learning. Learning is the means by which tacit knowledge (informal and subjective) is exchanged between individuals and between the learner and the learning resources. It is therefore both social and personal in nature. It occurs in both formal and informal settings, and includes connections and direct interaction among people. Learning is also the personal transformation from explicit to tacit within the individual through reading, observation, and reflective thought.

Organizations that are successful in the creation and management of knowledge cannot mandate that knowledge will be created, nor can they automate the process. The organization can, however, provide conditions (an environment) that will foster, nurture, and support this type of continuous learning, which in turn can result in peak performance.

It may seem that learning has been eliminated when in fact it has just faded from conscious awareness as it increasingly embeds itself into our products, services, tools, and technology. Learning takes its rightful place as a fundamental component of our day to day life. It is no longer always an event, an activity that is divorced from the rest of our life and existence. Perhaps this is the ultimate form of the much-discussed convergence we see happening in most other areas, such as technology.

Learnativity is much more than just a word or a term. It is literally a new existence, a new way of working, learning, and living. A new way of being who we are. Learning objects are one of the fundamental elements of this new "way of being." As we learn from the experiences of those reviewed in this book and begin to implement their ideas, this future full of learning objects and this new "learnativity" existence promises to be very bright and compelling for all. With the continuation of this type of exploration, with the passionate pursuit of these lofty goals, with people such as the authors of this book, and with readers such as you, we will continue to develop our shared vision and the velocity of its transformation into reality.

Welcome to the future. Welcome to the end of the beginning, and the beginning of the next phase of the wonderful world of learning objects. Please continue practicing the critical reflection, dialogues, and "learning by doing" activities that will determine how well and how quickly this future arrives. Perhaps the greatest challenge is how can we as people also become more effective and efficient as "learning objects" ourselves?

Acknowledgements

The author can be reached at: wayne@learnativity.com.

References

Bennis, Warren. (1997) *The secret of great groups.* Available: http://www.druckerfoundation.org/leaderbooks/L2L/winter97/bennis.html

Gerlertner, David. (2000) Conversation cited in The *Wired* Diaries 2000. *Wired* (January), 69.

Harrow, J. (2000). *Rapidly changing face of computing. RCFoC.* Available: http://www.compaq.com/rcfoc/20000717.html